Academic Library System

Second Edition

Academic Library System

Second Edition

Shri Nath Sahai

Ess Ess Publications

4837/24, Ansari Road, Darya Ganj,
New Delhi-110002
Tel. : 23260807, 41563444
Fax : 011-41563334
E-mail: info@essessreference.com
www.essessreference.com

Academic Library System
Second Edition

ISBN: 978-81-7000-583-4

Rs.900/-

First Indian Imprint 2009

Published by:
Ess Ess Publications
4837/24, Ansari Road,
Darya Ganj,
New Delhi-110 002.
INDIA
Phones: 23260807, 41563444
Fax: 41563334
E-mail: info@essessreference.com
www.essessreference.com

Printed and bound in India at Salasar Imaging Systems.

To

VIPULSHRI

my daughter

with love and affection

FOREWORD (FIRST EDITION)

One of the most valuable pieces of advice I ever received was from Dr Zakir Husain in the days when I was working as an educational administrator. As part of my work, I was expected to inspect colleges. As it happened, I never inspected any college as the routine prescribed, though I spent a lot of my time in the colleges. It was while I was telling him what I used to do or failed to do in this regard, that the eminent educationist told me, "If you are in a hurry, or impatient, and want to make a quick assessment of the quality of a college, walk into the library. Also, flip through the pages of the latest issue of the college magazine." I followed this advice, and passed it on to many others who were also involved in educational administration in one form or another. My experience has been that the state of the library invariably indicated the kind of institution that housed and ran it.

The regular user of a library does not have to be told of the thrill one experiences as one walks into a well-organized library, and conversely, of the depression that would fill one's mind while moving through a badly run library. These contrasts do not come about by accident. A good library takes shape through the learning, care and dedication of many. Most of the time, the clientele have no idea of the hard work that has gone into the apparently effortless streamlining of procedure. To ensure that every reader finds the book he wants to read, and that every book finds the reader who would enjoy and profit by it, is a facile slogan. To achieve this end, calls for the untiring labour of the library staff. Their own reward is the gratitude of the readers and the proud awareness of the contribution they are making to the high tasks of the transmission of culture, the extension of the frontiers of knowledge, the deepening and refining of sensibility and the correction of taste.

Dr Sahai's book is the outcome of his years of experience in academic libraries, and deep and extensive study of professional literature. While he deals with diverse aspects of the organization and running of libraries, he avoids the error into which far too many of his colleagues in the profession fall, of looking upon the library staff as a band of technicians and even technologists. The vanity of calling the management of libraries 'library science' could be condoned if it does not prevent recognition of the vital fact that it is principally an art.

That librarianship is an art should be evident to anyone who reflects on how one library differs from another. The adoption of common classification systems and other techniques of organization might suggest that every library is expected to be like every other library. But a keen user of libraries knows that every well-run library develops an individuality of its own. It will be a great service to the academic community if knowledgeable users of libraries could be induced to write profiles of their favourite libraries and make them available to the reading public. Dr Sahai's book contains plentiful suggestions as to what to look for, when one wants to attempt such a profile.

Is a love of books and of learning an adequate qualification for a librarian? Dr Sahai has thoughtful things to say about the adequacy or otherwise of learning in any academic field to fill the role of a good librarian. While it may not be wise to take any rigid positions in the matter, the case for rigorous professional training should always be kept in mind in any ambitious plans for setting up a network of academic libraries.

Jodhpur **V. V. John**
1990

Preface (First Edition)

Universities are the chief producers of high-level manpower. In a developing country like ours, a university has the primary role of producing and developing competent human resources for use at various levels of Government and non-Government functioning, and in the private and public sectors. To fulfil this obligation effectively, universities need to provide members of the academic community with easy and direct access to recorded knowledge, accumulated and conserved by libraries through years of acquired experience. The library is the most appropriate agency in an academic institution to collect, organize and disseminate such knowledge for use. In library, books are not only collected but conceived and comprehended as well—here, books become modules and integrated circuits, helping academic community at the university to interpret and advance knowledge and skill.

Further, in the post-independence era, there has been accelerated expansion of education in India. Number of schools, colleges, universities and institutes of higher learning has immensely increased. Recently, there has been rethinking and some shift in our education policy and planning to meet the countrys' emerging socio-economic challenges. This suggests renewed slant on library-oriented education with less emphasis on classroom lectures.

It could be possible, only when there is well-equipped modern functional library at the campus. But, present academic library system in India is deficient on many counts to become adequately modern and functional. We still lack in defining the university and library objectives properly and clearly and this creates varied problems of organization, administration and financial support to the library.

There has been no full-length text discussing the academic library system. Even the few books available, they are written for the librarians alone. This one is different in being addressed to, besides librarians, the university and government administrators and faculty members as well to enhance their understanding, interest and support so essential for the development of college and university libraries in India. As such, it is an attempt to meet the long-felt need of a comprehensive text-book on the subject at the graduate, postgraduate and research levels, besides being useful to the practicing librarians, their staff and to the policy makers and administrators in education in India and abroad.

I am profoundly grateful to the authors and publishers of the works I have consulted and cited in the text.

Jodhpur
1990

S. N. Sahai

PREFACE (SECOND EDITION)

Present is the second edition of the book Academic Library System. When issued from the press first in 1990, this text was well received by the library teachers, students, professionals, as well as the educationists. (Acceptance to add Foreword to this book by the educationist of Professor VV John's eminence speaks for the academic merit of this book) Soon the book went out of print, and has remained so until now, but still looked for and demanded. As such, in the fitness, it seems worthwhile to reissue this book to meet the professional needs and requirements.

In the present era of knowledge-explosion, technological development and social change, higher education is experiencing radical shift, both in intellectual content and the manner and mode of its delivery, communication and exposition. Students are in the midst of drastic pedagogical diversions; placing upon them heightened responsibility for their educational progress and achievement, on their own. Number of students is huge, and many of them are found more natured and motivated to equip themselves better than their predecessors. Necessarily, therefore, they bank upon the library much more than before.

Library is a 'memory of civilization'. Its repository showing, accompanied with reinforced task of constant updating the stock and resources, render this institution indispensable in the academic set up and learning; and that any neglect on this account is at the expense of education itself.

This book is addressed to, besides libraries and library faculties, to the educationists and education-planners as well, engaged in formulating and designing maps of education — since the library is a basic, cardinal component, constituent of the education, be it general, specific or specialized. It plays infinite role in successful functioning and fulfilment of the seat of learning; as also its neglect could be amiss, hugely. Therefore, a well-knit library needs to be well-placed and well-fed in the scheme of things. The present book will help share the endeavour in this regard, it is believed.

I am thankful to M/s Ess Ess Publications, New Delhi, for their undertaking publication of this edition. M/s Ess Ess Publications are a leader today in giving light to library literature and by placing this book in their hands, I feel extra delight.

Lucknow **S.N. Sahai**
Independence Day
(2009)

CONTENTS

1

LIBRARY IN ACADEMIC SYSTEM

Library occupies an important place in the framework of the academic system. It is not a mere storehouse of books, but is a dynamic instrument of education. Without active support of a library, the whole academic functioning will come to a grinding halt. The primary role of a library is not only to fulfil the "mission" of the academic institution to which it belongs to but also to advance its aims and objectives. It is a central place for study and research. To this end, the total functioning of the library has been geared. Catalogues and bibliographies are now compiled, classification system has been devised, and circulation work has been planned and designed. Library is fully computerized and connected with internet. Stressing the role library plays in a university, the University Grants Committee (UK) in its report of 1921 mentions :

> "the character and efficiency of a university may be gauged by treatment of its central organ—the library. We regard the fullest provision for library maintenance as the primary and most vital need in the equipment of a university." (Parry: 1968: 9).

For research work, a library is as much essential especially in the field of humanities and social sciences as the laboratory occupies in the experimental sciences. The functions of a library are:

(i) conservation of knowledge and information;

(ii) expansion of ideas and dissemination of knowledge with the help of interpretation, research and publications; and

(iii) dissemination of knowledge through teaching and extension services.

The primary objective of the library in the academic system is to function in such a manner as to achieve these aims.

The academic libraries include school, college, university and research libraries. All these cater to the needs of the academic community for supplementing the study and research programmes of the institution and help conserve and disseminate knowledge. Although these academic libraries share certain common features and characteristics, they differ enormously in the value and content from one another.

Universal Education

One of the aims of the Indian Constitution is that every citizen of the Union has the right to receive free and compulsory education up to the age of 14. The objective of this provision is that, for proper functioning of a democracy, every individual should be equipped with knowledge, skill and aptitude to discharge his duties as a responsible citizen of the country.

Knowledge is acquired through education. Formal education begins in school, which tries to develop the intellectual faculty of a child and transforms him into a good citizen. The Secondary Education Commission states that

> "the aim of secondary education is to train the youth of the country to be good citizens who will be competent to play their part effectively in the social reconstruction and economic development of their country" (India—Ministry of Education : 1952-53 : 5-6).

The role of secondary education in the socio-economic as well as cultural development of the nation is well recognized. It has been accepted as a programme which develops a child's skill and ability to face the day to day problems of life with ease and plan his work effectively and methodically. All this requires extensive reading of not only the prescribed text books but also other supplementary books, periodicals, pamphlets, maps, charts, newspapers, etc. The audio-visual programmes also help in acquiring knowledge and information. This exercise demands libraries to provide a variety of reading material in the form of general and reference books, besides textbooks. Here, the library becomes indispensable as a repository of such knowledge and helps in providing intelligent and effective service to pupils.

School Library

It is of utmost importance that today's boys and girls, who are the future citizens of the country, are helped to blossom out and meet the needs and the challenges of the country effectively. This is possible only if they receive a sound education, which in turn depends on the existence of a good school library. This fact has since been recognized universally.

Aims : The aims of a school library are linked with those of secondary education. The literary, artistic and cultural faculties of students have to be aroused for the full development of their personality and for the enrichment of the national culture as a whole; they have to be provided with practical and vocational guidance to harness their energy and improve their efficiency for contributing towards the national economy; they have to be trained to become economically self-supporting and independent and finally they have to be enjoined to actively participate in the development of the nation and bring about a new social order. To achieve these aims, the mind and body of the school students have to be properly developed.

Functions : A school library is not a substitute for formal education. It is a complement to it, rather it is an integral part of the school. The stock of the library consists of, in addition to textbooks, biographies of eminent men and women, works by intellectuals, reference books like encyclopaedia, dictionaries, atlas, maps and charts, magazines, journals, pamphlets, clippings, pictures and other up-dated information media.

The objective of maintaining such materials is to stimulate the intellectual curiosity and capacity of the pupil and reduce his dependence on textbooks alone. The standard of general reading and the level of intellectual curiosity are generally found to be low at the secondary school level and have to be raised by additional reading material. This is the real job of a school library.

The main functions of the library are:

(i) to acquire and display books and periodicals to meet the varying needs, demands and interests of school students;

(ii) to encourage reading habit amongst boys and girls;

(iii) to provides reading and audiovisual material to supplement the classroom work;

(iv) to provide them an opportunity for life-long and functional education; and

(v) to train them in the art of selecting the needed material and information in the library and thus make effective use of books and other resource materials. School children are of an impressionable age and their inclinations and habits can be moulded to create in them a life-long liking forbooks and a curiosity to learn more about things through reading. The school library is the proper place for this and has a fundamental role to play in this context.

The School Library System

There are three forms of school libraries, viz.;

(i) School Central Library;

(ii) Class Libraries; and

(iii) Subject Libraries.

A particular school library can assume any of these three forms.

School Central Library : It is a library which caters to the needs and requirements of the school as a whole. It functions under the charge of a whole-time qualified librarian. The facility of this library is made available to all the students and staff members of the school. It remains open all through the working hours of the school.

Under the modern trend of development of knowledge, when the subjects are crossing their traditional barriers, overlapping the boundaries of allied subjects, the centralized system of school libraries is more useful. There are many related and correlated and closely linked subjects such as History and Political Science, Geology and Geography, Mathematics and Statistics. If books relating to all these subjects are housed in one library at a central place in the school, the students will be able to derive maximum advantage of the study of the overlapping subjects and thereby widen their horizon of knowledge and understanding in a proper perspective. Scott mentions:

> "such a library, comprehensive in range, displays the range and extent of human experience and endeavour in a way impossible where the collection is dispersed." (Scott :1947 : 12)
>
> "dispersal of books results in intellectual segregation rather than cooperative development." (Viswanathan : 1957 : 11).

This enables us to conclude that arrangement of a school central library is a more practical way and would benefit the school children enormously.

At times, due to acute shortage of space to house the central library in the school building itself, the class libraries or subject libraries have come into use now a days in certain places.

Class Libraries : These are small libraries meant for the individual classes in the school. These libraries posses 50 to 100 books at a time and meant exclusively for use by class students. These books are specially selected for a particular age-group and is located in the class-room itself under the charge of the class teacher. The selection of books for class libraries is done selectively in such a manner that it would supplement the text books. This type of library is more useful for the elementary and junior class boys. For higher classes, this proves too small and limited for use of the subject coverage. The students do not have much choice of books for coverage of the individual subjects exclusively across their subject-border. As such, the variety of reading material that the children require is extremely limited and sometimes even missing in class libraries. If the collection of books is not renewed often, it becomes stereotyped and outmoded for children's requirements, who need newer titles to become up-to-date. It loses its value and the children's interest toward books get limited. Thus, such a library proves ineffective for imbibing the reading habit amongst children which is so necessary at this stage of their development. It is, therefore, necessary that the stock of the class library is frequently renewed by suitable newer titles so that it works as an attractive medium for students and becomes a reading centre.

Subject Libraries : It is a collection which pertains to the individual subjects like History, Geography, Physics, Chemistry and Mathematics. It is located in the respective subject rooms under the charge of the subject teacher. This library caters exclusively to the need and interest of a particular subject. The subject-books are revised and changed often. This is especially so in the case of science subjects where results of new researches are to be brought to the notice of students. To provide up-to-date knowledge on the subject, the stock of these libraries should be constantly replaced and supplemented with new standard titles. This would mean additional financial burden for maintaining such a library up-to-date. Lack of funds would cripple the subject libraries and make them static.

A well-stocked and organized central library for the school is quite important and, in fact, it is a necessity. Its efficient functioning is essential for the students. The other two types of libraries, viz., class and subject libraries may function as branches of the school central library and not as independent units.

Historical Perspective

Prior to 1947, provision of a library in every school in India was never considered essential. In 1942, Dr S.R. Ranganathan had advanced the philosophy of school library in his, book. School and College Libraries'. The first attempt on the educational planning in this country was made by the Sarget Report on Post-war Educational Development in India. But in this report there was no mention of the school libraries. For the first time, the Secondary Education Commission (1952-53), appointed by the Government of India, with Dr A. Lakshmanaswami Mudaliar as its chairman drew the attention of the Government and the country to the sad plight of school libraries in the country. The report highlighted the fact that in most schools, no libraries functioned worth the name. The collections of books in these schools were generally old, outmoded and unsuitable for the needs and interests of the school students. The collections were arranged in shelves and kept at a remote place in the school and attracted only a few students. The person under whose care the library was left was often not a professional. Very often the library was left to be managed by a disgruntled staff or teacher who worked on part-time basis. Thus a well-organized and efficient library service in the school was missing. Neither there was any planning nor imagination to inspire and stimulate children to reading book and cultivate the habit of love of books. This fact had still not been realized by the teachers and the educationists leading to further deterioration and lack of a useful service. To remedy the situation, the Commission recommended the following steps:

1. Physical Setting : The place of the library should be made quite attractive. It should be housed in a spacious, well-it hall (or room) with the walls suitably coloured and decorated with flowers, artistically framed pictures and famous paintings to present an inviting look so that the students could be drawn to it naturally. The furniture and equipments should be carefully designed. Free entrance to the library (without charge or subscription) as well as the open-shelf system should be provided to encourage students to make full use of the library service.

2. Rich Collection : Adequate care should be taken to equip the library with properly selected books, journals and periodicals. The guiding principle in selection of books should be not the teacher's own idea of what books the students must read but their students natural and psychological interests. If the student feel, "more interested, at particular age, to stories of adventure, travel, biographies or even detection and crime, there is no justification for forcing them to read poetry, classics or belles-letters. Of course, the teacher's kill and teaching efficiency will consist in being able to direct what they are reading now towards what they should be reading in due course. Literary education postulates the gradual elevation of taste and the refining of appreciation but the teacher's tact will lie in not forcing them but in unobtrusively guiding them on the way. In this endeavour, his own example and contagious enthusiasm can prove very potent allies." (India—Report of the Secondary Education Commission 1952-53 : 111).

3. Efficient Service : The next important factor is the efficient service. Unfortunately in most of the schools this factor is overlooked. To achieve the concept of providing an efficient library service, the first requirement is the provision of a highly qualified and trained librarian who should be "on a par with other senior teachers in pay and status" (*Ibid*: 111). Putting emphasis on this point, the Commission said further, "we definitely recommend that there should be, in every secondary school, a full-time librarian of this type. If his function is merely to maintain a register of books, keep the library open at odd hours and occasionally issue books to a few students, there should obviously be no need for a full-time and highly qualified librarian. But if the library is to be the hub of the academic and intellectual life of the school, if it is not only to meet but guide the reading interests of students, if it is to work as a centre of free and supervised study as well as group-work on projects undertaken by them—if it is to do all these things—the librarian will surely have all his work cut out" (*Ibid* : 112). The Commission also recommended for training of some teachers in the management of school libraries as part of their training course. These partially trained teacher-librarians will, working in co-operation with the professional librarian, gradually build up the central library and organize the library service, while working for the class libraries. The class libraries, the Commission mentioned, is an important and essential adjunct to the central school library and will prove useful to create the right type of reading habits and advance various other educational programmes.

4. Subject Libraries : The Commission also recommended creation of subject libraries under the charge of subject teachers. This would help enrich the teaching of subjects immensely with the help of a small collection of books on the individual subjects of their own. The collection should not be confined to textbooks alone. Advanced works, reference books, books on related and allied subjects, all should find a place in this collection so that the students handling them and browsing over them could get a wider perspective of the subject in all its bearings. The headmaster and the teachers both should make themselves concerned with the students' general reading habit and give them personal guidance in the selection of the right type of reading material. Record of the books read should be maintained and necessary guidance and encouragement given to each student individually for improvement and intellectual development.

The Commission said that in states where a library cess was levied, the proceeds should also be utilized to strengthen and improve school libraries. In the smaller cities and towns, it might be more economical to build the school library in a way that it also served the general function of a Public Library for the locality and thus avoid the duplication of expenses on buildings, furniture and the staff. Further the Commission observed that to overcome the acute paucity of books for children in general and adults in particular, especially in the Indian languages, the Centre and the State Governments should take well thought-out measures to encourage the production of suitable books. The books should not only be rich in content but also attractive in printing, binding and illustration. To this end, the organizations engaged in book production should be accorded financial assistance including the award of prizes to the best published works and also arrange for translations of good children's books available in English or published in various regional languages. The Commission believed that if school libraries were better financed to buy large number of books, the habit of reading could be developed in students initially and in adults eventually. With the increase in the purchase of books, better quality books would become available and would begin to be published.

In short, the Commission recommended:

(i) every secondary school should have a well-equipped school library backed by class and subject libraries. This was essential for the efficient working of every educational institution and for encouraging literary and cultural interests in students;

(ii) trained librarians possessing love for books and understanding of students' interests should be appointed in all secondary schools and all the teachers (of secondary schools) be given some training in the basic principles of library maintenance in the training colleges as well as through refresher courses;

(iii) where there were no separate Public Libraries, the school libraries should, possibly, make their facilities available to the local public and all Public Libraries should have a special section for children and adolescents; and

(iv) to improve general standards of work in school, necessary steps should be taken to produce textbooks as well as books of general reading of distinctly superior quality than those at present available.

Production of Text-Books

The Commission had also stressed the need to make available standard text-books for the libraries. To ensure publication of standard text-books of quality, the Commission made the following recommendations (India—Report of Secondary Education : 1952-53 : 233):

(i) A high power Text-Book Committee should be constituted consisting of a high dignitary from the judiciary of the State, preferably a Judge of the High Court, a Member of the Public Service Commission of the region concerned, Vice-Chancellor of a university in the region, Headmaster or Headmistress of a recognised school in the State, two distinguished Educationists and the Director of Education. The Committee should function as an independent body.

(ii) A fund should be maintained from the amount realized from the sale of publications which might be utilized for awarding scholarships and providing books and certain other amenities for school children.

(iii) The Text-Book Committee should lay down clear criteria for the type of paper, illustration, printing and format of the book.

(iv) The Central Government should set up a new institution or help some existing Arts school to develop training in the techniques of book illustration.

(v) The Central and State Governments should maintain libraries of blocks of good illustrations which could be loaned to Text-Book Committees and publishers in order to improve the standard of book illustration.

(vi) Single text-books should not be prescribed for each and every subject of study, but a reasonable number of books which satisfy the standards laid down should be recommended, leaving the choice to the schools concerned. In case of languages, however, definite textbooks should be prescribed for each class to ensure proper gradation.

(vii) Frequent changes in textbooks and books prescribed for study should be discouraged.

During the First Five-Year Plan, no allocation was made for the improvement of school libraries. Consequently no development took place during this period. The school libraries during this period were either non-existent or were mostly stocking old outdated and outmoded editions of books. They were managed by either non-professionals or by some frustrated teacher of the school. The professional expertise of a librarian was missing. Service of the library was poor. Books were also issued sparingly to avoid possible loss.

The Second Five-Year Plan also did not envisage any substantial improvement in school education. However, secondary school libraries increased. Funds were made available for purchase of books and library equipment. During the Third Five-Year Plan, primary education received better priority. Improvement in school libraries was proposed. In 1964-65, the Government of India chalked out a nation-wide plan for the improvement and strengthening of the school libraries in the secondary institutions. Central assistance was provided to various states for organizing training courses for the personnel in school libraries; appointment of librarians in schools and provision of stationery and other materials necessary for the school libraries. Dr. V.K.R.V. Rao said in his

Presidential Address at the 15th All-India Library Conference at Mysore (1965) that the position of libraries was much worse in the case of secondary schools in the country. Many high school libraries were having only four or five cupboards and there were hardly any journals available in these libraries. Thus, development of school libraries was not taken as an integral part of the school expansion programme.

The Education Commission (1966) suggested the method of 'circulation library' under the proposed system of a school complex. It also wanted the linking of the scale of pay of the librarians to that of teachers. The report also wanted proper upkeep and maintenance of the library and provision of spacious accommodation and adequate seats for proper reading. For teachers, provision of separate reading-desks in the library was envisaged. The Fourth Five-Year Plan envisaged creation of additional facility in the library for about a lakh of teachers and nearly 4 million students by the year 1973-74. The plan also provided for improving the quality of secondary education which naturally implied better and extended provisions for the school libraries. The secondary education aimed at developing the overall personality of the students, improving their vocational capability and widening their horizon of knowledge, skill and the overall capabilities to undertake independent work at the university level. To achieve these aims, provision of well-equipped libraries with a variety of reading materials was considered essential. This was all the more necessary in a country where the public library system was not properly developed. So, it was considered essential that a proper school library system was initiated. Further, with the increasing cost of books, common people found it difficult to purchase the much needed books either for themselves or for their children. This necessitated the provision of school libraries.

Modern education demands not merely a thorough reading of a single textbook but also the overall understanding of all the recent publications of merit relevant to it, both Indian and foreign, and also a wide variety of other reference materials. To meet this need, institution of a library in the school becomes quite essential. For this purpose, 10 per cent of the total expenditure on secondary education was to be allocated for proper development of school libraries. At least 50 per cent of the matching grant for the development of school libraries should be provided by the Central Government. In the Directorate of Education in the States, a library wing was to be set up to look after the development and organization of school libraries. Every school library should have its own building. It should function under a professionally trained librarian whose pay-scale should be at par with a trained graduate teacher. He should also be provided with adequate supporting staff.

The Indian Library Association organized a seminar in 1966 on the development of libraries and made the following recommendations:

(i) the Union Government, State Governments and the University Grants Commission should strengthen the facility for training school librarians;

(ii) a qualified librarian should be provided on a full-time basis by the education department;

(iii) for school children, attractive, inspiring and educative literature should be produced by encouraging the writers and publishers; and

(iv) to supervise and guide the school libraries, School Library Bureaux should be set up by the State Education Department.

Another seminar, held on November 19, 1973 regarding the optimum use of school libraries, recommended that the Indian Library Association should constitute a committee to determine school library standards for accommodation, furniture and equipment; the libraries should be equipped with books, periodicals, graphs, charts, photographs, slides, filmstrips, newspapers and paper clippings; each secondary school library should have a trained librarian with pay, status and promotional avenues equivalent to those of a teacher; the school library should remain open for extended hours—at least for two hours beyond the working hours of the school; the funds for purchase of books and magazines and the binding work should form part of the school budget; a book-selection committee should be constituted in every school with the Principal as the Chairman, any three teachers as members and the librarian as member-secretary. The Bureau of School Libraries should be headed by a qualified librarian with the rank and status of a Joint Director or at least a Deputy Director. The functions of the Bureau should be:

(i) to administer Government funds allocated for the libraries;

(ii) to circulate the approved titles amongst the libraries;

(iii) to deal with appointment, transfer and promotions of librarians; and

(iv) to determine the Job description of library staff. The seminar further recommended that an advisory committee should be constituted to advise the Director of Education on matters of libraries. Facilities should be available to the librarians for improving their academic and professional standards and refresher courses should be organized for the working librarians.

The development of school libraries in this country has not been quite satisfactory. The condition is apallingly poor. The authorities of school are not conscious of the proper role of school libraries. Therefore, the library service in the schools has remained very poor. It is high time that the authorities in the Government, especially the education department, should pay adequate attention to improve the conditions of school libraries in India.

College Library

College Education

As an institution of higher studies, the college imparts post-Secondary/Higher Secondary education. It offers a four-year course after Secondary (School) Examination and a three-year course after Higher Secondary Examination, both leading to Bachelor's Degree in India. Certain other colleges also impart post-graduate education leading to a Master's Degree. In India, there is a system of instituting affiliated colleges, besides the university college. The number of colleges in the country was estimated 4,886 during 1981-82. There has been an increase of 511 colleges between 1977-78 and 1981-82. These colleges play a vital role in the university education system. A bulk of the student population hare, especially at the first degree level, is actually enrolled in the colleges and thus the colleges cater to the needs of 87.9 per cent of the total enrolment of students at the undergraduate level, 55.3 per cent at the post-graduate level and 15.1 per cent at the research level. Also, there is a fair proportion of teachers working in the colleges. During 1981-82, it was found that teachers employed in the colleges constituted as many as 78.9 per cent of the total number of teachers in the universities and colleges in India. During the Sixth Plan period, therefore, the UGC formulated a policy for development of undergraduate and post-graduate education in the colleges, with a view to improving the standard and quality of higher education. This improvement, in fact, largely depended upon the adequacy of college libraries.

Objectives : Being the most important adjunct of the college, the library aims at the realization of the objectives and programmes of the college. It strives to transform itself into a working force for generating curiosity and eagerness among the readers and thus help them make use of the available reading material. The objective of the college library is to supplement the instructions imparted in the class. It aims to serve not only the undergraduate teaching but to function as an independent teaching agency, encouraging and promoting the use of books in ways beyond those suggested or required by the class room.

Functions : To fulfil its objectives, the college library functions basically to assist and support the study and teaching in the college. It helps to meet the reading needs and requirements of the students as well as the teachers of the college in pursuit of their knowledge. Occasionally, research is also conducted in the college, mostly by teachers. The college library provides the needed reading materials and documents for research as well. The difference in the functioning of a college and a university library however, is that while the former lays emphasis on the acquisition and dissemination of knowledge at the undergraduate and post-graduate levels, the latter also caters, besides the overall needs, the needs of research work and helps students and scholars to this end. W.M. Randall and F.L. Goodrich state that to meet the educational objectives of the college, its library performs the following functions (Randall : 1936 : 19):

(a) makes available to the students books and allied reading material relevant to the courses offered in the college;

(b) makes available the books and documents required by faculty members in preparation of their instructional courses;

(c) provides supplementary books and reading material to help study and teaching at the college;

(d) provides comprehensive selection of authoritative books and documents needed by the faculty members to pursue their research programmes;

(e) promotes the proper use of the reading material available in the stock; and

(f) trains the students in making use of the library properly and derive full advantage out of it, integrating the library with the educational courses.

D.L. Smith and E.O. Baxter have also enumerated the functions of college libraries in similar terms as under: (Smith: 1965 : 9):

(i) to acquire and provide text and standard reference books to the students, necessary for preparation of their examinations;

(ii) to train college students in the use of the library material and to encourage them to enrich their knowledge and outlook in a wider perspective through general and wider readings;

(iii) to help and assist the faculty members of the college in preparation of their instructional courses and in keeping them abreast of the current knowledge and concepts in different areas of study; and

(iv) to assist the teaching staff in the pursuit of higher studies and research and support them with relevant literature and information on the subject.

Historical Perspective: In the early 19th century, the college education became prevalent in India with the help of missionaries who set up schools and colleges in the country.

The college libraries came up along with these as their adjunct. In the beginning, however, the college libraries, attached to these institutions, were only keeping collections of certain stray books, which were not systematically arranged. There was also no systematic collection of these books. The books were just stacked in a few almirahs lying scattered in the college premises. They had been put under the charge of a teacher who worked more as a custodian of books than a librarian. No one knew what books and magazines were available. The collection was not put to proper use either by the students or even by the teachers. The availability of books to the students for reading purposes just depended on the mercy of teachers who controlled the collection. The circulation of books was restricted and highly controlled.

Certain colleges had good and useful collection of books but there was no provision or arrangement for their proper maintenance and upkeep. There was no catalogue for the library books nor was the collection kept in a proper sequence or subject-order.

Gradually, the idea dawned upon the authorities to systematize the books at one place in the college premises, under the exclusive charge of a low-paid employee of the college called book-attendant. Only a few of the colleges had good libraries. Even the best one available in the country at the Presidency College (Calcutta) was quite defective in many ways. There were a few good and old collections of interest at the Scottish Church College, Serampore College, Krishnagar College and Hooghly College but in general they were not up-to-date. Only a few used them. The libraries were inadequate to the needs of students and still less to those of teachers.

With the passage of time, the socio-economic and political factors made their impact on the society and this changed the very purpose and objective of higher education in the country. This had the impact on the objective and functioning of the libraries attached to the colleges, as well. Earlier the students of colleges, which lacked the facility of a lounge to spend their leisure hours, used the library as a rest room or a meeting place. During the 20th century, the concept of college library has changed considerably. Emphasis was laid on the educative aspect of the library, treating it to be a fountain of knowledge and information.

In 1882, the Government of India appointed the Indian Education Commission (Hunter Commission) to find out the effect of the Despatch of 1854 and to explore the measures to improve it further. The commission gathered data from 75 colleges which existed at that time and put forth certain measures to improve the working and functioning of those colleges, including their libraries and laboratories. Again in 1902, the Government of India appointed another University

Commission to investigate the functioning of the universities, set up under the British rule and suggest measures for necessary changes in their constituents to ensure improvement and progress in their working and "to promote the advancement of learning". Laying emphasis on the provision of an adequately equipped college library, the commission noted that in a college where the library is illequipped and disorganized, the students are deprived of the opportunity to cultivate independent and intelligent reading habits.

In 1916, a Commission of Enquiry was appointed by the Government of India to investigate the problems of the University of Calcutta. This enquiry was a very broad-based one and college education as well was included in its purview. The commission mentioned that in a poor country like India, libraries should not be made unnecessarily costly. An ordinary college library should not, like an Imperial Library, aim at having the maximum number of books on a subject, good, bad and indifferent, but should be content with having only the best of books. The report indicated that the commission viewed the college library with a limited scope. Then came the Radhakrishnan Commission (University Education Commission) which gave a strong fillip to the development of the college libraries (as well as other academic libraries) in India. While keeping a note of the inadequacy of the book-stock of the college libraries in the country, the commission strongly recommended that the college libraries should be well-stocked, and well-organized with trained staff posted to manage them. For this purpose the annual grant to the college libraries should be increased and fixed at 6.25 per cent of the total budget of the college (or Rs 40 per student) with special provision for non-recurring grants, once in five years, to cope up with the expenditure on arrears of books needed in the libraries. The commission further recommended that the libraries should function for 12 hours and be kept open on all days; open-shelf system should be introduced to enable undergraduate students to select books at their free will, and to go from one stock to another and browse the books in their free time.

A highly significant landmark in the development of the college libraries in India was the appointment of a UGC Library Committee in 1957 under the Chairmanship of Dr. S.R. Ranganathan to help develop libraries, their organization and management in the colleges and universities of the country. Some of the important recommendations of the committee were as follows (UGC : 1965 : 141-50) :

1. The entire finance for the library of a college should be provided by the Commission and concerned State Government together. The Commission and State Government should decide from time to time the proportion in which their respective grants to a college library should be determined. The Commission should not ordinarily withdraw or reduce the grant to a college library even if the State Government fails to provide the corresponding matching grant.
2. The college library fund should be maintained and operated in a separate library account.
3. The college authorities should provide a panel of experts on different subjects to help librarians make final selection of books and other reading materials.
4. Measures should be taken to promote reading habit among students. Reference librarians should be appointed to help the students with sympathy and understanding in selection of the reading materials.
5. Each college should encourage the formation of a bookshop within its campus through co-operative efforts or in any other manner.
6. The books having no permanent value may be weeded out once in five years.
7. Books worn out by use beyond repairs may be weeded out once a year.

8. The professional staff of a college library should be appointed in the following grades:
   (a) In a large college with an annual book grant of not less than Rs. 20,000, the scale of pay for the librarian should be in grade 2 (Readers' scale) with qualifications appropriate to it.
   (b) In a small college with an annual book grant of less than Rs. 20,000 the pay-scale for the librarian should be in the grade 3 (Lecturers' scale) with the qualifications appropriate to it.
   (c) The other staff in a college library should be in the grades 3, 4 and 5 (Lecturers' and Assistant Lecturers') or grades 4 and 5 as the case may be.
   (d) A person already in service in a college library without possessing the prescribed qualifications for the post, may be placed in the grade just below the one recommended for the post to which he is assigned. As and when the person leaves the service, his post should be brought in conformity with the qualifications and the scales prescribed for it.
9. The standards prescribed for the library buildings, fittings and furniture by the Indian Standards Institution should be followed by all the college libraries.
10. Any proposal for a new library building, fittings and furniture or the extension of the building should be examined and approved by an expert appointed by the UGC.

Another Education Commission (Kothari Commission) was appointed by the Government of India in July 1964, which laid emphasis on the academic libraries. This commission recommended that no new college should be opened without adequate provision for its library in terms of building, furniture, staff and books and journals. It also said that the foreign exchange required by the college libraries should be provided separately by the UGC. Further, provision should be made in the libraries to extend reference service to the undergraduate students.

During the plan periods, the college libraries have made significant progress. They have received comparatively more funds to meet their expenditure on books, journals and staff and building. However, it still needs much augmentation; especially in case of libraries of privately-owned colleges.

Organization

1. Building and Furniture : The building of the college library should be functionally equipped with provisions for proper lighting, ventilation and other accessories including comfortable furniture to give an inviting look and make the library atmosphere pleasant for reading purposes. Best library service can be provided only when the library building is of the latest design and plan. The building should also have additional space for students and faculty members who intend to work in groups with the new media of communication. Many modern library buildings today possess a small lecture hall and an auditorium. They are also provided with studios and theatres for exhibition of films and also adequate space for working on photo-electric communication equipment for organising exhibition of educational television and halls for exhibition and display of a wide variety of books.

2. Book-Stock : The collection of books in a college library should be adequately complete and up-to-date to meet the curricula needs of the college. Besides, the library should have rich non-textbooks and recreational material to create a wider reading interest in the students. Journals, proceedings of meetings and other transactions are the principal means of inter-communication of knowledge and ideas. Further, a strong reference collection is also essential for the college library. The size and content of the collection of the college library should be as large as it can meet the educational objectives of the respective college.

Kinds of Collection: College library should stock the following reading materials:

(i) recommended texts;

(ii) required reading material like the reserved books;

(iii) periodicals and serials needed for the curricula;

(iv) reading texts and other materials required for special studies and for doing home-work;

(v) materials for cultural, recreational and general reading which may not necessarily be related to the curricula but the titles considered desirable in content and in quality of presentation for college students;

(vi) materials needed by faculty members; the scope of which varies from college to college and it is difficult to define its area. Each college library should supply its faculty members some material needed for higher education;

(vii) materials to support the special curricula being pursued at the college; and

(viii) materials relevant to the local needs of the college-community. The factors which influence the choice or acquisition of reading materials in a college library are:

  (a) the field of operation of the college library is, in fact, wider than that of the curricula of the college;

  (b) the college curricula do not strictly limit the library's area of responsibility; and

  (c) the library has an obligation not only to meet the local needs but also has to contribute to the cultural resources even on regional, national and international levels.

Scope of Collection : The scope of collection of books in a college library is certainly limited as compared to that of the university or research libraries, whose primary function is to preserve knowledge, no matter how ephemeral the interpretation or how ancient the enquiry is, 'College libraries tend to be less various and more scholarly.' The following reading material is beyond the scope of a college library:

(a) rare and expensive books of research studies;

(b) major reference books, which are highly priced;

(c) complete sets and files of academic and scholarly journals;

(d) Government publications;

(e) college and university catalogues and bibliographies; and

(f) dissertations and theses. The college library should lay emphasis on acquiring such books as the college students need and as are essential for their intellectual development.

The collection of books in a college library should be systematically arranged. The college librarian, being a professionally trained person, should bear the responsibility to acquire, classify and catalogue the books, besides undertaking the work of reference and circulation. Dewey Decimal Classification Scheme is more popular with college libraries in India. The special college libraries, however, adopt Universal Decimal Classification Scheme. With regard to cataloguing, college libraries in India adopt mostly Anglo-American Cataloguing Rules. The libraries which adopt Colon Classification Scheme for classification of books, follow the Classified Catalogue Code by Dr. S.R. Ranganathan for cataloguing books.

Staff : The efficient functioning of the library is largely dependent upon the adequacy of the staff. It is desirable to keep the college library open for at least 12 hours a day and for this the basic minimum staff, consisting of one librarian, two assistant librarians, two semi-professionals and two book attendants should be provided. With limited staff, it will not be possible for the library to provide full-time service.

The librarian in a college is more a teacher as compared to the university librarian whose concern is more related to administration, organization and bibliography. He should have scholarly interest and understanding, including interest in education at the undergraduate level. He should also have the ability to move with the students and cooperate and work with faculty staff.

Finance : Finance is extremely essential for the functioning of a college library. It should be linked to the financial position of the college. The library should have a fair share from the budget allotted to the college.

Service : The college library should render the following services to the students and teachers of the college:

(i) Orientation of the Undergraduate Students

The freshers in the college come after completing their Higher Secondary or Secondary (School) Examinations. Majority of the students are not aware of the utility of the library and they do not know how to use the library effectively. Library orientation of such students is very necessary so that they learn to use the library properly.

(ii) Readers' Advisory Service

Sometimes students in the college face difficulty in consulting the library catalogue, locating the exact document required by them or consulting the relevant reference tools available in the library. To this end, students need the help and guidance of the library staff, who should readily help them to find the necessary material through the reference service.

(iii) Circulation Work

Most of the students and teachers visit the college library to select and get the books issued or to return the earlier receipted material. This is a major work that is done by the college library. The college library should ensure that the readers' time is not wasted on this work. Sometimes a reader in a college library, because of the non-availability of a certain document for issue in the library, wants to reserve it in his name for subsequent issue as and when the required document is returned to the library. Such a system of reservation of document helps the genuine readers and regulates the circulation work in the library. College libraries should provide this service to readers.

(iv) Bibliographic Service

The new additions to the library should immediately be brought to the knowledge of readers by providing them up-to-date 'list of new additions in the library.' Occasionally, bibliographies should be brought out by the library on the subjects and topic of special interest to the students and teachers of the college.

(v) Inter-Library Loan Service

Some of the readers, especially the research scholars, may need some documents which may be available in some other library. The college librarian should help the reader in this study by getting the required document for him from other library, on inter-library loan.

Newer Media

All media of communication should be used to help enrich the learning from audio-visual materials. Slow-motion and time-lapse photography have opened the door to entirely new and popular understanding of our natural world and helped, for the first time, the millions to know the true nature of our plants and animals. The departments of modern foreign languages are increasingly depending now on new media to assist both class-room instructions and individual study. Audio-visual media are more closely related, functionally, to books and they serve the same purpose. Naturally, therefore, the world by books should accept fully sight and sound to improve the functioning and services of the college libraries.

Philosophy of Self-Study

In the changing concept of the college education today, one feels that greater emphasis should be laid on the students, self-study by reducing the number of formal lectures. To ensure two-way participation in instruction, there should be individual and group assignments, seminar discussions and tutorials. Discussions require detailed knowledge of subject-matter to be discussed and something which the students can understand for themselves. This naturally suggests that the students should be made to use the library of the college and correspondingly the libraries should be better stocked not only with books (even other than textbooks) and journals but also with other visual and reading aids like micro-films, tape-records, gramophone records, music records, maps and manuscripts etc. Thus, with the changing collegiate objectives, the library in the college is increasingly becoming a strategic place in the education of the undergraduates.

A Necessary Adjunct : Thus, due to its effective and very useful role, the college library is now increasingly understood and accepted as a direct-service adjunct to the curriculum. There is apparent need to support the library as an integral and important part of the college.

University Library

Before coming to the university library, let us discuss, briefly, the university as such.

University : *Objectives and Functions* : A university stands for truth, reason, tolerance and humanism. It helps in the progress of the universe and thereby adds to the well-being of the nation and the people. The fundamental values which the university aims to achieve are related to the contemporary changing society. The task of the university is no longer confined to the two traditional functions of teaching and advancement of knowledge. The functions are assuming new dimensions and depth. In the modern world, the broad functions of the university are, briefly, as follows :

(a) to pursue the truth, explore and cultivate new knowledge and interpret the old knowledge and beliefs in the light of the contemporary needs and necessities;

(b) to strive to promote equality, liberty, fraternity and justice to the people and reduce social and cultural gap in the society by disseminating knowledge and information;

(c) to diffuse and foster the real values and attitudes amongst the teachers and students necessary for attaining good citizenship, create a happy and assuring life for the people, besides developing the society;

(d) to impart knowledge to the students (boys and girls) in the fields of science, arts, agriculture, engineering, technology, medicine and various other subjects and give professional and vocational training for the development of the nation and the people; and

(e) to generate and provide the right kind of leadership in all walks of life in the society for the uplift of the society and the nation.

In addition to these functions, the Indian universities have special responsibilities in the context of the existing socio-economic milieu of the country. These are chiefly to (a) develop and assist the schools and colleges in their attempt at qualitative self-improvement; (b) improve the standards of teaching with a view to shake off the unwarranted old myths and false beliefs and reduce the monotonous load on children in the early stages of their education and remove the undue prominence given to the traditional pattern of examinations; (c) develop the wide-ranging programmes of adult education by evolving a large network of part-time and correspondence courses; (d) serve as the conscience-keeper of the nation by unfolding the personality of the individual and encourage the diversity, variety and dissent within the helpful and limited climate of tolerance; (e) create and develop a few centres of higher study and research in the country itself, comparable to those of well-known universities in other parts of the world to help bring excellence of knowledge within the country.

Wilson and Tauber have described the functions of the university as (i) conservation of knowledge and ideas; (ii) teaching; (iii) research; (iv) publication; (v) extension and service; and (vi) interpretation (Wilson and Tauber : 1958:16).

University Library : The university library is there to strive for the fulfilment of the ideals and objectives of the university discussed above. It has to discharge its responsibilities towards undergraduates, postgraduates and research students. The Hale Committee (UK) on University Teaching Methods maintains in its report that "for the student, attendance at lectures and private study are, to some extent, alternatives, and it would be unfortunate if an insufficient supply of books made it necessary to offer lectures which would not otherwise be required. If one of the main purposes of university education is to teach students to work on their own, reading by student must be preferable to attendance at a lecture unless the lecture is superior in presentation or content to the available literature" (In Parry : 1968:11). The Committee says further: it is "of value in training him (the student) to work on his own and to read the literature of the subject with an alert and critical mind". And again, the introduction of mere teaching by discussion is beneficial only when it can be matched by a corresponding increase in the amount of private study done by the student (Ibid :10). The points highlighted by the Commission suggest that there is increasing need for the students to read extensively on their own. This has important relevance with regard to the increasing pressure on the stock and administration of the libraries. The undergraduate students should be invited and encouraged to make full use of the library resources.

For doctoral research and at the staff-level, the pressure on the resources of the library vary because individual researcher pursues his research and study in his own field of specialization. A well-stocked library having organized its collection for making it conveniently available to readers is a strong attraction for the students as well as the staff. Gelfand mentions that as a dynamic instrument of education, the library should feed the intellect of students, provide encouragement to the research studies and "invite all who enter its house to partake fully of its intellectual and cultural fare" (Gelfand : 1962:74). He further says that in this context library use becomes a method of teaching, taking its place besides the time-honoured lecture and the discussion group. The librarian serves as a teacher—guiding the student in the way of investigation and research—and the library actively serves the teaching and research needs of the faculty.

The above role assigned to the library has far-reaching implications with regard to the building up of the collection, organization of the library and provisions of services. The collection should comprise of not only the reading materials pertaining to the courses of studies in the curricula and the research programmes of the faculties but should be fairly representative of other subjects too not belonging to the prescribed courses of studies. The stock of books should also be well-equipped with reference books and specialized bibliographies. The organization should be such as to provide the readers easy access to the holding; free and generous borrowing facilities and necessary extension programmes to apprise the readers regarding the resources and services available for them. It is also implied that the building of the library should be functional and it should be manned by adequate professional and non-professional staff.

Nigel Cox analyses the functions of university library in the five headings: (i) control—covering acquisition, accession, processing and shelving; (ii) archive—building up collection; (iii) service—including professional guidance to the readers; (iv) co-operation—linking the local and national network of library resources; and (v) research and development to enhance the library techniques (In Thompson : 1970:10). Paul Buck also gives similar classification of the functions of the university library under the heads: resources; retrieval of information; co-ordination and staff capability. He summarizes them all in the word 'responsiveness' to the university needs (*Ibid* : 11).

Looking Back

In ancient India the universities were the leading centres of learning. They attracted students and scholars from all parts of India as well as other countries. In the medieval India too, there were certain famous centres of Islamic learning. Unfortunately, these traditional seats of learning did not survive for long. The modern universities were established, more than hundred years ago, 'as exotic institutions created in imitation of the London University as it then was.' The earliest universities set up in India in around 1857 were Bombay, Calcutta and Madras. These were followed by the University of Allahabad in 1887. They started purely as examining bodies and continued as such till 1902 when the Indian Universities Commission was appointed and the Indian Universities Act was passed in 1904. It was observed that India had no corporate existence like those of Oxford and Cambridge. The universities did not even possess a collection of buildings needed to house the different faculties; not even a site. They were only bodies which controlled courses of studies; set examination papers and held examinations for the students of affiliated colleges, which were not situated in the same city or even the same province.

The Government Resolution on Educational Policy realized and accepted the need for setting up more universities. It mentioned that although it was difficult to dispense altogether with the affiliating universities, it was necessary to restrict the area over which the affiliating universities had control. To this end, it was envisaged to set up a separate university for each of the leading provinces (now States) in the country. Also, in each of the province, a new local teaching and residential university was set up to ensure higher educational facility. Thus, between 1913 and 1921, six new universities were set up. Lucknow, a teaching, unitary and large residential university was established in 1920. Further, encouragement was also given to the informal agencies, institutions and to the eminent people in the country in their efforts to set up universities like Benaras Hindu University by Pandit Madan Mohan Malaviya in 1916 and the Aligarh Muslim University founded by Sir Syed Ahmed Khan in 1920. In the meantime two princely States like Mysore and Osmania established universities in 1916 and 1918 respectively.

In the year 1921, education as a subject was transferred from British hands to the Indian control. This change helped the development of the universities in the country at a much faster speed and during the next 26 years, nine more universities were established. After attainment of independence in 1947, higher education in the country began to develop at an accelerated speed. The number of universities increased from 19 to 64 by 1966. In addition, institutions of 'deemed universities' under Section 3 of the UGC Act also came up. Today, in India, there are 130 universities, 16 'deemed universities', 5482 colleges and institutions of national importance.

The University Library—Historical Perspective

The recorded form of knowledge is a book and books (*liber*) make a library. So, knowledge, scholarship and book go together. And, India has been a land of scholarship. The intellectual enquiry and philosophical speculation has been a tradition in this country that dates back to the dim past. This resulted in compilation of monumental works like the Vedas, the Upanishads, the Ramayana, the Mahabharata, the Arthashastra, the Manusmriti, the Kamasutras and the like. These monumental works of religious and philosophical treatises, the epics, the texts of socio-political philosophy and the aesthetic studies have been preserved from the remote past of the Vedic age. But, those were the days of memory-libraries and intellectual monopoly too; the learned pundits did not think of libraries as a source of disseminating knowledge. But inroads crept into the orthodox tenets of Brahamanism. Jainism and Buddhism marked a new socio-religious awakening among the people and they copied the religious manuscripts on a mass scale to propagate and spread their philosophy. That was the golden age in India from the view-point of literature and philosophy. Renowned universities like Nalanda and Vikramshila (in Bihar), Vallabhi (in Kathiawar) and Taxila (in Punjab) were established and those universities possessed big libraries. Nalanda University had a splendid and well-planned library for thousands of students and hundreds of teachers. Its library campus was known as 'Dharma-ganja' comprising three monumental edifices aptly called Ratnasagar, Ratnadadhi and Ratnaranjika. The Ratnadadhi was a nine storeyed sky-scraper with specialized collections of rare and sacred works. It was because of its library that Nalanda University became the highest citadel of knowledge in Asia. These facts go to show that this country has a rich tradition of universities and libraries. The rulers of medieval India displayed interest for learning and took personal interest in the development of libraries which were mostly attached to the palaces or mosques, maktabs, khanquah, madarsas and such other religious and educational institutions.

The origin of the present setup of the educational system, including the system of college and university libraries, dates back to the first half of the nineteenth century. In his despatch to the Board of Directors of the East India Company in 1854, Sir Charles Wood outlined the future pattern of Indian education and issued a blueprint for University Education in India. For the first time three universities; one each at the three presidency towns in the country viz. Calcutta, Madras and Bombay were set up on the pattern of the London University to conserve, disseminate and advance knowledge. They were also envisaged to be institutions of higher education and learning to pursue the courses of studies and to confer degrees in Arts and Science as evidence of the educational attainment. Since in the beginning, these universities were merely affiliating and examining bodies, the need for providing libraries was not realized then. Thus, truly speaking, the modern institutional university education and the university library system as its conjunct did not emerge in India simultaneously. To fulfil its defined objectives, the Calcutta University emphasized on the provision of laboratories and libraries saying that the availability of these two facilities were indispensable for teaching and research. Thus, the Calcutta University library was established in 1873 with a total budget of rupees six thousand only. The Bombay University library was set up with a donation of rupees 4 lacs for its building in 1864. The building was completed in 1878 and the library was inaugurated on 27 February, 1880. It contained small collection of books on library and biography presented by the East India Company. Thus the stock of the university libraries consisted of small collection of mostly official publications of the local and union governments and some books received through gifts.

The government appointed the Hunter Commission in 1882 to enquire into the working of the existing system of education. The commission laid stress on the libraries in the educational institutions. It took notice of the conditions of the libraries and felt that they needed improvement. The University of Punjab (Lahore) was established in 1882 and that of Allahabad in 1887. In 1902, another Indian Universities Commission was set up. This commission too highlighted the miserable plight of the university libraries and deplored the neglect by the universities. In 1904, the Indian University Act was passed. This Act conferred statutory rights on the universities to build, equip and manage university libraries. The affiliated colleges were required under the Act to provide for the libraries and to maintain them as a pre-condition for their affiliation with the universities.

The Calcutta University Commission 1917-19 (known as Sadler Commission) under the chairmanship of Dr. M.E. Sadler, the Vice-Chancellor of the University of Leeds, observed the inadequacy of the libraries. The commission maintained that neither the students nor the underpaid staff could afford to buy books and, therefore, the university community was more dependent on the libraries for availability of the books they required. During the period 1913 to 1921 six more universities were created. A teaching-cum-residential university was established at Lucknow in 1920. The introduction of Montford Reforms in 1920 brought changes in the character of functioning of the universities. The universities introduced and opened new departments of teaching and research which needed libraries as a matter of unavoidable necessity. The Hartog Committee brought out its report in 1929 and emphasised the need for developing the libraries and equipping them adequately with books and journals. This committee observed that most of the university libraries were inadequate. In 1938, the University Committee was set up to examine the financial provisions of the university libraries. The committee maintained that the financial conditions of the libraries were not sound, the provisions of funds were decreasing and, therefore, larger grants should be made available to the libraries. With the transfer of education as a subject under Indian control, its development began to be accelerated and nine more universities were set up during the next 26 years bringing the total number to 20 on the eve of the country's independence.

Till this period, the conditions of the university libraries were, however, quite discouraging. They were considered merely as part of the administrative section under the control of the Registrar or an Honorary Librarian with the result that "Libraries even in the most well-established universities were not properly organized and the status of the Librarian was pitifully low" (Banerjee : 1964:23). Professor S. Bashiruddin observed, "the word library merely implied a collection of books; it did not matter, however, where it was housed, how the books in the collection were arranged and who administered it nor was such a variety sought in the quality of the book stock. All that the Librarian had to do under the circumstances was to keep a watch over the wares in the custody and grudgingly leave the chair in order to let a stray reader have the book he wanted to read" (Bashiruddin : 1963:4). The reason for such a deplorable state of affairs was that there was a general impression that anybody can look after a library and the work of a librarian is one which does not require much ability or capability. The competence of the librarian was not recognized fully by the authorities nor was the work of a librarian considered to be an organised profession. When the Madras University library was organised, the staff was chosen from amongst the attendants of the Museum housed in the Connemara Public Library (Ranganathan : 1963:63). The pay scale of the librarian was very low and hence the academic qualification prescribed for this profession was only matriculation. His assistant was required to qualify only up to the lower secondary examination and the man below him had to study not beyond the primary school stage. The librarian had not been given the proper status and position and his scale of pay was miserably low. "In 1917, the Calcutta University Librarian was appointed in the grade of Rs. 100-10-150". Hardly any person of ability and brilliance was interested and attracted to enter this profession—the librarianship was not a profession at that time. The common practice was to request a senior teacher or professor of the institution (school, college or the university) to look after the work of the library on an honorary basis. Since the librarian was not usually a trained professional, he was considered only as a custodian of the books in the library. The libraries of schools, colleges as well as the universities were provided with meagre funds for purchase of only those books which were prescribed in the syllabus. There was only a skeleton staff provided. The library service was scanty and direct access to the shelves and the books was not freely given. The librarian was usually reluctant to permit readers access to the books or shelves as he was personally held responsible for the loss of books. The systematic management of libraries using modern methods and techniques to organize and arrange the collection of books and extending the necessary and essential library services to readers was conspicuously absent. The reference service to the readers was unheard of. Thus, in fact, the university libraries in the pre-independence era were given only a secondary role in the university structure and was not given any significant value or positive role in the academic life and functioning of the university.

Post-Independence Era

On attaining independence in 1947, adequate measures were taken to improve the state of higher education and research in the country. It was realized that the libraries were awfully ill-equipped in space, stock and staff. They were not managed by competent and imaginative persons. The allocation of funds were too meagre and, thus, they were utterly incapable of meeting the needs of the university education, which was, then, looked in a new perspective in the democratic set-up that the country had envisaged. The democracy attached high value to education. To suggest measures for improvement of education in the country, a Commission for University Education (December 1948—August 1949) was appointed by the Ministry of Education, Government of India, under the chairmanship of Dr. S. Radhakrishnan. By then, objectives and functions of the libraries had undergone change in consonance with the changing socio-economic and political order in the country. The commission took notice of the inadequacy of the university libraries and emphasized their importance in the educational system. The commission stated that teaching is a cooperative enterprise. The teachers must have the necessary tools for teaching purposes in the shape of libraries and laboratories as also the right type of students. Library is the heart of all the university's work; directly so as regards its research work, and indirectly as regards its academic work; which derives its life from research work. Scientific research needs a library as well as laboratories, while for research in humanities the library is both a library and a laboratory combined into one single whole. Training in higher branches of learning and research is mainly a question of learning how to use the tools and if the library tools are not there, how can the student learn to use them? The commission quotes United States President Truman's Commission on Higher Education which said that the library was second only to the instructional staff in its importance for high quality instruction and research. Both for humanistic and scientific studies, a first-class library is quite essential in a university (India—Ministry of Education: 1949:110).

Unsatisfactory Position

Pointing to the existing unsatisfactory position, the Commission observed that while at a few universities, the libraries were fairly well-stocked, grants for their upkeep and maintenance were more or less adequate, arrangements for lending books to teachers and students were efficiently managed and the reading-room space was reasonably adequate, it was distressing that in most colleges and universities the library facilities provided were quite miserable indeed. Not only was the provision for keeping the library up-to-date very inadequate, but also at one place no attempt had been made to weed out old and obsolete books or replace old editions with new ones of the same book. At another place different scientific journals had been subscribed for at different times and then abruptly discontinued, with the result that not a single set was complete or up-to-date. At still another place the library was just a mass of books stocked somehow, with no space or arrangement for seats where readers could sit down and have even a look at books with ease and comfort. But the poorest libraries were those of professional colleges, e.g., the medical, engineering and agricultural colleges. That many teachers in medical colleges care more for their private practice than for teaching and research is faithfully reflected in the grossly inadequate library facilities at almost all medical colleges in the country. The libraries at the engineering and agricultural colleges were also poor because teachers took little interest in research.

The Annual Grant : The annual grants for libraries in most of the universities were quite inadequate. On a comparative study of the provision for the library in the chief universities of the world it was found that the annual grant for a good library should be about 61 per cent of the total budget provided for the university or Rs. 40 per student. The commission compared the library grants of some fairly good university libraries in India and found that their annual grants for the year 1948-49 ranged from 2.7 per cent to 6.5 per cent of their total budget grants. That included the grant for books and periodicals as well as the expenditure on service, administration and maintenance. The American Library Association recommended Rs. 60 to Rs. 85 per student, while Truman's Commission recommended Rs. 65 per student.

The commission also mentioned that it had not been sufficiently realized that for advance scientific work, scientific periodicals were more important than books. As scientific books and periodicals were very costly and in science subjects a proper library had to be built in India, the commission recommended that universities and colleges should work upto an optimum of 61/4 per cent of the total budget grant or Rs. 40 per student as the annual grant for their libraries. As it would not be possible for a library to purchase the increasing number of useful publications which come out year after year out of its fixed annual allotment, a special non-recurring grant should be made once in five years to cope up and purchase the arrears of books and journals needed for the library. Manuscripts are also important for university libraries. As a good part of the research work in Indian Philosophy, History and Literature is dependent upon the examination of unpublished manuscripts, each university must attempt to obtain as many of the old manuscripts as it could manage and a special grant for the purchase of manuscripts has to be included in the budget of every university library.

The Open Access System : The commission observed that most libraries did not allow open access. It should be remembered that undergraduates have to be educated in the use of the library as in so many other fields. They should be allowed to go at will from one shelf of books to another and browse the books thoroughly in their leisure hours. Except for a few rare and precious books, all others should be made available to them. It is necessary that there should be only one entrance and exit and that a junior assistant should carefully check all books taken out of the library. In every university there should be a carefully planned open access system.

The Hours of Work : The commission mentioned that in many universities, the library was open only from 10 A.M. to 4 P.M. This was obviously wrong as the library should not close as soon as the college lectures and work ended. It was precisely after the lecture hours that the libraries needed to be kept open. The commission, therefore, recommended that all university libraries should remain open for at least 12 hours a day for seven days of the week and throughout the vacation, so that the undergraduates could spend a good deal of their time reading there and the staff and postgraduate students could get long and continuous stretches of time for their research work in the library. The library staff would naturally have to work in shifts and should be given their offs by turn.

The Organization of a Library : The commission observed that the exact organization of the university library would differ from place to place but the ideal to be aimed at was a large central library with departmental libraries attached to it. The central library should maintain a complete catalogue of all the books in the university, indicating clearly the books and periodicals available in the central library and in the several other departmental libraries. It had been found by experience that it was best that the departmental libraries should contain only those books and journals which were to be used by the teachers and the postgraduate students and that all books for undergraduates should be available in the central library.

The Staff : The library should have adequate and well-qualified staff. Each library required several varieties of employees. On top, there should be a man of the calibre of a university professor who had specialized in some aspects of library science after a full degree course and who had capacities for organization and management. In the next grade would be his deputies, who would look after the different sectional activities of the library like cataloguing, reference work, reading-room management, etc. Then finally there must be numerous assistants helping in all activities connected with acquisition, issue and receipt of books. The top man must have qualifications equal to a Doctorate in Library Science; the deputy librarians should have obtained a degree after undergoing training in a university, while the other assistants should at least possess diplomas in library science where the course of study should have extended to at least one year. We must have at least one university centre in each province offering facilities for education and training in library science for the diploma courses. We may not be able to start degree courses at one stretch in more than three or four universities at present.

The commission further observed that sufficient attention had not been paid to the reference service in the libraries of our universities. Reference service rendered by a qualified assistant was necessary to provide guidance to the proper volumes and pages in each volume, which might be useful to the students. The reference assistants could be a help not only to the students but also to the teachers in their special subjects of study. Bibliographical and documentation work had to be developed to make the libraries proper centres of research.

Making Students Book-Conscious : Even when the central library was fairly well-stocked and afforded necessary facilities to readers by way of a complete catalogue, long hours of work and unrestricted access to the book-stocks, it was necessary that the student himself must be made book-conscious. He must be encouraged by his teachers to possess his own mini library and educate himself by his private reading. Right from his school, he should be convinced of the value of book-buying. The joy of possessing books, including reference books, continually consulting it and making it a familiar reference tool by careful and constant reading, was something he must learn by the precept and example of his teachers. It was an essential part of university education to learn how to read and understand writings by educated adults and the only way to learn that was to read such writings.

Book-Grants to Teachers : A large number of teachers are not able to buy books or subscribe for journals to keep themselves abreast and uptodate. They had no libraries of their own. The commission suggested that teachers of lower grade schools should be given a grant of Rs. 100 annually for buying books with a condition that they supplemented that by an equal amount.

Creation of UGC: The establishment of this august body in 1953 (which became statutory in 1956) has been a very significant and favourable step in giving direction and assistance in the development of the university libraries. This was presided over in the beginning by Dr. CD. Deshmukh who was himself quite aware of the problems of the university libraries and was too eager to improve their conditions. The first step that Dr. Deshmukh took in this direction was to constitute an ad-hoc Library Committee in 1957 to advise the UGC on the various problems connected with provision of growth of the libraries, book-purchase, development of reading habit and help students in the use of the libraries. The terms of reference also included documentation work and service to research workers, departmental libraries and their function, classification, cataloguing and other technical work, library personnel, their qualifications, status, salary, strength and other factors connected with the development of the libraries of the universities. This committee was presided over by the vetern library scientist Dr. S.R. Ranganathan. The members were Mr. B.S. Kesavan, Professor S. Bashiruddin, Mr. K.S. Hingwe and Mr. S. Parthasarthy. Another important measure taken was to constitute another committee to advise the Commission on setting up of library training schools as a department of the universities. Some of the other important recommendations of the UGC were as follows :

(i) Subject to local variation, the grant to the university library books and journals should be given on the basis of Rs. 15 per student registered in the university and Rs. 200 per teacher. This should be revised periodically in the light of change in the cost of books and periodicals. A period of 17 months should be allowed for a proper utilization of the UGC grant,

(ii) A library may spend l/5th of the Commission's grant on books and journals and the staff required for processing the material.

(iii) The library fund of a university or college should be maintained and operated as a separate library account.

(iv) To enable the proper utilization of book funds and avoid the 'rush-purchase', the unutilized portion of the budget amount should not be returned but carried forward to the credit of the library and used later on or included in the next year's budget, in addition to the normal amount sanctioned.

(v) The practice of appointing a person without prescribed professional qualifications even as an honorary librarian should be done away with; and

(vi) The professional staff of the library should have designation, qualifications and salary corresponding to those of the professors, readers and assistant lecturers.

The acceptance of these recommendations, especially the last one, has been a very noteworthy development in the field of university librarianship. By implementing this particular recommendation, the UGC recognized and attached the importance, due to the library staff, to be equal in position and emoluments to the university teachers. Also, the other recommendations of the UGC went a long way to improve the conditions of service of the college and university libraries and this helped the promotion and coordination of higher education and maintenance of standards of teaching, education and research in the universities. Earlier, the college and university libraries were financially crippled. The amounts apportioned for library purposes in the university budget were so meagre that they could hardly meet the recurring expenditure of the library on salaries of staff and other contingencies. The grant meant for purchase of books was utterly negligible. Provision for availability of appropriate grant was made for equipping and developing the university libraries. It was made obligatory on the part of the universities to spend a reasonable share of the proposed and allocated grant from its own resources as the matching grant. Advice on standards of design of library buildings, fittings and furniture was also provided. With this treatment at the level of the UGC, the college and university libraries in the country received a new lease of life.

The Work-Flow Seminar : The University Grants Commission organized a seminar on "from publisher to reader"— work-flow in university and college libraries—which was held from March 4 to 7, 1959 at New Delhi. The chief objective of this seminar was to streamline the administration of the libraries in colleges and universities. The UGC had made, earlier, considerable grants for providing adequate library buildings in our universities and colleges and for purchase of books on science and humanities. They were, now, concerned with the technical aspects of the briefing, classification, cataloguing of books and use of reading materials on scientific lines, with a view to assisting the colleges and universities to improve their libraries and make them really effective in the total system of education. The UGC desired and expected the seminar to bring to light a workable arrangement for the smooth and efficient functioning of the libraries.

Inaugurating the seminar, Dr. C.D. Deshmukh said, "the students were the body of the university, the administration was, of course, the head, the teachers were the soul and the library, the heart" (UGC:1965:158). He further mentioned that "during the last four or five years of the existence of the UGC we have extended assistance to libraries for buildings and furniture as well as for the purpose of books and, latterly, for the engagement of part of the staff on a scale which is, relatively speaking, larger than could be found in many other countries, particularly the United Kingdom" (*Ibid*: 156). This statement speaks of the importance given and the interest taken by the UGC for creating libraries and developing them as necessary components to the institution of higher studies in India. In his presidential address to the seminar Dr. S.R. Ranganathan mentioned the vital role of the university education in the development of the nation and traced the five-fold role of the library in the new reoriented education. He said that the libraries had to feed the students in five stages, three of which are correlated to work in the class-room and in the libraries. He elaborated his points by saying that to arouse curiosity amongst the readers, the reading materials should be gathered, organized and attractively presented to the students as a preparatory study before the lessons. Next, to maintain the university, another set of reading materials should be similarly served for the parallel study immediately after the lesson. Then, for the follow-up study, still another set of reading materials should be served which should harness the curiosity of the readers to a greater degree. At the fourth stage, the library owes a social responsibility to feed the readers with entertaining and elevating books to use at their leisure. The college and university libraries should further habituate especially the students and adults to make use of the leisure hours profitably. At the fifth stage the libraries should take into consideration the students of advanced courses, research fellows and the teachers. The research-potential needed for this class of readers need to be conserved by picking up and organizing the nascent thought in every field of knowledge. A great amount of time and energy is wasted by the researchers in literature-search, which job should be performed by the library staff through documentation work and service.

Dr. Ranganathan observed that "the University Grants Commission is fully convinced of the need and intimate role of the libraries in the university and college life in our renascent India. They have a policy to give liberal grants to all library purposes—reading materials, library buildings, fittings and furniture and library staff. The UGC did not take long to realize that proper way to develop our library service along helpful lines is to entrust the planning of the whole affair to the library profession itself" (*Ibid*: 168). The seminar dealt with the period of rhythm of work, constants of the staff-formula, periodical publications, textbook collection, treatises and reference books, book selection and ordering, promotion of the use of books and periodicals and book fund. The details of these are found in the relevant chapters. In the concluding session, Dr. Ranganathan said, "Dr. Deshmukh has enabled the whole body of university librarians to step up to a higher level of vision, enthusiasm and delight in book-service. He has arranged this seminar to gather the initial momentum by collective effort. It is hereafter for each one of us to make sure that momentum swells from more to more" (*Ibid*: 213). Dr. P.J. Philip, who addressed the conference, said that if our libraries were to become potent instruments for the improvement and strengthening of standards of university education, they certainly had to play an imaginative and dynamic role (*Ibid*: 215).

India Wheat Loan Educational Exchange Programme

Under the Public Law 480 (1951) of the United States of America, a scheme was drawn up for a loan of $19 million to India for the purchase of wheat, with the provision that the interest of $5 million should be utilized on (i) the purchase of American books and journals; and (ii) grant of fellowship to twelve university librarians to visit important libraries in the U.S.A. The scheme provided a great opportunity for some of the librarians in India to observe closely the working of similar libraries in the United States and enrich their knowledge and outlook towards the profession. Between 1954 and 1961, 36 universities and 52 research libraries benefited from this scheme. Many libraries received sizable grants for purchase of books and back-volumes of journals pertaining to different branches of knowledge. Some of them also received different types of library equipment like microfilm and micro-cord readers etc. This helped university libraries to adopt modern systems of automation in the functioning and organize documentation service.

Education Commission (1964-66)

This Education Commission was appointed by the Government of India by a resolution dated July 14, 1964 to advise the Government on the national pattern of education and on general principles and policies for the development of education at all stages and in all aspects. The commission consisted of Professor D.S. Kothari, Chairman, University Grants Commission, and 15 members, one member-secretary and an associate secretary. It submitted its report in June 1966. The commission mentioned that with the ever-increasing enrolment in universities and colleges, the demand for the services of libraries has been constantly growing unlike in the past. The staff of the libraries have now to cater to the diverse needs of the students at the undergraduate and postgraduate levels as well as the research scholars. A new realization in the field was that the modern university libraries were to render the indexing and abstracting services to serve the various new academic departments that are coming up The demand was constantly growing. The commission observed that needs and responsibilities of the libraries being high, the existing grants for expenditure on books and periodicals were not adequate. It found that only in 4 universities, the expenditure on books and periodicals was more than 5 per cent of the total expenditure of the university. In 34 universities, the expenditure was 1 to 5 per cent and in 5 universities, it was less than 1 per cent. Although the universities were getting liberal grants from the UGC for improving the condition of their libraries, an equitable distribution of the funds was not made by the universities. Here, Professor John Weatherford's apt words may be recalled: "Poverty may force a university to have a substandard library, but not to give the library a substandard share of its resources. Here, then, is a test of the sincerity of university administrators, who so often say that the library is the heart of the campus" (Weatherford : 1965:5346). The Education Commission which observed the shortcomings in the libraries, made the following recommendations to improve their conditions :

(i) The heads of the departments and the library staff should cooperate and combine together to draw an integrated plan for library development. The factors like the anticipated increase in enrolment, distribution of students in the faculties, new subjects, areas of specialization and special research projects should be taken into consideration.

(ii) While establishing a new department, college or university, the needs of the library in terms of staff, books, journals and space must be taken into consideration. In no case the library should be neglected or given low priority in respect of a growing department; on the contrary the library should be developed as a centre of attraction on the college or university campus.

(iii) The grants of the library should be properly phased over a plan period for utilization. There should be a regular programme of strengthening the departments with the financial resources available, instead of overfeeding haphazardly a department in the beginning of the plan and starving it during the later period of the plan.

(iv) It is necessary to lay down the physical targets rather than the financial ones.

(v) Use of books by the students and the teachers should be ensured. Lectures should be supplemented by tutorial instructions and the students should be trained to find for themselves in the library the needed material.

(vi) The library services should be streamlined by making adequate provision of books (with multiple copies of textbooks), staff, better organization of the reading material, extending the library hours and providing separate rooms for the book-clubs, periodicals and reference books etc. The reading habit amongst the readers should be developed and library standard raised.

(vii) The traditional belief that a library is a conventional but more or less useless accessory, should be eschewed.

(viii) Although no definite pattern can be set forth for the development of university library programmes, some essential requisites are competent staff, adequate collection of properly and carefully selected books, their proper organization and well-planned physical facilities.

(ix) A collection of books, even though good ones, does not necessarily go to make a library. The essential requirement is the availability of enthusiastic teachers to teach with books and librarians to help convert the library into an intellectual workshop. "Even a comparatively small collection of sensitively chosen books may work wonders in the life of students." Even the most luxurious building or extensive book collection is unlikely to make any impact. The object of the library planning is rather to relate the book selection, organization and administration and other activities of the libraries to the daily needs of the academic community which includes both the professors and the students. Therefore, it is necessary that the book selection should be oriented towards supporting instructions and research.

(x) The library should aid the university teachers in keeping abreast of the development in their respective fields of studies and provide the necessary resources of their special interest.

(xi) The library should provide its services necessary for the success of all formal programmes of instructions.

(xii) Crossing the boundary of one's specialization, the library should open the doors to the wide world of books that lie beyond the boards of that specialization.

(xiii) The library should bring books, students and scholars together in a manner to encourage the habit of reading for pleasure, self-discovery, personal growth and sharpening of intellectual curiosity.

(xiv) The Commission observed that the expenditure on library in relation to total educational expenditure of the university had gone up from 1.88 per cent in 1951-52 to 4.04 per cent in 1960-61, by the time the grants provided by the UGC began to make impact. The University Education Commission had suggested about 6.5 per cent of the educational budget as reasonable expenditure on libraries. But this could vary from 6.5 per cent to 10 per cent depending upon the stage of development of each university library. It may also be suggested that, as a norm, a university should spend each year about Rs. 25 for each student registered and Rs. 300 per teacher.

(xv) The foreign exchange needed for university and college libraries should be allocated separately to the UGC.

Sidhanta Committee Report

This UGC report on Standards of University Education (1965) suggested encouragement to students to visit libraries, select books and make proper use of them. It would be more helpful if the teacher prepares a synopsis of his lectures containing bibliography of the relevant material and making it available to students for their guidance and use in preparing their lessons.

The recommendations go to prove that a well-organized and properly established library, manned by professionally qualified staff, is an integral part of the teaching process in the academic institutions. In the areas of higher education and research, the libraries play a dynamic role; it is an intellectual workshop. The job of a modern librarian is not a mechanical work of arranging the books on the shelves but organising the smooth flow of books by circulation amongst the readers. He is a professionally qualified man who can understand books as tools of learning and help the readers use them properly. Present-day libraries use their potentialities and resources in the field of research being done at the universities. This constitutes more than 50 per cent of the total researches made in the country as a whole. To perform this task, they have since developed the information retrieval system and they keep themselves in touch with the various day-to-day research activities in different areas. In this age of explosion of knowledge, the importance of documentation work has greatly increased. The library has also to be well-equipped, financially as well as from the point of view of the staff, providing the staff-members with proper salary and status on par with the university teachers. The staff-members should also possess a wide range of interest and scholastic activities to understand the problems of education and research and help the researchers in the pursuit of their investigation.

UNESCO Regional Seminar

The UNESCO Regional Seminar on Library Development in South Asia was jointly sponsored by the UNESCO and the Government of India. It was held at the Delhi University Library between October 3 to 14, 1960 under the directorship of Mr. A.G.W. Dunninghan, UNESCO Libraries' expert in Indonesia. The purpose of the seminar was to seek solutions, both on national and regional basis, to the problems involved in the development of public and university libraries in South Asia. About fifty experts in library science from Afganistan, Burma, Sri Lanka, India, Iran, Nepal, Pakistan and Thailand attended the seminar. Inaugurating the seminar, Dr. K.L. Shrimali highlighted the importance of selection of books in the libraries necessary for the maintenance of the national cultural values as well as the development of ideas. The books on classics and great works of eternal truths should find a place in the libraries instead of books of temporary and ephemeral value. The seminar discussed the vital significance of libraries in the educational systems of countries. To play the competitive role in the fields of science, technology and social development of the nation, the countries should be served with a proper and effective chain of libraries of all types, public as well as academic and special. It was also observed that some of the participating countries have tried to build up their library system on the advice and planning of the library experts drawn from abroad. The opinions and recommendations of such experts have often been found to be unrealistic because of their ignorance of the local realities like the physical financial and educational ones. The remedies suggested by such experts usually prove to be more theoretical.

The seminar discussed the pressing problems, administrative and technical in nature, which the libraries are facing every day. It was observed that adequate reading material was not available in the region. The countries are largely dependent on British and American books which are difficult to procure due to want of foreign exchange; especially the costly technical and scientific journals and periodicals. There is also dearth of technically qualified staff. The profession is not yet as lucrative and prospective as the other professions, are and, therefore, it fails to attract brilliant people. The pay-scale should, therefore, be made handsome enough to attract promising young-men. Otherwise they would be weaned away by other professions.

Seminar of University Librarians

The Rajasthan University, Jaipur, organized a seminar in 1966 with the active support of the UGC in which about 40 delegates from various parts of the country and abroad participated. The seminar made certain important recommendations which are as follows :

(i) The practice of appointing Professors as Honorary Librarians should be abolished.

(ii) The university librarians should be given statutory recognition, making them ex-officio members of all academic bodies and make them directly responsible to the Vice-Chancellor of the university. They should be accorded the rank, status and privileges of the Head of a postgraduate department of the university. The Library Committee should function only in an advisory capacity with the university librarian working as its Member-Secretary.

(iii) The designations of the staff of the library should be equal in status to the teaching members of the faculties and their scales of pay should be on par with the teachers. If any university fails to implement such a scale, the UGC should withhold the financial grant.

(iv) A separate library wing should be established at the UGC with a professionally qualified librarian as its head and a standing library committee be constituted to advise the commission on all matters concerning the working and development of university libraries.

(Since then, the university librarianship has made considerable progress in the developed universities of the country. The honorary librarianship has more or less been abolished, except in a few libraries, and some librarians also enjoy faculty status and representation on the university's academic bodies. The University of Mysore has stipulated that the university librarian would be an ex-officio Professor and Head of the Department of Library Science. Certain other universities like Aligarh Muslim University and the University of Kerala, Trivandrum, have also made similar provisions. Noteworthy progress has been made in the areas of administration and organization of the libraries as a result of researches made in the discipline.)

Further, the seminar also made its recommendations regarding various aspects of organization and administration of the university libraries like allocation of the budget grant for libraries, mode of procurement of books, journals and other reading materials, library services and the loss of books etc.

(v) The university budget upto the extent of 10 per cent should be set apart for the library.

(vi) The grants for purchase of books should be treated as non-lapsable.

(vii) The policy of calling for tenders for the supply of reading materials should be dispensed with to encourage competition.

(viii) The restrictions imposed by the Government on the import of research materials like maps, globes, atlases etc., be lifted.

(ix) The duty-free import of films, filmstrips, slides, linguaphones and longplaying records of educational value should be allowed freely.

(x) The university libraries should be allotted sufficient foreign exchange for the duty-free import of books, periodicals, audio-visuals and reprographic materials.

(xi) The UNESCO coupons should be made available freely in the libraries for procurement of reprographic and audio-visual materials without restriction.

(xii) Postal rates for books sent on inter-library loan be reduced in order to promote the maximum use of available book resources in the country.

(xiii) The system of getting the security bonds executed for purposes of lending out manuscripts and other rare items to institutions or libraries be abolished.

(xiv) A separate textbook collection should be provided for the benefit of the teachers and students who can borrow books at the nominal charge for full academic session.

(xv) Extension libraries should be set up and where such libraries already exist, they should be allowed to function effectively.

(xvi) The university library should be regarded as depository centre for all Union and State Government publications.

(xvii) The academic libraries should compile, publish and circulate comprehensive catalogues of theses and manuscripts available with them.

(xviii) Reprographical facilities should be made available in the academic libraries.

(xix) The INSDOC has compiled and published the Union Catalogues of Serials in Science and Technology. Similarly, a suitable institution or organization should take up the work of compiling the Union Catalogues of Serials in Humanities and Social Sciences also. (The Union Catalogues of Social Science Serials and Periodicals of certain States have been compiled and published by the Social Science Documentation Centre, ICSSR, New Delhi).

(xx) Regarding the physical verification and stock-taking in the library, the seminar recommended that sample stock-taking should be done only on a quinquennial basis and the normal loss of books be written off.

(xxi) A librarian be nominated on quinquennial visiting committees of the University Grants Commission to scrutinize plan proposals submitted by the universities.

(xxii) A standing library committee be appointed to advise the commission on all matters concerning the working and development of university libraries.

(xxiii) The earlier practice of allotting 20 per cent of the book grants for the appointment of additional temporary staff etc., be revived.

(xxiv) The UGC should finance the seminars and refresher courses in library science held by the universities at regular intervals.

(xxv) The forecast of the finances involved in a planned development of university library system in the country for the decade 1966-76 be undertaken.

(xxvi) The term 'university library' in the above recommendations would apply also to those institutions which are 'deemed to be universities'.

(xxvii) The Indian Academic Libraries Association should be revived.

The recommendations of the seminar are quite appropriate and useful. When practically adopted, they will add to the development of the university and college libraries.

The academic librarianship in this country has not yet acquired the desired standard as compared to the developed countries. There are many deterrents and obstacles to their development and progress. We will discuss in the succeeding chapters the various aspects of their functioning.

References

1. Banerjee, P.K. 1964, Reflection on the University Libraries in India, in *Indian Librarian*, V. 19, Nl.
2. Bashiruddin, S. 1962, Education for Librarianship, in *Indian Librarian*, V.17, N3 (December 1962).
3. Bashiruddin, S. 1963, Twin Requisites of Modern Library, in *Journal of Library Science* (Nagpur University), V.6.
4. Gidwani, N.N. Indian University Library: Problems and Prospects, First Seminar of University Librarianship in India, V. 1 and 2.
5. Grelfand, M.A. 1962, University Libraries for Developing Countries. Paris, UNESCO.
6. India—Ministry of Education 1949, Report of the University Education Commission (December 1948—August 1949), V. 1, Delhi.
7. India—Ministry of Education, Report of the Secondary Education Commission (October 1952—June 1953), New Delhi.
8. India—Ministry of Education 1966, Report of the Education Commission 1964-66 (Education and National Development), New Delhi.
9. Neal, K.W. 1971, British University Libraries, Wilmslow (author).
10. Parry, Thomas (Chairman) 1967, Report of the Committee on Libraries, London, Her Majesty's Stationery Office.
11. Randall, W.M. and Francis, I. 1936, Principles of College Library Administration. Chicago, American Library Association and University of Chicago Press.
12. Ranganathan, S.R. 1963, University Library—then and now, in *Library Herald*, V.6, N2-3, July-October 1963.

13. Sharma, J.S. 1978, Library Organization, New Delhi,, Vikas Publishing House.
14. Thomson, James 1970, An Introduction to University Library Administration, London, Clive Bingley.15. University Grants Commission. 1965, University and College Libraries, New Delhi, University Grants Commission.
16. Viswanathan, C.G. 1957, The High School Library, Bombay, Asia Publishing House.
17. Viswanathan, CG. 1972, University Libraries of India-Principles and Policy, New Delhi (author).
18. Weatherford, John 1965, A Visit to U.S. Average Library, in *Library Journal*, December 15, 1965.
19. Wilson, L.R. and Tauber, M.F. 1958, The University Library: the Organization, Administration, and Functions of Academic Libraries 2nd ed., New York, Columbia University Press.

2
LIBRARY GOVERNANCE

The university library functions within the framework of its university. The various university bodies viz. Academic Council, Senate and Syndicate formulate and adopt statutory provisions in the form of university Acts to determine the position and status of the university library in the general set-up of the university; depending upon the policies enunciated by these bodies. The chief objective in formulating and enacting such a law is to ensure the existence of the institution of library, define its broad principles and objectives, provide for organizational and administrative machinery and guarantee the necessary resources as in the case of other departments of study and research of the university.

Library Statutes

The statutes for the university library spell out briefly the following structural provisions:

1. Nomenclature : In a university there may be a number of libraries pertaining to colleges, faculties and departments. But the university library is the central one. Therefore, exact nomenclature (like University Central Library) is determined under the Act. In certain universities, where the department and faculty libraries are made integral parts of the central library of the university, it is termed as University Library System.

2. Objective : The fundamental objectives and aims

with which the university library is set-up are briefly stated.

3. Jurisdiction : The statute delimits the area of operation of the university library. It lays down specifically whether the university library is going to serve the university community alone or it aims to render service to a larger clientele comprising the general public and the government.

4. Budget : The statutes make provisions for providing funds and other resources needed for the functioning of the library and place specific responsibility to this effect on the university.

5. Staff and Status : Statutory provisions are made to define the rank and status of the University Librarian and his staff. The University Librarian is categorized as one of the administrative officers of the university. He is an administrative head like the President or Vice-Chancellor, Provost or Pro-Vice-Chancellor, Registrar and other such officers of the university. The statutes of the developed universities also entitle the University Librarian to be a member, *ex-officio*, of the governing and academic bodies like the Senate and Academic Council of the university.

Also, the statutes spell out the comparable academic ranks and scales of the other professional staff of the library and lay down the qualifications, responsibilities and other conditions of service.

Such statutory provisions for university library help the authorities formulate policy and plan the structure and services to the members. With the expansion in university education and research, the scope of activities and services of the university library has tremendously widened. The library has now to play a more important role in the academic programming. To meet the new and emerging challenges, it is necessary that this institution is strengthened and backed by legal sanction in the form of university Act; as is done in the case of public libraries which are governed under the Public

Library Act enacted by the State Legislature.

In India, the idea of managing the university library through a faculty committee came first on March 1, 1873 when the Syndicate of the Calcutta University constituted a committee for preparing the list of books to be purchased in the university library. The performance of that committee was so useful, commendable and encouraging that the university decided to place the affairs of the library under the management of a committee consisting of not more than five resident fellows. Subsequently the said committee was officially termed as Library Committee. Since there was no librarian appointed at that time, that committee assumed the administrative function over the library. This is how the idea of a library committee came up. The other universities by and by followed suit.

Until 1950 the university acts did not make any provision to recognize the university librarian as one of the authorities. Later on, however, necessary provisions in the Acts were made to treat the librarian as a statutory officer. Such a statutory provision enables the library authorities to formulate and determine the library policy and plan the structuring of the library services. Therefore, it is a matter of prime need and necessity that the university Acts should essentially make such a provision.

Library Governance

There are generally two forms of governance to organize and administer the library service. These are :

(i) library committees which are vested with statutory powers to maintain and administer; and

(ii) a competent specialist viz. professional University Librarian. For the functioning of the library, if the library committee is keen on taking forward-looking decisions, that may be of positive help to the librarian. Otherwise if the librarian lacks the authority, he has to seek instructions and approval of the committee on every issue and this results in stagnation in the growth and development of the library. As such, the traditional method of managing the library through the library committee is losing significance in modern university education. This is the second stage in the governance of a library viz. the professional librarian which proves to be more effective and relevant in the changed context of the university library's role. Chosen specially for this task on the basis of his scholastic performance, specialization and administrative competence, the librarian is delegated with the powers of governance and management of the library, which were previously vested in the committee.

College Library Authority

Purpose

To control, govern and administer the functioning and service of the library in a college, a Library Committee is appointed under the college regulation or by an executive order of the principal.

Composition

It is a small committee comprising nearly 8 to 10 members. It is constituted by Principal of the college, who presides over the committee, as its chairman. College Librarian functions as Secretary of the Committee. Other members are appointed from amongst the faculty members of different departments of the college. The present demand is to include representation from students in the Library Committee. This is a healthy idea. The student representation on this committee would provide them with better opportunity to ventilate their reading needs and grievances.

Role

Although, the role of this committee should be advisory

and recommendatory, in most of the colleges and for all practical purposes, it acts as an administrative authority. The committee provides a useful function and liaison between the Faculty members and the Librarian. The student representation on it would mean further liaison between the student community and the institution of library.

Function

As the function of the college library is to help realise the educational objectives enunciated for the college, the Library Committee ensures to achieve these. The budget proposals, acquisition programmes for books, circulation activities and service to the readers are all scrutinized and directed by the committee. The Library Committee also frames rules for the functioning of the library.

Status of a Librarian

Time was when professionally trained librarians were not available to manage the college library and in such a situation the college library was managed by a few non-professional and incompetent people, with a person from the teaching staff heading it and assigned the additional burden to look after the general administration and control of the library and its staff. Such a head was designated as an Honorary Librarian or Professor-in-charge of the library. The situation has now entirely changed. College libraries are now managed by qualified and professionally trained librarians. Therefore, there is absolutely no need to appoint Honorary Librarians or Professors-in-charge of college library. The Library Committee appointed by the University Grants Commission, New Delhi in 1957 under the chairmanship of Dr. S.R. Ranganathan to advise UGC about the development and organization of the University and College libraries in India, recommended that the system of appointing non-professionals as Professors-in-charge of the library or head of a library on an honorary basis should be abolished. It would be in the fitness of things that a professionally trained person alone is appointed as a college librarian and is vested with all powers to manage the affairs of the library. A small library committee may be constituted to formulate policy matters in an advisory capacity but the college librarian should be given faculty status and rank. This will enable him to voice his views on the needs and problems of the library more effectively and serve the student and teaching community better.

University Library Committee

To enhance and execute the enunciated policies of the university library and to realize the objectives so formulated, a library committee is constituted by the governing body of the university empowered under the University Act. While the aims and objects of this committee are almost the same in all the libraries, its nomenclature varies at different places and in different universities. It is named as 'Library Board', 'Library Trustees', 'Board of Directors for Libraries', and 'Curators of the Library', etc.

Constitution

It is a statutory body constituted under the statutes and ordinances adopted by the Senate or the Academic Council of the university. The Parry Committee Report on British University Libraries mentions that this is most commonly a Senate Committee, although in a few universities, it is a joint committee of Senate and Council (Parry: 1968:141).

Size

The size of the committee, however, differs from country to country and from one university to another as usually there is no fixity or rigidity with regard to its size. The idea is that it should have a manageable size. In India, the size of the library committees at present varies from 5 to 50 members. Thompson mentions that the total size of the committee in Britain tends to be in the region of a dozen or so (Thompson: 1970:12). Walker's survey indicate that the size of the committee varies from university to university. The committee of the Newcastle's University consists of the Vice-Chancellor, Pro-Vice-Chancellor, Librarian, 11 Professors, 6 other Academicians and 3 students. The University of Reading has a comparatively smaller number in the committee consisting of 5 members viz. Vice-Chancellor, 3 members of the Council and the Librarian (Neal: 1971:6).

In India, certain universities constitute a large committee including all the Professors, Deans, representatives of teachers, students and other officers of the university like the Vice-Chancellor, Pro-Vice-Chancellor, Registrar, Finance Officer, Development Officer, and the Librarian. Such a large body becomes unwieldy and at times proves unhelpful for transacting business and taking quick decisions. For active and smooth functioning, there should be a small committee with its members reflecting a happy balance between different disciplines and faculties of the university. Inclusion of the officers of the university like Registrar, Assistant Registrar, Finance Officer and Development Officer affect the very nature and purpose of the committee; it becomes more administrative and executive than academic and advisory. It is commonly felt that this is not a desirable goal.

As mentioned earlier, the first Library Committee constituted in India at the Calcutta University comprised, in the beginning, of five resident fellows only but later all the heads of departments were included and with the rapid expansion and proliferation of subjects the membership of the committee became large enough to prove cumbersome and unwieldy in its functioning. In Delhi University, a small library committee was created in 1922, which later grew into a large body of 42 members comprising every head of the department, as *ex-officio* member and two members nominated by the Vice-Chancellor. The library committee is a specialized body and, as such, in contrast to other bodies of the university, which are usually large, it should be small in size. Further, there are certain universities which have more than fifty departments and big universities like Benaras Hindu University possesses more than 100 departments. Naturally, therefore, a committee consisting of such a large contingent of members, one from each department, would not be helpful in taking administrative decisions for the library. To overcome such a situation, the University of Delhi appointed a "Standing Committee of the Library Committee" in the year 1959. This committee comprised 9 members and the librarian. Functions of this committee was (i) to prepare the annual budget (after having known the needs and requirements from the heads of departments) for consideration by the Library Committee; (ii) to allocate funds for different departments for books and periodicals; (iii) to make recommendations to the Executive Council with regard to the staff of the library; (iv) to prepare the Annual Report for consideration of the Library Committee, and (v) to advise the librarian in matters of administration and other such matters.

Later, the nature and composition of the library committee of Delhi University was changed on the recommendation of Carl M. White. It was composed of (a) three persons each from the faculties of Science, Social Sciences and Arts, nominated by the academic council (these persons were not necessarily members of the council); (b) one person each from the faculties of Mathematics, Education and Law (again not necessarily members of the council); (c) three persons nominated by the Vice-Chancellor; and (d) the Librarian as *ex-officio* member-secretary of the committee (White: 1965:184). Several other universities also found this recommendation useful and they adopted it.

In British universities, the library committee is comprised largely of representatives of the faculties, with *ex-officio* membership for the Vice-Chancellor, Pro-Vice-Chancellor, Treasurer, Bursar, Secretary or Registrar (invited to attend only). The Vice-Chancellor is usually Chairman and the Librarian or the Registrar acts as Secretary of the committee (Parry: *op. cit*: 141).

The library committee should be presided over either by the Vice-Chancellor or Pro-Vice-Chancellor. Sometime a senior Dean or the Professor is appointed as Chairman of the committee. Being influential members of the academic community of the university, their opinion matters and their presence facilitates implementation of the adopted policies.

The university librarian acts as the member-secretary or the convener of the committee. He prepares agenda and convenes the meeting. In British libraries, where the size of the library committee varies, one noticeable uniformity is that the librarian functions invariably as secretary of the committee. But in India, it is surprising that the regulations of certain university libraries like Allahabad, Berhampur, Bhopal, Sambalpur and Lucknow are still silent about the status of the professional librarian in the library committee. Thus, in fact, a great anomaly persists in the composition of the library committee in India which needs study and remedy.

Student Participation

To make the committee more broad based and representative, now students are also allowed representation on it. A recent trend in the university library administration is to pay greater attention to the students' views in matters concerning them, In British libraries, the library committees have made various arrangements to elicit students' opinion and views through their representatives. The representatives convey, meet and discuss their suggestions with the chairman of the committee before the meeting is scheduled and the chairman conveys their views (on the items) to committee members for consideration. Direct representation of the students on the committee is also gaining currency. In case of the representatives being appointed by the students' union, it is necessary to include representatives of the postgraduate students. The Parry Committee has welcomed such a system (of the student representation) through which the students are extended opportunity to express their views on library matters and suggest changes in the policy (Parry: *op. cit*: 146). The American Library Association also suggests setting up of a student committee on the library where possible (Withers: 1970: 159). In India, most of the universities have still failed to make provisions for the student representation on their library committees.

Other Staff Participation

In the meeting of the library committee, the university librarian is generally assisted by his deputy librarian. Regarding involvement of other library staff in the library committee meetings Thompson says, "there is not a great deal to be said for involving other members of the library staff; for one thing, such membership would unbalance the composition of the committee, the chief merit of which after all is that it represents an outside control on and interest in the affairs of the library." The library staff will already have, or should have, ample scope within the library's ordinary organizational structure to express their views on its functioning and policy matters. An additional reason is the need for the university librarian to present a single official library view in public, not (as could happen) a set of contradictory and discordant 'Library' opinions which would only serve (especially if they were on technical matters) to bewilder the lay members of the committee (Thompson: *op. cit*: 12). For involving the deputy librarian in the meeting, Thompson advances two arguments: first he will act as minutes-taker as the university librarian remains too busy and is actively involved in the discussion and secondly, he will provide the precise details on the matters of agenda which he is in a better position to do because of his close involvement in the routines and day-to-day functioning of the library. Thompson's views look practical.

Tenure of the Committee

The tenure of the office of the committee is usually fixed for a specified period varying from one to three years, depending upon the local conditions of the different universities.

Functions

The library committee performs the following functions:

(i) Formulation of library policy, keeping in view the emerging needs and requirements of study, teaching and research in the university.

(ii) Preparation and presentation of the budget of the library (annual and quinquennial) for approval of the higher authorities.

(iii) Framing rules for the library and adopting changes where necessary to ensure adequate service to the reading community of the university.

(iv) Making necessary provision for building, furniture, equipment, reading material and staff etc. in the library.

(v) Advising the university authorities regarding the adequacy of the staff and their appointment.

(vi) Prescribing necessary regulations for security and preservation of manuscripts and rare documents in the library, as also for reproduction of the copyright reading material.

(vii) Preparation of annual report of the library (an yearly account of the library activities) for presentation to the Senate.

(viii) General development of the library and its functioning.

Sub-Committee

Sometimes, the library committee delegates its powers to a sub-committee or standing committee constituted for the purpose. This is a smaller committee which functions as an executive body of the larger one. Usually this committee consists of the chairman and a few senior members of the library committee and the librarian. The Parry Committee recommends that the sub-committee or the joint committee set up with a view to considering special problems like planning the new library buildings etc. should always include the librarian amongst its members (Parry: *op.cit*: 146). This committee is convened by the librarian. It meets as often as the occasion demands to transact the business expeditiously, which is mostly of the following sort :

(a) preparation of library budget and allocation of funds under different heads;

(b) allocation of funds to various faculties and departments of the university for purchase of books, journals and library equipment, etc.;

(c) consideration of needs and requirements of the faculty and departmental libraries to make recommendations for their staff, furniture and equipment, etc.; and

(d) extending advice to the university library in matters concerning the different libraries of the campus.

The library sub-committee presents its deliberations and recommendations to its parent body viz. library committee to seek full approval and sanction before implementing and executing its decision.

In British universities, matters relating to library policy are discussed in the meeting of the library committee and its recommendations are sent to the Senate or the relevant Council Committee (for building, staff and finance, etc.) for being processed and approved. The proposal so approved are then sent to the Council for ratification. Such proposals as are raised directly in the Senate or in the faculty are referred to the library committee for consideration. The Parry Committee on libraries has no comment to make on the existing arrangement. This committee feels that each university will organize the library and its administration to suit its own circumstances-(Parry: *op.cit*: 141).

D.G.F. Walker's survey of the governance of university and university college libraries in Britain, done in 1968-69, brought forth that forty-eight out of fifty-one such libraries had library committees and, of these, forty-two reported to Senate but six direct to Council. Mostly, there were ten to fifteen members in the committee comprising faculty members, representatives of the students, Vice-Chancellor, Pro-Vice-Chancellor, Registrar, Librarian and Deputy Librarian. The size, however, greatly varied from university to university. For instance, the library committee of Newcastle University composed of 14 members comprising the Vice-Chancellor, Pro-Vice-Chancellor, Librarian, 11 Professors, 6 other academicians and 3 students (one post-graduate). The University of Reading had comparatively a smaller committee comprising the Vice-Chancellor, 3 members of the Council and the Librarian. There is, however, one noticeable uniformity that the librarian acts invariably as secretary of the committee (Neal: *op.cit*: 6). The recommendation of the Parry Committee is also identical regarding librarian's inclusion in the committee. The American Library Association suggests that as a rule there should be a library faculty committee, acting in an advisory capacity, to interpret the problems and policies in library to the academic community. The librarian may serve as its chairman (Withers: *op.cit*: 159).

Viswanathan states that the experience of some of the universities established in India after 1950 has shown that "fuller the powers and responsibilities vested in the librarian, the larger and better are the library services that accrue to the university community." (Viswanathan: 1972:16).

Scope

An awfully controversial but pertinent and moot point arises regarding nature and scope of the library committee. The point is whether the library committee should have an advisory or the executive role i.e., whether the deliberations of the committee should be obligatory and mandatory or only advisory and recommendatory in the functioning of the library.

Half a century before, the library committees were more of administrative than advisory in nature and scope. The reason being that the university librarian then was not an academic personality as there had been little professionalization of the institution of librarianship in those days. Now, this profession has undergone sea-change and the library organization and management has become a specialized job to be tackled by highly qualified persons backed by their professional training. The status and position of the university librarian and his professional staff have also since been recognized and equated with the faculty members of the university. As such, in the whole gamut of the functioning of modern university, the traditional system of administering the library through an executive committee bears no significance now.

Woledge and Page remark that depending upon the administrative capability of the librarian, the role of the committee will be advisory rather than executive. It will uphold, maintain and support the librarian's point of view to enable him to further and "to elaborate his plans in the light of detailed criticism and in enlisting on behalf of the library a body of enlightened opinion within the university." (Quoted in Thompson: *op.cit*: 10).

Besides playing the role of trusteeship and supporting the librarian's decision, the library committee can serve as a useful and sympathetic forum for the librarian to examine his proposals and test his new ideas and thereby enlist the members' views. Thompson states, "very rarely does a library committee resort to voting procedure; very rarely does it override the librarian's expert and professional recommendations. More often it enables him to formulate and improve his plans and so inform and sharpen his own performance." (*Ibid* : 14).

Highlighting the supporting role of the library committee,

Thompson cites an example of a British librarian who, on his appointment, quickly managed to constitute a library committee "mainly to provide himself with a shield" as there was none already existing (*Ibid*: 13). The author of these pages also subscribes to this view which is based on his own experience provided the committee functions as advisory alone; not tending to usurp administrating.

The American Library Association presented that the duties and authorities of the library committee should be concerned with general policy only. The librarian should be responsible for administrative and executive matters. He should be responsible directly to the president, the head of the university or college (Withers: *op.cit*: 159).

The Parry Committee states that presently the library is administered by the librarian with a library committee playing a role somewhere between an advisory and executive one depending in part on the personal qualities of the librarian and in part also on the tradition of the university (Parry: *op. cit*: 6). This committee makes no recommendation as to which definite role, viz., advisory or executive, should it perform. Carl M. White in his survey of the Delhi University Library in 1965 proposed formation of a library committee as a liaison agency between the university community and the library. He suggested that the appointment of staff and formulation of library rules should be kept outside the purview of the library committee.

The committee should be concerned only with the matters of formulating policy decisions leaving the organizational, administrative and financial issues to the librarian, whose rank, status and value are recognized to be equal to the faculty heads in the modern universities. In most of the American universities, while the library committee is responsible for making decisions in the matter of education and policies, those relating to finance are dealt with by the librarian and the Vice-Chancellor. In case the library committee assumes the executive role in affairs of the library, a situation arises when it proves to be a hindrance in the progressive development of the institution. Elaborating this situation, Viswanathan mentions, "one comes across members who either refuse or are incapable of seeing eye to eye with the librarian in matters of library administration. This is bound to result in stagnation in the growth of the library and frustration to the professional librarian, who remains bound by the decisions of such a committee. The librarian, who is the chief executive in the management of the library, lacks authority in taking decisions over the problems of readers and has to seek the approval of the committee which may or may not be inclined to view them in the same perspective" (Viswanathan : *op.cit* : 15-16).

As such, attaching undue importance to the library committee is not in consonance with the spirit and concept of university library. The committee should lend a helping hand in the functioning of the library and the best way to achieve this is to assign an advisory role to the committee. The powers and responsibilities be vested in the librarian—a specialist on the job who, with his knowledge, administrative experience, and professional competence, can manage the library well. To facilitate his functioning and enable him to acquit himself more effectively, the librarian should be allowed direct access to the highest authority in the university viz. Vice-Chancellor and made responsible to him directly for his decisions especially those connected with the affairs of the library. As a safeguard against misuse of his position, a small library committee with Vice-Chancellor as *ex-officio* chairman and librarian as its member-secretary should be set up. Further, well-meaning and competent persons alone should be appointed as librarians. With these discussions, we conclude that the second form of the library governance viz. that a professional librarian is more relevant and suited to manage and govern a university library in its new setting. The library committee should be renamed as library advisory committee.

References

1. Gelfand, M.A., 1962, University Libraries for Developing Countries, UNESCO Manual for Libraries-14, Paris, UNESCO.
2. Neal, K.W., 1971, British University Library, Published by author at 7 Church Road, Wilmslow, Cheshire.
3. Parry, Thomas (Chairman), 1967, Report of the Committee On Libraries. University Grants Committee, Her Majesty's Stationery Office, London.
4. Sharma, Chandra Kant, 1977. University Library: Its Management and Organization Metropolitan Book Co., New Delhi.
5. Thompson, James, 1970, An Introduction to University Library Administration, Clive Bingley, London.
6. University Grants Commission, New Delhi 1965, University and College Libraries, containing the Report of the Library Committee of the University Grants Commission and the Proceedings of the Seminar from Publisher to Reader held on March 4-7, 1959.
7. Viswanathan, C.G., 1972, University Libraries of India: Principles and Policies. Published by author, New Delhi.
8. Wilson, L.R. and Tauber, M.E-, 1958, The University Library, 2nd Ed., Columbia University Press, New York.
9. Withers, F. N. 1971, Standards for Library Service, UNESCO, Paris (Mimeographed).

3

Library Finance

Library Grant

Adequate provision of finance is an essential pre-requisite for a library. It is necessary for its day-to-day functioning and maintenance. Good library management depends on the financial footing; inadequacy of funds leads to its sluggishness. Therefore, it is the bounden duty of the authorities to assure adequate funds to the library.

Where from to procure the funds? The university authorities, viz., the Senate or the Academic Council do not have any income of their own, except the meagre fees received from the students. As such, the onus rests with the governments of the Union and the States, depending upon the tax-structure prevailing in the country. It is also dependent partly on how higher education is viewed as an agent of socio-political change under the existing political milieu of the country. In a developing country, socialistic pattern of education is favoured to meet the growing demand and, as such, cost of education, including higher education, is met out of the public funds. It seems impracticable to prescribe a common pattern regarding funding-source for the university education and its library; it varies with countries and time.

In India, the entire cost of education in general and that of the college and university education in particular, is met by the government grants. Under the existing structure of taxes in the country the major share of the revenue is taken by the Union Government, which is given back to the States in the form of various grants. Thus, in India both the Central Government through the University Grants Commission (UGC)and the State Governments provide funds for university education as grants. Under the existing system of grant sharing, the State Governments should place adequate financial resources at the disposal of universities and simplify the rules and procedures for operating them. The University Grants Commission should provide both development and maintenance grants to State universities. There should be some reasonable sharing of the developmental expenditures of the universities between the University Grants Commission and the State Governments. The University Grants Commission should take steps to resolve the problems faced by some universities on account of non-payment of committed grants by some State Governments. The system of grants-in-aid from the State Governments to the universities should be recognized on the basis of a suitable system of block grants. The finance of universities be placed on a sound footing on the basis of advice given by the University Grants Commission to State Governments and universities after periodical review. Further, it would be desirable to keep the universities immune from direct governmental intervention and also from direct public accountability.

Kinds of Grants

The three kinds of usually sanctioned grants to the library are: 1. Recurring; 2. Non-Recurring; and 3. Ad hoc or Special Grants.

1. Recurring Grant : This is a recurring fixed annual grant, especially to meet recurring expenditures like subscription to newspapers and periodicals, grants to purchase text-books for students and other items of routine and sundry nature in the library. This kind of grant helps the librarian to plan his budget of expenditures. The sub-committee of National and University Library (SCONUL), U.K. has indicated the following important criteria to evaluate recurring grant for a library :

(i) the number of students and the branches where teaching and research work are undertaken at the university concerned;

(ii) the number of research projects operating and the programmes undertaken at the university;

(iii) the scope of interest of the individual researcher, teacher and the department in which the subject is being studied and investigated;

(iv) the special collection of specific subjects, the manuscripts or the archives needed at the university;

(v) need for setting up outlying subject libraries and the extent to which duplicate reading material is required; and

(vi) responsibility of feeding the local institutions like jail, hospital and the centres of research in the different areas like education, health, agriculture, medicine and technology etc.

The recurring grant should be increased to enable the library to meet its regular commitments as well as the extended service to the members. The Parry Committee has recommended that the recurring grant for libraries should be increased to enable them to meet their responsibilities and develop their service (Parry: 1968:164).

2. Non-Recurring Grant : The non-recurring grant is sanctioned only once for a specific item of work or equipment and that has to be spent within the specified period of time. For instance, for construction of the library building or its extension; for purchase of book-stock for a new building and for building up book collection for a newly created faculty or the school. The Parry Committee has recommended for sanction of such a grant saying, "each institution must from time to time make non-recurring grant from its own funds to provide for the special interests of the new heads of the departments for subjects newly established in the university" (*Ibid*: 149). Neal mentions that despite Parry's recommendations, the non-recurring grants are not provided (in British libraries) for new subjects or new departments or for buying special collections (Neal: 1970:20). The Parry Committee has recommended non-recurring grant to university libraries to deal with even backlog of binding and repairs to damaged books and journals.

The non-recurring grant is meant to provide special funds for the following needs :

(i) To create and equip collection of books for undergraduate students.

(ii) To equip research collection of books and back volumes of journals and serials for a newly established department or faculty.

(iii) To fill the gap in the holding of the library especially in respect of the department whose demand for reading material has remained unfulfilled during the past, (iv) To acquire specialized collection in the library needed by the university departments.

(v) To purchase documents of rare value from the library of distinguished scholars or from second-hand book market.

(vi) To meet the cost of retrospective binding as in most of the libraries this work remains pending for funds which is fully utilized on purchase of books and journals.

(vii) To purchase library equipment. The new technology developed in the field of management has influenced the routines of the library practice in the recent years. The modern library now needs micro-film reading equipment; data processing equipment; computer consoles and equipment; closed circuit television; photocopying equipment and tape-type writers etc. Further, certain libraries also need library-bus or the library-van for its active and speedy extension services. Availability of these modern equipments in the library and their use will enhance the efficiency of service to the readers. To have them, the library will need non-recurring grants to meet the initial cost involved and thereafter the recurring grant for their maintenance and running cost.

(viii) The library also needs office furniture, racks, catalogue cabinets, shelves, charging and discharging trays etc. which require non-recurring grants for their purchase.

3. Special or Ad Hoc Grant : The special grant is a once-for-all grant. Parry Committee cited the special grant sanctioned by the University Grants Commission for purchase of basic book stock for the libraries of seven British universities viz. Sussex, East, Anglia, York, Essex, Lancaster, Warwick and Kent. The committee stated that for purchase of substantial special items for the libraries or those of distinguished scholars, a special central fund administered by the University Grants Commission or some other appropriate body should make available funds.

Price Rise of Books and Journals

The price of learned technical and scientific journals has increased tremendously due to rise in cost of papers, printing and binding materials besides the increase in labour charges for printing and binding work. Added to these are the increased inland and overseas postal rates. This has, in effect, led to reduce in real terms the year by year grant resulting into the drastic pruning of the subscription lists of journals. The report of the National Book League, London, for 1969-75 reveals that the book-buying in universities has slumped over the past two years. During the years 1972-73 and 1974-75 the purchasing power of the pound fell to more than 40 per cent and 16 universities spent less on books per student in 1974-75 than they did in the year 1972-73 and only 4 universities proportionately raised the grant amount. 25 per cent universities spent less than £12.73 per student because of the book purchasing capacity had decreased due to inflation and the largest percentage of grant was spent on salaries for the staff.

There has been 9.2 per cent annual increase in 1977 in the average subscription rate of periodicals in the US over those of 1976. Similarly, there has been 9.9 per cent increase in 1977 in the average serials published in the US over those of 1976.

In India, the cost of books and journals, especially scientific books and periodicals has been rising steeply. There was an overall increase of 75.76 per cent in the cost of periodicals and 93.7 per cent in the case of books in 1970. The increase in the postal rates of books has made matters worse. Thus the amount sanctioned as ad hoc grant by the library committee is quite meagre. Even the norm of Rs. 40 per student suggested by the Radhakrishnan Commission is miserably low with the rising cost of books and periodicals. There has been lack of proper guidelines and approved standards for arriving at the financial commitment of college and university libraries and, therefore, provision of funds has been irrational and disproportionate to the individual needs of the department and the library as a whole.

The British universities spent on an average 3.8 per cent of their income during 1955-56 to 1964-65 on their libraries. The expenditure, however, varied widely between the different libraries viz. Birmingham (2.3 per cent), Manchester (2.9 per cent), Leicester (6.5 per cent), Oxford (7.9 per cent) and Essex (a new university) 10 per cent. By 1966-67 the average percentage increased to 4.2 and during the period 1969-70 to 1974-75, the expenditure on the university library increased further to 4.3 per cent.

It is evident from the figures that during the recent years the British universities have been allocating more and more funds to their libraries and the percentage of the library's expenditure to the university's total recurring grant has increased though it is still below the norm suggested by the Parry Committee.

Determining The Library Finance

The Victorian Pattern

Under this pattern, the quantum of grants-in-aid to an educational institution is determined on the basis of a fixed ratio of the fund that the recipient institution provides from its own fund. This condition will not apply to a university library as it does not possess any source of income from which it could provide funds to be eligible for the grant. The alternative to this is the State Government who could provide funds to meet the recipient's share. Thus, if the above pattern is followed, the grant of the UGC to the university library will depend upon the amount the State Government provides to the library. And, due to numerous pressing demands of different sorts of other departments and institutions, the State Government remains too much preoccupied to provide funds to the library and the case of a university library for funds goes by default of the State Government. As such, this system does not ensure adequate funds to the university library and hence it is defective and holds no good.

Functional Approach

To determine the financial requirements of the library, it is necessary to take into account the size of the various faculties, the number of departments and the nature of study and research being pursued at the particular university. This is known as the functional approach.

Per Capita Approach

Another method to evaluate the financial needs of the university library is on a per capita basis which is a more realistic and equitable.

During the pre-war period the grant of books for university library used to be assessed on the basis of Rs. 15 per student and Rs. 200 per teacher and research fellow of the university. The annual cost of expenditure on other items in the library including that on administration and reference staff used to be estimated as equal to the ratio of expenditure over books, periodicals and other reading materials. The rising inflation in world economy since the World War II, has necessitated periodical revisions in the amount.

Before independence, the universities in India were too few in number and too small in size. After independence, the number of universities increased rapidly to meet the peoples, surging demand for higher education and they became active centres of teaching and research. This necessitated creation of well-equipped libraries with adequate financial resources. Also, the old and traditional universities had to be transformed and brought on a wider base by adding the newly emerged subjects in the field of knowledge to the courses of study. Every additional subject meant a new faculty and department; followed by a strong collection of books and journals to help study and research. All these needed money in the form of non-recurring and recurring grants. In India, the university library finance did not receive the attention it deserved and the libraries remained ill-equipped in respect of stock and staff. The sanction of grant lacked rationality; it was mostly ad hoc and arbitrary and, therefore, majority of the libraries lacked adequate finance. The University Education Commission appointed in 1948 under the chairmanship of Dr. S. Radhakrishnan took notice of the inadequacy of resources of the university libraries. Emphasising upon their importance on education, this commission recommended that (a) about 6 1/4 per cent of the total annual budget of the university or college or Rs. 40 per student should be allocated for their libraries; and (b) this grant should be augmented by non-recurring special grant for purchase of back stock of journals and books every five years.

Dr. C.D. Deshmukh, who was chairman of the University Grants Commission, gave special attention to improve the conditions of the libraries. He constituted a Library Committee in 1957 to advise the UGC about development of libraries and their organization. The important recommendations of the committee regarding the financial provision of the libraries in universities and colleges were the following:

(i) The UGC and the State Government should provide the entire finance of the university and college libraries.

(ii) The question of grant should be determined on the basis of per capita formula. For the time being, this formula should be as follows: subject to local variation, the grant for books and journals should be Rs. 15 per student registered in the university or college and Rs. 200 per teacher and research scholar.

(iii) In case of a new university or the new department created in the existing university, a special initial library grant should be sanctioned.

(iv) The university or college libraries should be helped also by additional grant at a rate to be determined by local conditions.

(v) The grant for the following year should be estimated normally on the basis of the statistical data of the preceding year, without prejudice to any unexpected and special demand coming up in the course of the year of grant, and the funds should be allocated.

(vi) The university and college libraries should decide between themselves from time to time the proportion in which they provide their respective grants. For the time being, the committee suggested that the UGC share should be four-fifths of the total grant and the State Government should provide the remaining one-fifth. These two authorities should have gentleman's agreement for prompt payment of their respective share of the library grant.

(vii) In case of failure on the part of the State Government to fulfil its obligation in payment of the share, the UGC should not withhold or reduce its grant and vice-versa.

The Kothari Commission appointed in July 1964 made a survey of the entire field of education and laid stress on adequate development of the academic libraries. It said that for a growing department, nothing could be more damaging than neglecting its library or giving it a low priority. The commission recommended that the new university, college and department should be set up only after taking into account (along with other items) the needs of the library in terms of staff, books, journals and space. Further, the foreign exchange needed by the universities and college libraries should be allocated separately by the University Grants Commission.

The commission also suggested that 6.5 per cent of University Budget or Rs. 25 per registered student and Rs. 300 per teacher should be allocated for the library. That, the ratio of expenditure on reading materials, staff and other items should be 4:5:1. The expenditure over staff and books should be in the ratio of 40:60.

Provisions equal to 10 per cent of the book-budget on furniture and equipment; 5 per cent of the book-budget for building and 8 per cent of the library budget for miscellaneous items should be made.

The amount suggested by the UGC Library Committee is considerably lower than that suggested by the first education commission (Radhakrishnan Commission). The recurring expenditure on books and journals, including building, has increased in the libraries in India at the ratio of 1.5 to 2.3 per cent of the total expenditure of the college and universities but still the ratio remained much lower to the norm of 6.25 per cent recommended by the Radhakrishnan Commission.

Control of Expenditure

The process of keeping control over the budget of the library is simple but essential to make the spending of the grant useful. The practice may vary in different libraries. The grants of books and journals are divided amongst the faculties and departments of the university to ensure equitable distribution of funds to each department. This system acts as a control over the unusually voracious departments and keeps the expenditure on an equal level for each department; it leads to a close contact between the library and the department and helps the librarian to visualize the pressing needs of a particular department and justify its budget proposal.

This is, however, a traditional system and inherits certain disadvantages too. By whatever criterion it is distributed, the department wise allocations, in truth, become arbitrary and unrealistic. The factors like student population, strength of academic staff, intensity of research, popularity of subject, the amount previously spent, price of books on the subject in question, richness of the existing collection and the score of other such factors hardly lead to any fair allocation between different departments. Secondly, there is danger of 'unspending' and 'overspending' as while one developing department has to limit its demands within the allocated quota even at the cost of its expanding programme, some departments, on the other extreme may spend its quota non-purposively just to consume its share. Again, if a certain department chooses to spend its grant on specialized literatures of limited interest, the general collection on the subject will adversely affect; creating imbalance in stock which is detrimental to the larger interest of the readers. And, Woledge and Page mention, "any such departmentalization of funds is apt to mean a departmentalization of the library itself; a professor is apt to refer to his books in the library" (Quoted in Thompson : 1970 : 17).

These points suggest that the traditional system of allocating the grant departmentally need to be liberalized and made flexible. Thompson advises to promote a less possessive interpretation of the word allocation and, instead, use the term 'target figure', which will carry the idea of suggested figure of expenditure which the department should aim at (*Ibid*).

Further, a substantial part of the book-grant should be kept in reserve and placed at the control of the librarian to be used for purchase of reference books, bibliographies, printed catalogues, and special collection offered for sale by some scholars. In special cases, this reserve fund can also be used to help equip a newly created department of a specific area of knowledge. The American Library Association prescribes that the library budget should be planned and administered by the librarian.

While distributing the grant, factors like size of the department (student population and strength of academic staff); popularity of the subject, number of research projects and cost of books and journals in the discipline concerned should be taken into consideration. A separate sheet may be maintained for each subject in the ledger of the library which should indicate the allocation for each subject. Each item of expenditure should be entered departmentwise and the running total should be maintained to show the balance of amount available for each department. Similar account need be maintained for the grants under the other budget heads. It is also necessary that separate accounts should be maintained for the grant of the library to prevent its diversion for items other than that of the library.

The figures of expenditure in the library should be got tallied and reconciled periodically with those maintained by the development and accounts branches as these departments also check and compile the expenditures besides keeping a watch over the progress.

The grant or the part thereof which is not fully spent by the end of the financial year (31 March of the respective year) is generally treated as unutilized and lapsed amount. In case of the grant for the five year plan period or quinquennial grant, it continues till the last year of the plan or the quennium.

In India, the UGC report mentions that "provision for the revival of unspent balance, in the next year's budget, is quite essential" (UGC : 1965 : 22). Each library should "spread the utilization of the grant received from the Government for reading and kindred materials as uniformly as possible over the entire period of 17 months allowed for the purpose" (*Ibid*: 142). Acquisition of standard texts, research material, back volumes of professional journals, and other scholarly treatises take unduly long time. This is particularly so in the case of a country whose book trade is not developed and where a thorough and extensive search is to be carried out to trace good publications. The UGC report again recommends that "to make the spending of book-fund useful and to avoid its being dissipated on the rush-purchase of any materials readily available in the nearby market, the unappropriated amount of the budget should not be lost to the library, but should be carried forward to the credit of the library and be available for inclusion in the budget of the next year, as an addition to the normal allotment" (*Ibid*). As such, the revival of the unspent grant and its addition in the next year's library budget are an imperative.

Staff

The following factors determine the staffing pattern of a library :

(i) the size of the grant for books, journals, equipment, furniture and fittings;

(ii) number of documents acquired and the rate of their accession;

(iii) increase in the student population;

(iv) pattern of the library-use in vogue by the members and the kind and scope of services provided by the readers;

(v) seating accommodation for the students and faculty members of the college or the university;

(vi) scope of the technical service to the readers of the library viz. classification and cataloguing systems followed; charging and discharging methods, regulations governing the borrowing and loan system, kind and scope of the reference services provided to the members and the amount of time the library functions to render service to its members;

(vii) number of service points created in the library and quickness with which the disposal of work is done and the amount of service rendered to the members; and

(viii) the kind of the library building i.e., whether it is an inherited and traditional building causing inconvenience of service to the readers and in use by them or whether it is a modern functional building.

In considering the library staffing, it is important to take into account the fact that 'library growth, unlike growth in most other parts of a university, is cumulative'. "Students come and go but books remain on shelves and have to be served" (Parry : *Ibid*: 268). There should be corresponding increase in the staff with the total increase in the student population in the university. Otherwise there would be fall in the standard and efficiency of the library.

The basic standard prescribed for staffing a library will always be subject to change on account of the special factors. If the library has acquired some major special collection, extra staff will be needed to acquire and catalogue them. The following of the pattern of depth classification and extensive cataloguing would require more classifiers, cataloguers and typists. Similarly, the extended library hours would entail engaging additional staff to be put on duty at different service points. Structure of the library building and degree of dispersal of service points are also the factors which affect the library service and consequently the staffing pattern of the library.

The ratio may vary greatly according to the size of the library and scope of the service offered. With the increase in the service to the readers, the estimated cost on the staff will essentially be higher and may be even greater than the cost of acquisition. This accords with the view expressed by SCONUL in their supplementary report that the ratio between book grant and salaries should be of the order of 50 : 50 (Parry : *op. cit*: 151).

Withers stated that a good college library spent usually twice as much (or more) for services as for books (Withers : 1970 : 160).

"Too many libraries have arrears because of parsimonious staffing—not least in the higher levels—and larger establishments are needed. New university libraries should be saved from slipping into arrears, otherwise unprocessed arrears will become in due course an unnecessary 'inherited burden' (in Parry : *op. cit*: 269). Most of the libraries in India are suffering from this kind of inherited burden.

The SCONUL report mentions that the sub-committee was unable to formulate a criteria for constant relationship between members or readers and the requirement of staff. The statistics produced by them earlier in the first report indicated ratio of 100 : 60 between book grant and salaries. This was a "purely notional ideal for a unitary library of a certain size, housed in a modern well-planned building, and with no 'inherited burdens' of old-fashioned methods or records incomplete or in need of revision." The committee further says, "probably no existing library conforms to these conditions." Cramped or rambling buildings, multiplication of service points, legacies of uncatalogued or imperfectly catalogued gift collections, out-of-date and cumbrous procedures afflict the older libraries; the newer ones have special problems in coping with exceptionally rapid development. In the present circumstances, therefore, the sub-committee feels that a ratio of 50 : 50 or even 45 (book grant) : 55 (salaries) is probably more realistic. The committee further observes that "they are not, however, persuaded that the cost of services will always bear a fixed relationship to the cost of acquisitions" (*Ibid* : 277).

Book Fund

The conventional term 'Book Fund' is used to mean the grant for purchase of books as well as for the periodicals, serials, newspapers and magazines. More loosely, it also includes the cost of binding and rebinding of the reading materials. In most of the libraries, the funds for periodicals, journals and binding and rebinding of books are usually treated together as part of the general budget of the library instead of being allocated separately to each department of the university. This practice has been adopted to avoid the number of broken sets. It has been experienced that when one department controls the subscription to the periodicals and serials, the number of broken sets is reduced as compared to the cases in which the subscription is controlled by the individual department separately, in which case cancellations frequently occur due to change in the departmental personnel or such other causes. When the university library controls the subscriptions and their renewal etc., centrally, "cancellation is practised only in the case of publications which have seriously lessened in their importance to the educational programme of the university." The latter practice makes for a consistent policy and insures complete sets of journals (Wilson and Tauber : 1958 : 99). Similarly, the control of grant for book-binding work centrally by the university librarian yields more uniform results than what otherwise happens if the grant is scattered and distributed separately, to the department libraries.

There are different practices followed in the different

libraries with regard to the distribution of book-grant, received centrally, to various departments. Certain university libraries prefer to control this grant centrally while most of the libraries consider it necessary to apportion the grant amongst the different departments separately. The responsibility of distribution lies with the librarian who usually gets it done through the library committee. This practice helps the librarian to spend the book-grant uniformally according to the needs and requirements of each department and subject and assures the expenditure more objectively. But it is necessary that if funds are distributed, there should be provision for the re-apportionment and adjustment of the grants wherever need be. This brings about flexibility leading to better utilization of the funds. "Rigid systems of allotment make it difficult for institutions to take advantage of special bargains which appear on the book market or to meet varying requirements of academic departments" (*Ibid* : 100). To make the allotment of the grant amongst the departments more objective and impartial, factors like the courses offered, student population, teaching method, recency of the department and its requirements, adequacy of the present collection of the department, the publication rate in the respective subject-area of the department etc., should be taken into consideration. The local conditions play an important role in the assignment of funds to the departments and, therefore, it is neither advisable nor practical to establish a formula in this regard to be used indiscriminately by all the university libraries.

Miscellaneous Expenses

Besides the provisions for books, periodicals, non-book and audio-visual materials, a part of the budget is also set apart for miscellaneous expenses like stationery (which includes the catalogue cards); communication, such as telephone, telegraph and other postal charges; insurance; printing of library forms; hot and cold weather charges; travel; entertainments; and institutional membership etc. Provisions for these items of expenditure are made in the budget based on the previous year's expenses and visualizing the likely increase, if expected.

Binding

The cost of binding books, journals, serials and other such reading materials is rising; even more rapidly than that for books and serials. But this is an essential item in the budget of the library. The SCONUL has mentioned that the proportion of the total book fund spent on binding appears to vary between 12 to 20 per cent. This allocation is considered inadequate and, therefore, the sub-committee recommends that 25 per cent of the grant for books and journals (excluding the grant for multiple copies or any special collection) should be regarded as essential for binding work (Parry : *op. cit*: 151). Further, the Parry Committee has viewed that the university libraries should be given non-recurring grants to clear up arrears of binding.

The Council for Arts and Science—learned and scientific libraries, Federal Republic of Germany—suggests that 25 per cent of the book fund should be allocated for binding.

Insurance

The collection of a college or university library is a treasure and its loss, if it occurs, means a considerable loss, much more than that of any other ordinary store or the collection. As such, the entire collection of a university or college library should be properly protected under a comprehensive insurance cover. The librarian should inform the estimated value of the library's collection, reading materials, equipment and furniture, office records, store articles and the building etc. The librarian should also make himself conversant with the methods of establishing loss for the purpose of insurance, when occasion demands.

Sundry Expenditure

The items under sundries include generally stationery, transport expenses of books and other reading materials, cost of postage stamps, telephone and other communication charges, minor office equipments, travel and other contingent expenditure and petty cash etc. The SCONUL recommends that 10 per cent of the book grant will be a reasonable proportion for sundries and funds to this extent should be set apart by the libraries.

Duplication of Text-Books

It is essential that a strong collection of text-books and the recommended reading is built up. This is all the more necessary in view of the high cost of the books which the poor students of the underdeveloped and developing countries can hardly afford to possess or purchase, especially in science, medicine, technology and the law. Also the seminar and tutorial teaching needs the library to provide a wider selection of multiple copies of the titles needed for a stipulated period for intensive use. The seminar programme of postgraduate classes will also demand duplication of texts. Further, the area and scope of certain subjects of humanity and social sciences are such that they need wider range of material to be used.

Some libraries keep one copy of the text-book in the issue section and deposit the second copy in the reserve section of the text-book, not for loan. A more common system is to buy multiple copies of the popular reading-texts and keep some of them in the reserve section for use within the library.

It would be impracticable to suggest what percentage of book-grant should be on purchase of multiple copies of the text-book as it will depend largely on the local conditions of the university. However, it is also necessary to encourage students to buy standard books for themselves. Thompson says the students are under some obligation to buy them. The amount specified in the SCONUL model is generous: "Multiple copies at £3 per student for 4000 students." At Reading University Library, for example, "reading-room collections built up over quite a few years still do not number above 7000 titles, and an annual sum not exceeding £ 5000 for the purpose of maintaining these collections would not seem inadequate" (Thompson : *op. cit* : 18).

The question of spending funds on duplication of textbooks in college and university libraries in India assumes all the more significance since the students in this country are by and large poor. Therefore, it is advisable to provide multiple copies of the text-books in the libraries of the college and universities and the residential halls. The extent to which a particular text-book should be multiplied should depend on the conditions prevailing in the respective college and the university from year to year and the college and the university should decide it by holding a meeting of the librarian and the department of teaching in each term for the books needed to be duplicated in the next term. The UGC report (1965) has not prescribed any specific norm in this regard and says, "the commission can do no more than keep on emphasising the problem of maintaining a fair amount of multiplication of textbooks as one of its intentions in giving the grant" (UGC: *op. cit*: 25).

Growth Rate of Documents

As per estimates in Germany and USA and also confirmed through the figures of Great Britain, the production of scholarly books and learned periodicals is rising at the rate of 4.5 to 5 per cent every year and in the nearly 15 years the learned publication will be doubled. The publications of serials, Government publications and literature of general interest is also increasing steadily. Therefore, to keep abreast of the developing knowledge and maintain its relative position in the world of scholarship, the library needs corresponding increase assets resources in terms of grant as well as storage capacity.

The physical burden on the library can be reduced by electronic devices and photography etc. but this will not help much the rising expenditure of the library.

Growth and Diversity of Indian Publishing

Today, India is one of the top six publishing countries in the world. In publishing English books, this country ranks third, following USA and UK. And this publishing industry is all set to grow further here. Internationally, this country is looked as the growth-centre by the foreign publishers. They consider India potentially achievable for their business enterprize. Harper Collins, a major publisher has acknowledged, its business in India has been growing at around 30 per cent annually over the past three years; outbeating the prevailing slowdown. And, if the unorganised sector is tackled and exploited adequately, the growth openings will further be reinforced. Presently, "only about 20 per cent of the industry comprises the organized sector but contributes to about 70 per cent in sales."

For Indian writing in English, a calling has created, requisitioning its demand, in the recent years, on a scale that never existed before. Country having vast youth - population, after immense scope in the area. Adding to it, factors like the outstanding and wondrous growth in Indian economy; fast growing literacy in English; the changing perceptions of people and the consumer's liking for different varieties of products and goods. With widespread globalization; upsurage of the new middle-class constituency as a potential buyer of books are the contributory contours, shaping and impacting the book-production focus here. With recently developed liking for English language (due to globalization), English literature is now amagingly popular with Indian readers, that did not happen before mid-1980s. Increase in the number of Indian fiction-writers in English has made positive impact on Indian readership. (Prabhakar Sinha : Publishing biz to grow in India : *The Times of India*; 9 Dec., 08).

Professor Tapan Basu, in his paper presented at the London workshop, states that the popularity of Indian writing in English in India has almost been affirmed by the two recent studies conducted in respect of English language book-industry in India viz. one by the Khullar Management and Financial Investment Services (1999) and the second by the British Council (2003). (Tapan Basu : Contemporary Indian writing in English : Is there a Market In India for this text; Presented at London workshop; The open university ; U.K.).

Pushing behind the so called impact of satellite television, computer and internet etc. the reading habit among Indians has increased. The National Readership Survey 2005 revealed that "The time spent on reading by people in India had gone up significantly — from 30 minutes per day to an average of 39 minutes per day over previous three years. The increase was sharp in urban India (from 32 to 42 minutes per day) as well as rural India (from 27 to 35 minutes per day). This speaks of the likely state of book-market in India — bright indeed.

Another determinant operative in this area is that, even though English-language-literate section of Indian population comprises only about 7 per cent of the country's population, but this small percentage actually ends up to account for nearly 65 million persons, because of the country's possessing a vast population. Comparing with the West, it is second only to 215 million English-literate population in USA, and more than about 60 million grass population of Britain and 20 million of Australia. This shows, India is possessing very large population that hunts for books in English language ; making this country a potentially promising book- market for English books. David Davidar (Penguin, Canada) says India is "the fastest growing English language market in the world today." In the coming decade, book-market of India could be bigger than Canada.

Here a noticeable feature is that while publishing in English in this country is more active, writing in regional languages too is equally prospering in India, comprising about

80 per cent of the book-market. The federation of Indian Publishers (FIP) estimated the total number of titles published in India in various Indian languages and in English during the year 2004 as 82, 537. Besides, other books published in all minor languages on the subjects like folk literature and religion (which do not have ISBN numbers) may be nearly 25000. Of these, Hindi books counted largest 21,370 (25.9%) in numbers ; followed by English 18,752 (22.7%); Tamil 7,525 (9.1%) ; Bengali 5,538 (6.7%) ; Marathi 5,475 (6.6%) ; Telugu 3,482 (4.2%) ; Malayalam 3,358 (4.1%) ; Gujrati 3,213 (3.9%) ; Urdu 2,172 (2.6%); Kannada 1,998 (2.4%) ; Punjabi 1,298 (1.6%) ; Assamese 1,285 (1.6%) ; Oriya 763 (0.9%) ; Sanskrit 749 (0.9%) ; Sindhi 176 (0.2%) ; Kashmiri 140 (0.2%) and other languages 5,243 (6.4%). This shows, only two languages - Hindi and English carried double-digit percentages ; and other languages remained restricted to one digit only.

The per capita book-output for India as a whole has been about 8 titles per 100,000 population. This number is much lower, in comparison to those of the countries like UK, USA, France and Germany. As for the language-speaking population, English language books are the highest at 23 titles per 100,000 speakers of this language, followed by Tamil at 11 ; Malayalam 8.7, Marathi 6.9 ; Bengali 6.3 and Gujrati 6.2. All these language books are higher than Hindi books being at 5. Kannad is 4.8, Telgu 4.2 and Urdu 3.9. Assamese at 7.7 is higher than many of these languages. Considering the fact that Hindi language speakers are greately higher in India, Hindi publishing is found less enthusiastic and deficient than English. Tamil and Malayalam publishing are similarly most active than other Indian language publishing ; although in terms of speakers, Marathi, Bengali, Telugu, Gujrati and Kannad are the larger languages. Assamese publishing is far ahead of these, despite its lower speaking number.

An striking point here is that in a growing economy, the increasing GDP calls for more educated, informed and knowledgeable persons in the work-force, who will need more and more books and allied literature, as a source to obtaining knowledge; enhancing their ability and understanding.. This situation digs up and impels demand for books. Further, the growing GDP generates higher income, which in turn, results in the increasing consumption for diversified products ; which includes books. There is positive correlation between the GDP growth and outgrowth (increase) in the book-production.

Looking at the growth in GDP per capita and the number of books, per capita, published in major publishing countries like USA, UK, France and Germany, it is seen that in USA, the growth in per capita book-title output increased from 7.6 per 100,000 people in the year 1950 to 43.2 per 100,000 in 2000. In this period, the corresponding figures for Britain increased from 19.8 in 1950 to 212.2 in 2000. And in Germany the per capita book title output, per 100,000 people, during the year 2000 was 100 and in France, it was 87 in this year. But, the relevant projection of book-production in India is found a marked low. The per capita book-title output was 6.3 only, per 100,000 Indians during the year 2004. In China, this figure was 9.9 in 2005.

To catching up the present level of book-production in the developed countries, India needs to go far ahead and increase its per capita output of books to draw a level with the GDP growth rate, set for 8 — 10 per cent per year; as also to meet with the developing consumption and the emerging urge for knowledge-books of the countryman. Sale of books is no deterrent as it has been growing at 30 per cent per year. The needed augmentation reasonably deserves government's assistance ; treating book-publishing as industry. (60 years of Book Publishing in India 1947-2007 ; Federation of Indian Publishers (FIP) ; New Delhi ; And certain data obtained also from Net).

Sources of Library Finance

The sources of colleges and universities for getting grants can be viewed under two categories, viz.

1. Primary Sources; and
2. Secondary Sources.

1. The primary sources of income in the college and university libraries are the following :
   - (i) The University Grants Commission (UGC);
   - (ii) The Governments (Union as well as State);
   - (iii) Endowment Funds;
   - (iv) College or University Grant; and
   - (v) Grants from Agencies (other than college or university).
2. The secondary sources of income in the college and university libraries are the following:
   - (i) Membership fee;
   - (ii) Fine;
   - (iii) Membership Fee by Non-Students and Teachers;
   - (iv) Refrographic Service Fee; and
   - (v) Fee for Inter-Library Room Service.

1. Primary Sources

(i) The University Grants Commission (UGC) : The universities are private institutions supported by public funds. The bulk of the university funds comes from the Government via the University Grants Commission.

In the United Kingdom, the UGC was set up in 1919 to act as a buffer between the State and the universities to safeguard the latter's autonomy likely to be interfered with increasing involvement of the State in education and in the financing of the university. It is non-statutory in character and surely not a Government department. It arranges for the allocation of grants and distributes the funds received from the States, amongst the universities.

In India, the University Grants Commission was constituted in 1956 by the Government of India under Act 3 of 1956 of Parliament with the objectives of promoting and co-ordinating the university education and determining and maintaining their teaching standards. The commission is empowered to assess the financial needs of the universities, allocate and provide grant for maintenance and development of the established universities or for any other general or specific purpose; keeping in view the development of the university concerned, its financial needs and the standard attained and the national purpose that is going to be achieved. The commission also advises the central and state Governments on the allocation of grants to universities for any general or specific purpose out of the consolidated funds of Indian Union and the State. The grants sanctioned by State Governments are usually in the form of recurring grants received annually by renewal. The allocations are usually done for a plan period spreading over generally a span of five years.

The University Grants Commission has been providing substantial grants to colleges and universities in India for various purposes like construction of new buildings, addition of annexes to the existing buildings, construction of building for their libraries and for buying books and subscribing to journals necessary for teaching and research and computerization of various library equipments and know-how.

The University Grants Commission has been making very significant and substantial contribution for maintenance and development of the libraries in the colleges and universities in the country.

(ii) The Governments (Union or State) : These are the largest providers of funds for the university and college libraries. The funds are received in the form of recurring grants (to be received every year) or a lump-sum grant provided by the Governments (usually the Union Government in respect of the centrally-governed universities and the State Governments with regard to the State-controlled universities) in the general budget of the university. Rarely the Governments directly sanctioned funds to the libraries. Sometimes, detailed schedules for the break-ups like building and equipment, furnishing and fittings and staff etc. are provided precisely by the Government in the budget. These grants are sanctioned for a definite period on financial year basis.

(iii) Endowment Funds : Such funds are generally donated by some philanthropists interested in the development of education. The donor expresses his wish whether the endowment should be used for a general cause or for a limited purpose. In case of general use, the income derived from the endowments can be used for a variety of purposes including the library. Sometimes, the endowment is received for a specific cause like development of libraries. Such funds are usually deposited in the university treasury. The librarian is authorized to withdraw funds from it in accordance with the terms set for its use.

(iv) College or University Grant : The primary responsibility of feeding the university library is that of the college or university. The university sanctions funds to the library by providing these in the university budget. The provisions are met as a lump-sum amount as well as in the form of providing the specific item individually. In certain cases the university allocates funds direct to the research or the academic unit, instead of the library. But this system is not conducive for co-ordinating the library resources and putting effective control over the grant.

(v) Grants from Agencies : Occasionally, special grants are received from certain sources other than the Governments or universities. Such sources are international agencies like the UNESCO, the UNO or the private and individual foundations. The grants are routed through the university and the Government.

2. Secondary Sources

(i) Membership Fee : Usually universities make it compulsory for every student to pay a membership fee for making use of the library service. Such fees are to be paid on a semester or yearly basis. It is highly unreasonable to ask students to pay for the library services. In fact, the university should provide the library service free of cost to students as in the case of a lecture-room or laboratory and other facilities. In fact, the income from the fee meets only a small part of the total cost of the library service and, therefore, should be considered insignificant.

(ii) Fine : The library charges a fine for the overdue books and for the books lost or damaged and for supply of duplicate borrowing-cards lost by the members. These are the secondary sources of library income. A fine is also imposed on members for violation of library rules with regard to maintenance of discipline in the library. The intention of effecting fines on the readers is not to earn or make it a source of income but to use it as a corrective against the violation of the library rules, warn them for any such indiscipline and make them aware of the sanctity of the library. The fine is collected by the library and then deposited into the account of the university.

(iii) Membership Fee by Non-Students and Teachers : Certain universities or colleges make provisions for special membership for such persons as may not be bonafide students or teachers of the university. They charge a special membership fee from them for making use of the library. The fee may be in the form of a certain amount to be paid annually or a lump-sum one; sometimes refundable too like the caution money. In fact, there is no uniform policy in this regard and the provision varies from college to college or university to university as per the prevailing practice. The fee is deposited into the university account. However, the fee, so realized, for such special membership does not meet the total cost of the service provided by the university. As such, this kind of a special fee is relatively an insignificant source of income.

(iv) Reprographic Service Fee : For providing photostat copies or reprographic service, the library charges a fee. In some universities, the charges are only nominal since the university contributes to the expenditure to encourage the availability of research material to the researchers.

(v) Fee for Inter-Library Loan Service : Many libraries ask the members to pay for the cost of postage or other such expenses for the documents requisitioned from the other libraries under inter-library loan service. As the postal rates are rising day by day, this cost may be high enough in some cases to prove to be a deterrent and discourage the intending members to requisition reading materials from other libraries on inter-library loan. Thus borrowers are deprived of such material, sometimes essential, for furtherance of their research work. Reasonably the library should assume the responsibility to incur this expenditure on its own to help encourage the researchers to derive full advantage of the inter-library loan facility so necessary for study and research.

Library Budget

A Budget is the financial statement of the library for a definite period. It is based on the estimate of estimated income and expenditure of the library concerned during a stated period of time. Drawn in the best interest of the service to the academic community of the university, the library budget presents a financial analysis of the logical, comprehensive and progressive policies of the library and tends to apprise the authorities with the needs as also the means to fulfil these commitments.

Objectives of Budget

The purpose behind preparing a budget for the library is to achieve the following primary objectives:

(i) to co-ordinate and correlate the resources with the expenditure scientifically;

(ii) to ensure a planned and purposeful spending;

(iii) to control the overall expenditure of the library; and

(iv) to serve as an instrument for planning the expansion of the library.

Thus, the need for preparing a budget for the library is very clear. Its absence leads to the uneconomic and unplanned expenditure and consequential loss of funds which are quite meagre, limited and scarce. Further, the budget-making provides an opportunity to review the existing plan and functioning of the library and redesign the future programming in consonance with the changed policy and the availability of the resources. And, occasion for such changes frequently arises. Therefore, it is indispensable for the effective management and administration of the library economy. Its utility, however, depends on how best the architect (librarian) plans his budget.

Budget Planning

The planning of the budget takes into account factors like funds already available and the likely grant and the revenue that might accrue from all possible sources on one side, and the estimated expenditure over maintenance of the existing services as well as implementation of the future policy and schemes designed on the other side. Depending upon the nature of planning, the budget can be a short-range (annual) or long-range (five-year duration) one. It differs from the annual financial report inasmuch as the report is only a statement of the financial targets achieved during the previous year whereas the budget speaks of the financial position and commitments of the ensuing year(s).

Usually there is a target date fixed by the authorities for submission of the library budget. Therefore, it should be planned sufficiently in advance. The budget is required to be prepared in the form and procedure prescribed by the university and the Governments. The librarian may like to consult the faculty members and departmental heads for a more purposeful planning of the resources in their particular area of study and research and to enlist their interest in the programming of the library. In the case of a university librarian being responsible for co-ordinating the services of other branch libraries of the faculties and departments of the college or the university, he may also wish to consult the in-charges of these libraries regarding their schemes. The budget should be approved by the competent body at the university and the Government well in advance. This would provide appropriate time and assure the university librarian to go ahead with the future year's programme.

Classification of Budget

The items of expenditure under the budget may be classified on the basis of the following characteristics :

1. By Periodicity;
2. By Objects; and
3. By Departments.

1. By Periodicity

(i) The budget is prepared for a stipulated period of time, may be for the current financial year or annual (for one year); for two years; and for five years etc. Accordingly, the expenditure can be classified as Current or recurring which includes expenditure on staff, salaries, postage, telephone charges, stationery supplies, heating and cooling, light and water charges and other such expenditure on consumable items on a recurring basis.

(ii) *Non-Recurring or Contingent Expenditure* : There are

certain allocations of grant in the budget by spending which some physical and tangible assets are created in the library. For example, purchase of books and other documents, audio-visual aids, periodicals, equipment and furniture and construction of buildings. These are called 'non-recurring' or 'contingent' expenditures and are included in the 'capital outlay'. These allocations are not essentially included in every year's budget. Though funds for purchase of books and periodicals and other equipments are generally provided in the budget every year, in a particular year it may not also be considered as an essential item for the budget and further, the amount of grant for these items may also vary from year to year; and

(iii) *Repayment of Debt* : This is a non-recurring expenditure, although the payment is made in instalments every year and, therefore, it may be included under the 'recurring' head.

2. By Objects

Another way of classifying the items of expenditure is by the nature of the materials acquired or the kind of services derived out of them. For example, purchase of documents (which include books, periodicals and the reading and audio-visual aids); preservation and maintenance (which include binding of books and journals etc.); building and equipment (which include construction, extension and maintenance of the library building, purchase of equipments, furniture and fittings etc.); salaries and wages and miscellaneous expenditure on postage; telephone and stationery items and other contingent expenditure for arranging book-exhibition, seminars and conference etc

3. By Departments

The various items of expenditure in the budget may be

classified departmentwise as well, as under :

(i) Acquisition;

(ii) Classification;

(iii) Cataloguing;

(iv) Reference;

(v) Circulation;

(vi) Periodical; and

(vii) Administrative.

The advantage of this method of classifying the expenditure is that every section gets an opportunity to participate in the preparation of the budget by assessing their estimates by themselves and helping the heads of the respective sections to exercise necessary watch and control over the expenditure. It also helps each department to provide funds to their every activity in the proposed budget.

Preparation of the Budget

The preparation of budget needs proper planning for making provisions of the necessary items. This planning needs to be done in advance. In fact, a well-planned budget needs preparation all the year round. To be more practical in this regard, the following steps may be taken :

(i) Opening a general budget file : All policy decisions on various aspects of the budget items taken from time to time, should be recorded subjectwise and maintained properly in a file.

(ii) Estimating the Income : Details of the sources of the estimated income should be maintained and noted from time to time.

(iii) Sectional budget file : The different sections of the library should maintain respective files of their financial needs to be incorporated in the total budget of the library.

(iv) Exploring the new sources of revenue : Efforts

should be made to explore the new sources of income to meet as far as possible the estimated expenditure and minimize the deficit.

(v) Justifying the items : To make the budget comprehensive as well as convincing, the proposed items should be properly explained, argued and justified; giving reasons for the increase or decrease of the estimated expenditure.

(vi) Working out the exact expenditure : To make the budget realistic, the exact and actual amount of expenditure should be explained showing the sources of revenue and then the actual amount required be worked out.

An ideal budget should consist of forward-looking financial programmes and co-ordinate the various commitments of the different sections working in the college or university library. To make the budget more useful, comprehensive and broad-based, it should be designed methodically.

Methods

Before discussing the methods, it is worthwhile to mention that the librarian should keep himself abreast with certain information like the period or duration upto which the current budget exists, the time by which the preparation of the next year's budget should start and the date by which it must be submitted to the authorities for consideration. The duration or the validity of the existing budget depends upon the dates of tried fiscal year, the particular university is following. The next year's budget starts immediately after the current year's budget ends. Therefore, it is always advisable to start the preparatory work of the next budget well in advance. Sometimes, the budget needs revision at different stages and, therefore, the margin of time for all these procedures is an important factor in its preparation and must be taken into account to avoid submitting an unplanned budget.

To make the budget more useful, comprehensive and broad-based, it should be prepared by adopting the following methods:

1. By comparison with Previous Expenditure

Except in case of the newly set-up library, every library has its budget of the previous year. Therefore, the budget figures of the previous year, the appropriations done during "the current financial year and the estimated expenditure of the next year should be put on a comparative table before finalizing the budget. The budget estimates of other similar and comparable libraries should also be looked into. To highlight the inadequacy in respect of a particular item and convince the administrative authorities, the support from other departments of the university as well as that from the other libraries be cited. This is necessary as the administrative officers are generally found unaware of the library provisions of other libraries. This method of preparing the budget by way of comparison helps the librarian analyse and evaluate the estimates of various items correctly and also, strengthens his proposal because of the citations of other libraries contained therein.

2. By Budgeting according to the Work Programme

The needs and requirements of the library should be assessed in terms of service to be offered and the work to be accomplished; keeping in view the broad objectives of the university.

Then, the items of the budget be drawn and formulated according to the programme envisaged. In case of any modification in the programme, necessary changes be affected in the items of the budget. The librarian should keep himself abreast of the changes that occurs affecting the library budget. The items under this head generally include:

(a) Fixed Charges : These include the maintenance of the catalogues and other records; reading-room expenditure;

binding cost; office expenditure; communication charges and expenditure on maintenance of the building including the insurance premia against fire, theft and other damages.

(b) Modified Expenditure : Consequent upon the re-organization of the library and its services, certain items of the budget get revised and changed. Also, certain items have to be deleted and some new ones to be added. This results into the modification of the estimated budget which should be taken into consideration while finalizing the budget.

(c) By Adopting the Accepted Norms (against arbitrary standards): Every profession follows certain generally well accepted practices. Subsequently, when these practices are approved commonly, they are recognized as the norms and standards of that profession. The library profession is no exception to this rule. These norms and standards are generally followed until certain other improved and more useful methods are discovered. Such a process of standardization leads to development and progress in the profession.

In the functioning of the university and college libraries also, the library profession, in consultation and collaboration with the financial administrators, educationists and the educational associations, has tried to work out and establish the set norms and standards for their different services. Attempts have been made in the areas of working out the ratio between the total institutional expenditure and the library expenditure and the per capita expenditure over the library staff, university teachers and the students. Many studies have been made (little in India but quite a deal in the developed countries) to work out the set norms and standards for the different aspects of the library services but results have been found to be varying and incomparable. One potent reason for the difference is the varying local conditions, the different universities or colleges are working in. To quote Wilson and Tauber, "it should be apparent that, because of the many variables which are involved and the variations in the needs of different institutions, no arbitrary standards will exactly fit a particular library. The nature of the curriculum, the status of the library's holdings, the amount and variety of the research carried on, the number of personnel and the efficiency of the library organization, the physical layout of the library building or buildings, the availability of endowment and other funds, the nature of the library programme—all have to be taken into consideration in determining what the budget of a given university library should be at a given time" (Wilson and Tauber: *op.cit*: 98). This discussion leads to the conclusion that the standards and the norms of the expenditure on library's functioning may be used keeping in view the varying local conditions while preparing the budget of a particular library.

The Grant from Government

The university receives its grant in blocks from the Government. Now, it depends upon the generosity of the university to allocate the share of the library out of the total grant of the university. Putting up the library financing on a sound footing is the prime obligation of the university. To highlight this fact and throw emphasis upon this point, the Parry Committee Report opens its chapter on 'finance' with the following paragraph, "We have had in mind throughout this Report, on one hand, that adequate provision for libraries is of central importance to the universities and indeed to the national system of higher education and to the intellectual standing of the nation; on the other hand, that library costs are rising steeply, that no end to this rise can be foreseen, and that the quality of provision in individual institution and nationality will always depend on the skilful use of financial resources which lag behind the demands made on them" (Parry : *op. cit* : 148).

In India, the financial provision for the college and university libraries has been totally disproportionate to their needs and requirements and the demands of service made on them by the students and the faculty. On our achieving independence, it was realized, during the course of improving the conditions of higher education in the country that our libraries were awfully illequipped and that the allocations of funds were too meagre. There were no norms and standards to work as basis for the allocation of grants and, as such, the sanction was mostly irrational, arbitrary and ad hoc. The Commission for University Education appointed under the chairmanship of Dr. S. Radhakrishnan recommended that about 61/4 per cent of the total grant of the university or college or Rs. 40 per student should be allocated for their libraries (in USA the corresponding figure being Rs. 60 to Rs. 80) and that this allocation should be augmented by special grant for books and journals every five years.

With the establishment of the University Grants Commission under the chairmanship of Dr. CD. Deshmukh, this point received better attention and the commission suggested for higher allocation of grants to the libraries for books, staff, building and equipment. The commission further recommended that 20 per cent of the book grant might be spent on the staff and this expenditure should be allowed as long as the book-grant lasts.

The Education Commission Report 1964-66 (Education and National Development), Ministry of Education, Government of India, under the chairmanship of Dr. D.S. Kothari observed that with the increasing enrolment in universities and colleges, while the demand for library service has been Constantly growing, the position of expenditure over books and periodicals was not satisfactory. 5 universities were spending less than 1 per cent; 34 universities were spending between I to 5 per cent and it was only in the case of 4 universities that the expenditure on books and periodicals was more than 5 per cent of their total expenditure. The committee emphasized upon drawing up an integrated plan of library development from a long-range point of view and mentioned that there was no formula for estimating with precision the amount of money to be invested by the university in its library. It was found that the expenditure on library in relation to the total educational expenditure of the university had gone up due to the impact of the UGC grants. The Education Commission suggested that about 6.5 per cent of the educational budget should be reasonable expenditure on libraries but that could vary, depending upon the stage of development of the university library, from 6.5 per cent to 10 per cent.

In fact, it seems unrealistic to compare the expenditure of one library with other as it depends considerably on the local funding capacity as well as the needs and requirements of the particular library. Students' enrolment figures, curricula of study and teaching, pedagogy, research programmes and the fields of specialization etc. are the factors to be taken into consideration for the allocation of grants. Further, a newly created library will need basic grant for the basic collection and setting as well as development grant for the expansion envisaged. Similarly, an old library in the process of re-organization and expansion will also require more funds. Cost of implementing the academic programmes also varies at different places. As such, application of fixed and uniform norms will not be workable in all cases.

Dealing with the standards, Gelfand observed that 5 per cent is now quite commonly set as a minimum standard for college and small university libraries. But such standards should be used with caution. It depends upon the condition of the library. A new and growing library will need far more than 5 per cent and an old one in the process of re-organization and development may require even more.

The Parry Committee viewed that the annual library expenditure of a university with total annual budget of £ 3,35,000 should be approximately 6 per cent of the total university expenditure. The said committee states, "the annual cost (on the SCONUL model) of the library provision in a university of medium size should amount to about 6 per cent of the budget of such a university. Circumstances vary and it would be undesirable and impracticable to, impose standards centrally; but we believe that this represents a standard below which British university libraries should not be allowed to fall" (*Ibid*:156).

The expenditure on university libraries in the United Kingdom has been gradually increasing.

The Standing Conference of National and University Libraries (SCONUL) has presented a model annual budget for an established library with 500,000 volumes for a university of 3,000 undergraduate students, 1,000 research students and 500 teaching staff :

Books — 40% (of the library budget)

Journals — 21.4%

Multiple copies — 13.10%

Binding — 15.50%

Sundries — 10%

The above book-grant assumes a unitary library with no departmental or branch libraries, nor having any amount for special responsibilities. Major subjects have been covered. The grant will increase with the number of subjects in which teaching and/or research is conducted (*Ibid*: 267).

This model was drawn keeping in view the prices prevalent in June 1965. After that the pound sterling was devalued and also the prices have risen and the cost of books, periodicals, binding work as well as salary bills have increased tremendously.

H.F. Dammers has presented break-ups of the budget of an average British university library as follows : (Quoted in Thompson : 1970 :15)

(i)	Salaries	50 per cent
(ii)	Books	25 per cent

(iii) Periodicals 13 per cent

(iv) Binding 6 per cent

(v) Sundries 6 per cent.

Thompson says there is no need to explain the allocation on salaries since this percentage is a 'wellnigh standard.' The SCONUL in the supplementary report on the standards in university libraries states that the Sub-Committee was unable to formulate any constant relationship between number of readers and requirements for staffing. In their first report the committee suggested an ideal ratio between book-grant and salaries at 100:60. It now elucidates that no such formula was intended; it was purely a notional ideal for a unitary library of a particular size established in a well-planned building and credited with up-to-date records and the modern methods, carrying no inherited burdens. But hardly any library conforms to these conditions. "Cramped or rambling buildings, multiplication of service points, legacies of uncatalogued or imperfectly catalogued gift collections, out-of-date and cumbrous procedures afflict the older libraries; the newer ones have special problems in coping with exceptionally rapid development. In the present circumstances, therefore, the Sub-Committee feels that a ratio of 50:50, or even 45 (book-grants) : 55 (salaries) is probably more realistic. The Sub-Committee, however, amply clarified that "they are not persuaded that the cost of services will always bear a fixed relation to the cost of acquisitions" (*Ibid*: 277).

US Libraries

The norms and standards observed by the libraries in the United States are sufficiently of a high level; even higher than those obtained in the British libraries.

The American Library Association suggests that the library budget should be determined in relation to the total budget of the college and university. The library service, based on the prescribed standards, would normally need a minimum of 5 per cent of the total educational and general budget of the university or college. With the rise in student population, expansion in the courses of teaching and addition to the new programmes of studies and teaching the above percentage would also increase (Withers: op.cit: 159).

The Budgeting and Fiscal Management

Budget of a university library is a formalized statement of all accounts showing the amount available for a specific period (usually a year) allocated under the various heads and categories (books, periodicals, equipments, binding, travel) or the operating units like administrative section, technical section, reference section, lending section etc. of different unit libraries like arts faculty library, science faculty library or the engineering faculty library etc. As a substantial portion of the budget is devoted to the staff, the individual names of the staff and their salaries are also mentioned in the budget.

The budget-administration or the fiscal management is a round-the-year operation and, in fact, quite difficult. The procedure of preparing and presenting the budget is a continuous process, which requires thorough consultations and discussions through the year in advance of the respective financial year.

The university library functions and operates with certain defined objectives and set goals. Accordingly, the factors of budgeting require certain assumptions as inflow of materials, work-loads, service and staffing. As such, in a library where the objectives and goals are distinctly laid down in the form of clear-cut programmes, its budget is also found to be exact and precise making promises with greater assurance and speed than otherwise would be in case of the university with confused goals and programmes. If the programmes are drawn with active participation of the faculties and the university administration, much of the defence of the budget is built-in and proper attention is ensured.

The Budget Process

Preparation of a budget needs a 'base' as a reference point. It comprises general university funds, specific income from the library endowment appropriated by the governing authority for library purposes. The miscellaneous gifts, grants and the anticipated income from fines or sale of duplicate materials do not form usually the part of the budget base. The general practice is to group the increase to the base in the following three categories: (i) Maintenance Funds; (ii) Improvement Funds; and (iii) Capital Funds.

(i) Maintenance Fund : It is necessary to maintain the current level of operation with no expansion of the programme. This head includes increase in the percentage of living affecting the salaries of the present staff, increase in book-costs (assuming no increase in the number of volumes acquired) and the corresponding increase in the supplies and services due to rise in the cost of forms, stationery, postage and telephones etc.

(ii) Improvement Funds : Under this category such funds are accounted as are needed for an improved level of operation or the new services. Funds to buy more books, increased staff to process enlarged acquisition intake, staff to set up new branch and unit libraries and a new provision for the full-time secretary are a few examples of the items of improvement funds.

(iii) Capital Funds : These are one-time expenditures to add to the library's tangible assets and these usually relate to new buildings and major reconstructions; major items of equipment in the library like installation of sizeable number of catalogue cabinets, book shelves and almirahs etc. an extensive and large collection of books in a specific field that is needed for a new academic programme for study and research in a given area, gifts, grants and contract funds, un-anticipated or for a limited duration, which are not considered part of the base. The activities carried out with such funds of this nature have a terminal date and can be managed and controlled without disruption of the normal functioning of the library or the long-term staff commitments. The procedure, however, varies in the different universities.

Depending upon the process of university budget followed in different universities, the requisition for the proposals of the budget is received in the library a year or more in advance of the respective financial year. Anticipating this call, the librarian should have canvassed from all his departmental officers for a statement of their requirements. It is better for the librarian to lay down certain guidelines for requests from departments rather than to leave them unguided for preparing their requirements and the demands widely without having the possibility of their fulfilment. The officers of the various departments and the sections may be instructed to explore the possibility of making savings that could be utilized elsewhere in their departments or in some other needy section. It would be more effective if the librarian asks for a response on the specific points enumerated by him. The officers in charge of the acquisition and cataloguing sections may be asked to study the economics that may be realized by combining the work-load of order-searching and pre-cataloguing searching. Similarly, the officer of the binding section may be instructed to explore the alternative sources of binding at lower cost without sacrificing the quality or prolonging the time taken in the binding work. Similarly, the officer of the inter-library loan services may be instructed to examine the requests for the loans to find out whether an unreasonable pressure and work-load is being generated by certain institutions. In the budget of the faculty library, it would be advantageous to involve the faculty library committee in budget-making and seek its general endorsement and support. This strengthens the hands of the library in seeking its budget requirements which are to be approved at the levels of the Vice-Chancellor or Pro-Vice-Chancellor.

The priorities in the budget proposals should be determined and this helps finalization of the budget quickly and intelligently. Certain items of the proposal are found to be interdependent and, therefore, to determine the priorities is not an easy task. The estimates should be based on accepted norms and standards for service in the college or university library. This facilitates budget-presentation and its justification. The library staff should explain each item with sufficient clarity and details to enable the university authorities to understand the proposals and realize their importance and the necessity with a view to approving them.

Preparation of Quinquennial Estimate

The budget proposal of a library is prepared in the form of annual or quinquennial estimates. It is divided under different headings and contains detailed analysis of the present expenditure and future commitments. Full description of the development plan and the expenditure involved is given. It also shows the items of income, existing as well as perspective, and indicates the resources of the library. The proposals are examined by the university and their financial allocation of funds are made annually in the library budget which forms part of the whole university budget. In the case of a Five Year Plan to be sanctioned by the UGC, the proposals are first considered by the university and included as a part of the whole and comprehensive plan of the university for submission to the UGC. The UGC appoints advisory panels to examine the budget proposals. Generally, the panel visits the library to ascertain its needs and requirements and then makes recommendations to the UGC. The UGC considers and approves the recommendations depending upon the availability of funds and finally sanctions the budget of the university which includes the library grants and provisions as well.

The university library has to perform this exercise every year for its annual plan and undergoes the same process for the quinquennial estimate (in India it is called Five Year Plan) as the UGC sanctions grant in a quinquennial cycle. It is common experience that library estimates are rarely met in full. So the librarian has to underline his priorities carefully under each budget-head. He has also to advance all sorts of arguments in support of his proposals; giving relevant datas and comparative figures. The estimates in the budget should be need-based. The librarian has to foresee well the future of the library and should draft a plan in relation to the growth and development of the library and the university.

The librarian sends his budget proposal to the development section of the university where it is examined, processed and submitted to the finance committee of the university. Then, the budget is presented to the appropriate body of the university and passed finally. At every stage, the proposals are generally subjected to pruning which, more often than not, results in clipping of even the necessary items; of course to the disappointment of the librarian. In the circumstances, the librarian has to re-draft his budget 'cutting a lesser coat from reduced amount of the cloth, and tailor his needs proportionately. In some cases, he again presents a revised budget to the library committee or any other appropriate body of the university empowered for the purpose and seeks approval before acting upon them.

Special Budgeting Techniques

In an institution, specialized financing has to be adopted to meet the contingencies arising from time to time. In this connection, the following three points need to be taken in view:

(i) Capital Liquidating Funding : At times, the library is faced with a situation when funds are not available to meet the new programmes involving sizeable expenditure. For example, to provide books for completely new departments, to provide extra hours of service and to create additional service points for widely-spread student community, while the university comes to the rescue of the library by providing funds once or twice, it shows its reluctance, to come forward all the time. The library has, therefore, to find out the means. This can be done on a capital liquidating basis. Contrary to the programme approach, it is a technique in which a special support of sizeable amount of fund is obtained which is spread over several years and phased out according to financial needs and commitments of the library. The funds are sanctioned by the budgeting authority. Five year is a usual span but it can vary between two to ten years depending upon the circumstances and the needs. The sizeable funds received in the form of foundation grant, gift or special allocation etc. from Government or the university can be utilized for this purpose. It was found that during the first five year plan, the entire expenditure was met out of the grant or the special fund or gift provided for the purpose but subsequently in the second year only 75 per cent, in the third year only 50 per cent and in the fourth year only 25 per cent expenditure was met and the library itself had to build up and increase its resources gradually to meet the balance of expenditure in the second, third and fourth years and to sustain the full expenditure in the fifth year. This procedure activises the implementation of the plan quickly.

(ii) Contingency Fund : Every institution has to face some unanticipated expenditure for which it has no pre-allocated budget. To meet such a contingency, the institution has to arrange for some general fund as its financial support for emergencies. This grant is always meant to meet any unforeseen expenditure and usually it is a small amount, as compared to the total budget, say 1 per cent to 3 per cent of the grant or even less depending upon the institution and its budget.

(iii) Revolving Fund : It is a kind of fund which provides working capital for certain activity in the library. Sometimes, this term is used, loosely. Income derived from a source other than within the scope of library's main activity but over which the library maintains certain control is called 'Revolving Fund'. The characteristics of such a fund is that the income and expenditure in this account should theoretically balance or wash each other out at the end of the year to leave a zero or nil balance of the available fund and, as such, it is sometimes called a 'zero' or 'wash' account.

An instance in point is the photocopying and photostat service provided by the library to readers. For this purpose, capital expenditure is incurred to purchase photographic equipment, payment of salaries and wages to the staff employed to provide this service, and also for setting up an office for this work which involves expenditure on items like chairs, tables, almirahs, registers and other such items. All these expenditures are credited to the account of the revolving fund. Fees realised on photoduplicating service from readers are credited to this account. Similarly, a publication account can also be operative out of the income from the sales of university publications. The cost of printing, editing, advertising and mailing is charged to this account. The person dealing with the budget in the library should be conversant with all the problems involved so that he may take appropriate decisions, although on certain other items, the final decision rests with the librarian. Unless the person, dealing with preparation of the budget, knows the fact that whether the impending proposals would affect the budget, favourably or adversely, he will not be in a position to include these items. As such, an appraisal with the details of the proposal and their financial—-implications is a pre-requisite for the official entrusted with the task of budget making. He will have a watch over different allocations and alert the librarian about the deficit or the surplus grants as the case may be with regard to the particular items of the budget.

The 'position of funds' in a large library should be reviewed periodically. First reading should be given at the end of the first quarter of the financial year to examine whether the progress is satisfactory. At this stage, necessary changes may be visualized and the final procedural outline may be drawn. As the year progresses, the review should be done more frequently and during the final year, monthly review is desirable to ensure the full utilization of the grant.

Library Book-keeping

Purpose

The purpose of book-keeping in the library is to exercise control and supervision over the funds of the library; to ensure proper utilization of the funds under different budget-heads; and keep a watch over the misuse of funds to maintain correct information in the form of statistics regarding the grant and its position and help prepare the next year's budget more accurately and objectively. Proper maintenance of these financial records serves as a mirror to reflect the exact position of the income and expenditure of the library, as also its future needs and requirements.

Procedure

For adopting a proper procedure of book-keeping for the library, the following records are essential :

(a) Allocation Register;

(b) Invoice File;

(c) Bill Register;

(d) Stock Register;

(e) Imprest Account Register;

(f) Caution Money Register;

(g) Miscellaneous Income Register; and

(h) Duplicate Record File.

(a) Allocation Register : The lump-sum grant received as book-fund is usually distributed amongst the faculties and the departments. These allocations should be noted properly in a register. Otherwise it would be difficult to verify and control the grants of different departments and the subjects. Writing the total grant on the top of the first page of the register, separate pages should be allotted to each department arranged faculty wise and then the allocation of the respective departments should be mentioned. A subject-wise index with page number should be given in the beginning of the register. Two separate such registers for (i) Book fund and (ii) Periodicals and Magazines grant be maintained. Each and every amount spent on purchase of books or journals should be entered under the respective subject and the progressive total should be given, showing the balance under the grant. This register is necessary to keep a watch over the allocation and expenditure for the various departments so that the latter does not exceed the ceiling.

(b) Invoice File : The supplier submits the bill in duplicate and sometimes in triplicate. One copy (original) of the bill is sent to the accounts section for payment after due verification. The duplicate and triplicate copies of the bill should be filed properly in the file kept in the library. For each financial year a separate file is opened and the invoices are filed.

(c) Bill Register : It is a register in which all the bills received from the supplier is entered showing maximum details. It contains the following information:

(i) Serial number;

(ii) Name of the supplier;

(iii) Bill number and date;

(iv) Nature of the reading material purchased;

(v) Budget-head and the account;

(vi) Date of the bill received;

(vii) Stock register entry number;

(viii) Date of the bill passed for payment;

(ix) Date of the bill received in the accounts section for payment; and

(x) Signature of the official receiving the bill in the accounts section for payment.

On receipt of the bill in the library, it is properly checked and verified with regard to the items received, their prices and the conversion rates, if any, condition of the supply and stock entry etc. and then a certificate is given for payment. The serial number of the bill register is also entered on the bill which is generally called the voucher number. This helps to find out the reference and details of the bills and its payment.

(d) Stock Register : Every item that is purchased in the library is entered in the stock register. Separate registers are maintained for the article of reading materials and the store and stationery. The books are entered in the accession register. Similarly, separate registers may be maintained for the periodicals and journals. The back volumes of journals of previous years with complete volumes are treated as books and, therefore, entered into the accession register of books. Stationery items, furniture and equipment etc. are entered in separate registers or separate pages in one register allotted to them. Every bill, before it is passed for payment, has to be certified by the stores-in-charge to the effect that the article was received in good condition and that it has been duly entered into the stock register; stating the serial number and page number of the entry.

(e) Imprest Account Register : In every library an imprest account register is maintained to show the day-to-day petty and contingent expenditures incurred for un-assigned budget items. A petty cash amount is usually sanctioned by the university to meet such day-to-day contingencies and petty cash expenditures. All the necessary details of the vouchers are shown in this register which is also called 'petty cash register'. The amount spent in this regard is immediately recouped. It is easier to prepare it weekly. It is a weekly job consisting of the following work:

(i) *Petty Cash Account Writing* : All the petty expenditures incurred during the week should be entered showing the details of the vouchers therein.

(ii) *Petty Cash Account Closing* : At the end of the week, the week's account should be closed in the petty cash book.

Certain libraries prefer to maintain this record on a monthly basis.

In some universities, the imprest money is created by converting the library income like fines and cost of replacement of the lost or damaged books etc.

(f) Caution Money Register : The library collects caution money from students to guard against loss or damage to books borrowed by them from the library. This amount is reimbursable to the students when they complete their course of study. Therefore, all details of the students who deposit the caution money are recorded in the register to help verify the claims for return of the amount later.

(g) Miscellaneous Income Register : The library gets income in the form of membership fee, fines and overdue charges of books and other reading materials borrowed by the library members. This is realized from the members as a fine for the violation of the library rules and procedures and to check such future default. A formal cash-receipt is issued for the amount realized in this way by the library. These 'cash receipt books' are kept in the library in the safe custody as a permanent record. Besides the receipt books, record in respect of such income should also be maintained on a separate register containing the following details: Serial number; Borrower's name; Class; Details of the book; journal and other reading material lost or made overdue; Period of the overdue; Price of book; journal or reading material (if lost); Amount realized and signature of the official concerned. This account should be kept month wise and report should be sent to the finance section of the university every month.

Similarly, if there is an income in the library for supply of photostat copies to library members or income from any such sources, detailed information should be given in the register and proper records maintained for purposes of audit or for future reference.

(h) Duplicate Record File : The carbon copy of each order (usually termed as office copy) should be properly filed date-wise. It is better to maintain this record separately for each subject, showing the allocation of the respective subjects on the top of the first page of the file. On receipt of books, the bill should be placed on the respective file for being processed after proper verification and passed for payment.

Budget Statistics

This is related particularly to heads: 1. Income; and 2. Expenditure.

1. Income : The items of income generally consist of the following:

(a) University Grants Commission (under Five Year Plans);

(b) State Government (Plan);

(c) State Government (Non-Plan);

(d) University or any other Agency;

(e) Membership Fee;

(f) Fines;

(g) Gifts and Donations;

(h) Sale of Publications or Photostat Copies etc.;

(i) Sale of Waste papers and old Magazines; and

(j) Other sources.

2. Expenditure : The items of expenditure in the budget consist of the following :

(i) Purchase of books and journals, which also includes back volumes of journals, antiquated and rare books and manuscripts;

(ii) Subscriptions to current journals and periodicals;

(iii) Purchase of library equipment and furniture;

(iv) Salaries:

  (a) Basic Pay;

  (b) D.A.;

  (c) House rent and other allowances; and

  (d) Provident fund.

(v) Contingencies:

  (a) Stationery including catalogue cards and book processing materials;

  (b) Printing of library forms etc.;

  (c) Binding of books and journals;

  (d) Electricity charges;

  (e) Telephone charges;

  (f) Postal charges;

  (g) Overtime and other allowances;

  (h) Insurance premium; and

  (i) Other unforeseen contingent expenditures.

Punch-Card System

Relatively a new system in maintaining the financial records and exercising administrative control over the income and expenditure in the university library has been the introduction of Punch-Card System. It is being used more extensively in developed countries. This is a simplified financial administrative procedure in which the punch-card equipment is used. For each transaction or the group of data-information, tabulating cards are used. The code of operation or the expenditure classification, account and other items are punched on the cards. To ensure complete integration of the accounting processes and the system, the information and data are first arranged so that the cards may be coordinated with those used for other processes.

Cost Control

For the sake of achieving efficiency in the financial administration of the university library, it is necessary for the librarian to collect and organize the various data showing the cost of such services as acquisition, classification and cataloguing, processing, circulation, reference services and binding etc. This is absolutely necessary to justify the proposals of the budget submitted to the university. This information presents an exact picture of the relation between the funds spent on a particular service and the units produced by the expenditure. This process provides not only knowledge of the total cost over a particular service but also indicates adequately what is being done in that area of service. This information is necessary for envisaging any change or improvement in the service.

Many university libraries, especially in the developed countries, have started organizing their data with regard to cost-studies on punch-card system. Whatever the system adopted, it is a necessary job to be done in every college and university library to justify its budget and strengthen its arguments for the increased grant. The information helps to advance answers to questions about the utility of the library and the advantages of the services extended by the institution.

The Financial Standards

Different standards have been laid down for the libraries of the different colleges in UK, USA and Canada.

Federal Republic of Germany

The Council for Arts and Science—Law and Scientific

Libraries (1964) recommends that students are increasingly dependent on libraries for their text books and other recommended readings. Therefore, every university library should build up a separate collection of text books with sufficient number of copies. Additional copies should be provided in the reference collection. The council recommends that funds to the extent of 20 Deutsche mark (DM) per student for purchase of books for the initial collection and 4 DM per student annually for maintenance (i.e. on the collection of text books) should be made available.

The council says that the number of periodicals subscribed is the influencing factor in assessing the funds needed for purchase of books. The expenditure on periodicals represents a fairly constant proportion of book-fund. The expenditure on continuations and series works out at 50 per cent of that on periodicals and the expenditure on books comes at 75 per cent of that on periodicals.

The council further mentions that the requirement of the total number of periodicals increases by 5 per cent annually. The increase in respect of German and foreign periodicals will be 35 per cent in general university library and 40 per cent in technical university library over a period of eight years. The prices rise by four to five per cent annually. There has been annual increase in book production by five to six per cent since 1957. Therefore, to admit of the expansion of the collection and to meet the increased cost, there must be an annual increase of 10 per cent in the book-grant.

The ratio between the allocations of periodicals, continuations and series and purchase of books and others should be 7:4 in the general university library and 8:4 in technical university library.

The council further suggests that funds should be provided for the improvement of its bibliographical apparatus to increase the efficiency of the library.

To Sum Up

Withers mentions that it is difficult and complex to prescribe standards for book stock and other materials in universities and other institutions. However, the model annual budget proposed by the SCONUL to the Parry Committee of the United Kingdom and by the Council for Arts and Science in Federal Republic of Germany for general and technical universities are significant and useful.

Withers also considers as valuable and considerably interesting the concept stated in the British, American and Canadian documents that the university library budget should not be less than a certain proportion of the total budget of its university and that this proportion should be between 5 and 10 per cent. In 1962 the UNESCO organized a regional seminar at Mendoza (Argentina) on the development of university libraries in Latin America. This seminar recommended that every institution should allocate not less than 5 per cent of its total budget for the library service (*Ibid*: 186).

The Cost Determinants

The following factors determine the cost of the provisions in the library: amount of literature published in each subject pursued in the university; extent to which the library renders service in a particular area of knowledge; average cost of publication in the subject; depth of research and range of interest of the researchers in each subject; special collection of manuscripts and archives; development of subject-library, geographically remote from the main library and special responsibilities to outside bodies, if any. The special collection proves to be of greater interest to the specialized members of the reading community and it attracts them to the library. At certain universities, such collections are especially built up as area of specialization under the national programmes. In United States, Germany and Scandinavian countries such schemes are operating. In India also, certain libraries possess specialized collection of Sanskrit and Arabic literatures and the manuscripts. Generally, these collections remain ill-equipped and the libraries are starved for want of maintenance grant because the immediate needs claim the major share of the funds. This fact should be taken into consideration while allocating the overall grant to the library.

The financial standards of university libraries should be considered in relation to the steady rise of prices of documents as well as the increased growth-rate of publication of the reading materials. Along with the increase in specialized and technical literature, prices of books and journals in general have been increasing. The SCONUL investigation indicates that the annual rate of increase in prices of books and journals is about 10 per cent. The German Wissens chaftsrat considers that since the flood of literature is increasing at an annual rate of 5 per cent and the annual inflation rate itself is 4 to 5 per cent minimum, the book-grant should also be increased annually by 10 per cent to allow for the increase in price as well as the increase in the rate and number of publications (Parry: op.cit: 264). The Council for Arts and Science—Learned and Scientific Periodicals (1964) —has recommended that the availability of funds in the library must keep pace with the expansion and increase in the book-price.

References

1. Gelfand, M.A., 1962, University Libraries for Developing Countries, UNESCO Manuals for Libraries-14, UNESCO, Paris.
2. Neal, K.W., 1971, British University Libraries, published by the author at 7 Church Road, Wilmslow, Cheshire.
3. Parry, Thomas (Chairman), 1968, Report of the Committee on Libraries (University Grants Committee), His Majesty's Stationery Office, London.
4. Sharma, Chandra Kant, 1977, University Library: Its Management and Organization, Metropolitan, New Delhi.
5. Thompson, James, 1970, An Introduction to University Library Administration, Clive Btngley, London.

6. University Grants Commission, 1965, University and College Libraries containing Report of the Library Committee of University Grants Commission, UGC, New Delhi.

7. Viswanathan, C.G., 1972, University Libraries of India —Principles and Policy, (author), New Delhi.

8. Wilson, L.R. and Tauber, M.F., 1958, The University Library—the Organization, Administration and Functions of Academic Libraries, 2nd ed., Columbia University Press, New York.

9. Withers, F.N. 1971, Standards for Library Service, UNESCO, Paris (Mimeographed).

4

Library Building and Furniture

The Library Building

There has been accelerated growth and development in the area of university education. Several new campuses have come up with a host of new library buildings. These new buildings are radically different from their predecessors. The library building of a university is a complex and specialized structure and needs careful designing, structuring and furnishing.

The Building Committee

This committee usually consists of the architect and consultant of the university buildings (if there is one), the librarian, one or two members of the university governing council (syndicate) and a representative of the students. It is presided over by the vice-chancellor or some senior member of the faculty. The committee makes a thorough study of the needs of the library and collects relevant data for planning a suitable structure. It takes into account the educational plans of the library. The committee consults the representatives and determines the local needs. To draw upon the experience of other institutions and acquaint with the present situation, the committee also visits the recently constructed library buildings of other universities and institutions. It studies their plans and discusses the details with the librarian and other members of the building committee. The committee works out with the assistance of the university librarian and the consultant the detailed estimates and requirements of the various units of the library.

Planning the Library

As a first step towards planning, the librarian should define the functions of the library and determine the services it has to render. Once the functions are defined it would be easier to design the library building to fulfil the commitments. Keeping in view the present design of the building he has to consider its future design, architecture, layout and methods of functioning. It is wrong to presume that the new building will provide greater accommodation than the existing building. He should realize that the new building will attract more readers and inspire them to make use of the space economically.

Next, the future development of the university as a whole should be assessed and estimated. Here, factors like rate of increase in the student population as well as that of teaching staff and setting up of new departments may be considered and, thus, the likely size and nature of the demand over the next fifty or hundred years may be estimated. In case, the position obtaining at a distant future seems unimaginable, then the details of the next twenty years may be considered. An intelligent plan will ensure that the library building is adapted to the local needs and conditions.

Architect's Role

The Architect is the leader of the team of designing the building. He creates the building which meets the requirements specified by the librarian; besides being an attractive piece of architecture. He is a professional to assess the needs and analyses the various problems in different fields of service. His work begins after the librarian has outlined the basic needs of the structure. He is not merely a draftsman of the plan but makes positive and fundamental contribution towards designing the different sections and placement of various units. Godfrey Thompson comments, "to leave an architect without an adequate brief is not to liberate his genius, but to limit his potential: an architect is a specialist in designing to meet client's "requirements, not in guessing what these requirements are or should be" (Thompson: 1977: 17). It is, therefore, very important that both these professionals should work with understanding for each other and in collaboration at all stages so that the skills of both of them may be utilized.

The architect has to explain and elaborate his ideas to the librarian so that the functional provisions can be appreciated by the latter. He (librarian) may not accept the modern solutions to old problems as he may not like the changes brought out by the modern technology. This can be overcome by repeated meetings between librarian and the architect and understanding each other's aims and intentions.

Librarian's Role

The librarian plays the prime role in the planning of the building. He works closely with the building committee and tells the architect by means of a brief or programme what the proposed library has to accommodate and what functions it has to perform. He discusses about the various units of the building and takes particular care of such matters as the function of the different rooms, relationship among them and the probable use of the building, flexibility of its interior and provisions for future expansion. He makes sure that each room is planned well with the desired layout and its appropriate equipment. He is the person who equips the architect with the actual needs and purposes of the building and appropriate design which can meet the local needs. The library building should be aesthetically appealing and should conform to other buildings existing at the campus or the institute.

The librarian's planning begins with his assessment of the library's total contribution to the community, securing a viable and sizable financial grant, drawing up priorities and relationships with other social, cultural and educational services; looking to the detailed organization of the library's resources particularly the reader's service. He develops a working relationship with the architect.

The point to be noted is that when the construction is completed it is the architect who gets the credit for it. He is the architect and creator of the building. The architect's goal is to derive visual satisfaction, and make the structure functional.

He should first understand the details and the exact functions the library has to perform. Similarly, the building, besides being functional, should be impressive and attractive. The librarian should appreciate aesthetic beauty and the combined understanding and cooperation of both these professionals are essential to make the structure satisfactory both from aesthetic as well as utility viewpoints.

In India, unfortunately, the librarian is not taken into confidence and is not consulted. The architect alone designs the building. A look at any library building bears testimony to this fact. The gap is apparently visible. Either it is an attractive showpiece which just does not work as a library or it is suitable as a library building but gives an ugly look. This will make it clear the distinct role the librarian and the architect has to perform.

Library Building Consultants

In some countries, it is common to make use of the services of a librarian as a consultant to a library building project. His great value is that he can bring to the notice of the authorities his wide experience of the number of library buildings that he has the knowledge of. With his knowledge of architect's work, he has a better grasp of the needs of the architect and later the librarian-consultant will be better equipped to guide the architect and properly evaluate the plans and proposals. He becomes an expert interpreter between two highly specialized professions. Though he is not in a position to devote his time at every stage of the project because of his preoccupations and commitments, he carries on and keeps in mind the librarian's viewpoint in continuous discussion with the architect. The fee of the library consultant is of course a small addition to the total cost of the project. But this is compensated many times over by the large savings obtained and the possible mistakes eliminated in the construction stage. The Parry Committee in the UK has highlighted the need for the appointment of library building consultants whenever a new library or a substantial extension of an existing building is contemplated. It observes that the best possible advice should be taken by the architect when large sums of money is to be spent over the project. The committee proposes, therefore, that "the UGC should draw up a panel of consultants who would be university librarians with considerable experience in planning library buildings. Any librarian asked to begin the planning of a building would be given the choice of any member of the panel to assist him in preparing the architect's brief and in all subsequent phases of the operation until the building is completed. The fees of the consultant would be included in the total cost of the building" (Parry: 1968: 92).

Architect's Brief

The librarian considers all the matters, discusses with his colleagues and others and gathers information by visiting several libraries in India and abroad to draw up his own needs and requirements comprising the building programme. This programme is called architect's brief or the client's requirements. This document is important and necessary because it makes the librarian think long and carefully assess the needs, which he conveys to the architect. The brief not only contains the details and requirements of the library but also explains the necessity for the proposed items. It reminds both the librarian and the architect of the provisions for the building.

The process of the librarian supplying details of the building programme to the architect is necessary because the architect knows very little about the library and no specialization is done by him (architect) in the area of library designing. Secondly, the conditions, needs and requirements of different libraries and factors like site, number of students and characteristics of the clientele vary. K.W. Neal quotes, "an architect is likely to spin out of his innards a sticky web that will entrap, rather than help, the library user" (In Neal: 1971: 134). However, handing over the architect's brief alone is not enough; there should be a continuous dialogue between the librarian and his staff and the architect and the library committee. Several copies of the architect's brief should be made available for discussion.

The architect's brief should comprise of the following sections :

(i) a table of contents;

(ii) summary tables of the space requirements;

(iii) a short history of the library;

(iv) a brief survey report outlining the directions of the library's future and the emerging needs, its functions, operation and the expansion;

(v) emphasis on the stack area according to the proposed acquisition of documents and their location;

(vi) the reading-rooms and research-rooms proposed for the students and teachers;

(vii) notes on important features like flexibility, lighting, heating, air-conditioning, ventilation, carpeting and acoustics etc;

(viii) notes on open access to stacks with necessary and

adequate safeguards of seating arrangement near them;

(ix) details of the specifications of areas like entrance, reading space, work-rooms, stairs and lifts etc.;

(x) notes on rooms for display of current periodicals and storage of their back volumes;

(xi) details of the room for the audio-visual aids in the library;

(xii) details of the ancillary services like refreshment room, office, tea, coffee and milk bar for readers and staff etc.;

(xiii) notes on the provision of cloak-room;

(xiv) janitorial and security staff accommodation in the library; and

(xv) index to the brief.

Planning the Library Building

The university library building is a complex and highly specialized structure. It is intended for a particular purpose and its success depends on how nicely its various sections function to meet the needs. The first requisite for building up a library plant is, therefore, its careful planning.

Planning the library building is a supreme task for a librarian as it measures not only the depth of his knowledge of librarianship in general but also the imagination and foresight. It is a highly skilled, complex and prolonged job and any one doing it for the first time is likely to commit errors. This is why in some countries, this task has been entrusted to a small building committee. Neal suggests that the interests of librarian and architect must largely merge in the planning of a new library building. Both should understand each other's view points and for successful fusion of ideas, the librarian must "learn how to read architect's plans and be able to draw up a brief for the architect on the functions, processes and needs of the library" (Neal: 1971: 116).

Planning Procedure

There are three major areas of activities in planning the library building:

(a) preparation of the building programme;

(b) development and approval of the preliminary plans; and

(c) approval of the final plans and specifications.

The librarian should associate himself with all the three activities, especially the first two. The objective of the institution is explicitly stated and their implications on library service visualized and outlined. Then, the plan of the library service is drawn stating the details of the spatial and technical requirements. Keyes Metcalf summarises its purpose as follows: (In Thompson: 1970: 113).

(i) it is the best way for the librarian, his staff and the administration of the institution to determine the actual and essential needs of the library;

(ii) it provides with an opportunity to the librarian to stress upon the administrative officers and the authority of the faculties the physical need of the library and obtain formal approval to the plan; and

(iii) it forms the basis and works as a foundation for planning a satisfactory building.

Importance of this part is real. Unless the librarian works out actually his library needs in detail with regard to book capacity, reading space, space for staff and the space required for other purposes, the university authorities would refuse to accept them seriously for consideration. The other two points follow.

Description of the interior of the building is also given. It should specify the desirable general characteristics to be expressed in the interior, discuss the aesthetics, colour, space dimensions, ceiling lights, lighting fixtures, sun control, noise and traffic control, wall treatment, floor coverings, fittings and furnishings, elevators, stairway and book lifts, security and fire protection etc.

The architect should also know the cost. The description of the site should also be provided. The plot-plans, master plans and other graphic devices showing the relationship of the proposed building to the existing structure may be closely indicated.

The above programme is essential for the architect inasmuch as he must be aware of, before designing the building: (i) what type of the library building is needed (i.e. Academic, Special or Public Library); (ii) the kind and quality of the reading material to be housed (viz. books, journals, pamphlets, maps, music records and other audio-visual materials); (iii) what type of services the library is going to provide (i.e. lending, reference or research); (iv) the appropriate number of users of the library and their classes; (v) the appropriate number and type of staff of the library and the accommodation required by them; (vi) the size of the auxiliary accommodation required (cloak rooms, lavatories etc).; (vii) average growth of readers expected; (viii) expected increase in the book stock and collection of other reading materials, and (ix) probability of future changes within the library. The architect should be provided with these details.

Having the building pragramme prepared by the librarian, now comes the turn of the architect. He studies the programme in detail and then prepares the outline plans and proposals. If the architect gets the librarian's point well and he is able to grasp and interpret the proposed needs and requirements intelligently and accurately, so much the better. But in case the architect has failed to note down the actuals and has proceeded erroneously on his own, the librarian's responsibility increases. He has to persuade the architect to start afresh or "the librarian will end up with what will be from his point of view a totally unsatisfactory building".

After the architect's outline proposals are accepted by the librarian, the final stage comes for establishing the details and approving the specifications. This is an arduous task. The librarian and architect both have to work upon this task jointly. List of topics sometimes becomes endless because every item of work, big or small, has to be taken into account. By the time, the construction begins, frequent visits to the site of the building are also worthwhile.

An architect or a group of architects and engineers is involved in all the three stages of planning, including the building programme. It is essential that the librarian is involved fully in all the three activities. The library consultant assists the librarian. If this procedure is followed closely, the success of the building is assured not only for the day of its opening but for the future years to come by.

Phasing of Construction

The plan of the library building should make an over all provision for the needs of the future also; the construction should, however, be staggered over a few phases. Adequate space may be kept vacant for future extension of the building.

The UGC Committee (India) recommends that university library building should be constructed in four phases. The first phase should provide accommodation for 1,00,000 volumes, second for 2,00,000 volumes, and third and fourth for 3,00,000 volumes each. The postgraduate college library should, however, be constructed in five phases. Its first phase should accommodate 50,000 volumes, second 1,00,000 volumes, and third to fifth 3,00,000 volumes each. It is advisable to build, in each phase, the stack-room to the full height of four tiers so that when necessary all the four tiers may be extended.

This will not disturb the work of the stack-room when extension is constructed.

This committee further recommends, that "any proposal for a new library building, fittings and furniture or for the adaptation of an existing building or for its extension for library purposes; should be examined by a library expert appointed by the Commission" (UGC: 1965: 117).

Design for the Open Access

At the construction stage of the library building, it should be decided whether the library will follow 'open' or 'closed' access system for its readers. The library design meant for the closed access system cannot serve for the open access, if desired at a later stage. The modern trend is to keep the library as an open access one which involves the following implications:

(1) One entrance and one exit should be provided for the readers and public. This should be at the counter and placed under the control of the circulation staff.

(2) The doors and windows of the library should be well protected with wire fabric for the safety of the books. There should be no means for passing of books between the readers within the library, at the entrance or exit.

(3) The height of the book-rack should be such as conveniently approachable for a reader of normal height so that he is able to pick out the book from the top-most shelf-plank of the rack.

(4) The reading area should be so placed that it does not get disturbed by the traffic. The catalogues and stack-rooms should be placed in its close vicinity

Monumental versus Functional Building

Before 1920, the architectural effect in the library construction reigned supreme and little attention was paid to the functional requirement of the building. The university libraries were generally monumental buildings constructed with architectural beauty, impressive external appearance characterised by big enterance hall and stairway, massive interior walls, lofty reading rooms and multi-tier book stacks of low ceiling height. But those buildings were not suitable to the actual needs and purposes of the present day libraries. The neo-Gothic building designed by Sir Gilbert Scott which formerly housed the library at the Glasgow University is a fine example. In the United States also, a comparative look at the Low Memorial Library and Butler Library at the Columbia University Campus show the sharp differences between the two older ideas of the library designs. While the former construction, with octagonal interior is an architect's monument to symmetry and balance, the latter one, rectangular in shape is indicative of an effort to have a functional building to meet the needs of a large university.

There were many factors responsible for change in the attitude against the monumental buildings. The most important one is the growing realization of economy to be pursued both in construction of the building as well as the administration of the institution. A major defect in the working of the monumental buildings has been that they have fixed functions and are not flexible for any other purpose i.e. each area is designed with a purpose of meeting one specific functional or operational need and that there is no room for any interchange. As an instance in point, the stack of such a structure can be used only as book stack and a reading-room only as a reading-room.

The UGC Committee in its report (1965) on university and college libraries in India has observed that it is not the sightseers who visit the inside of the library but, in fact, it is an intellectual workshop which functions inside the library. Further, it is not the people in general who are interested to visit the library. The intellectual features are needed most inside the library which may provide quiet and comfortable environment for study and research instead of the impressive beauty of the building as looked for by the tourists. The report emphasises further that overlooking of this principle reduces the library service to a mockery in a university library. "A big high rotunda with excellent echoing qualities, the hanging of huge portraits in the inside, and the outlook of the authorities, used to bring in to the reading-room crowds of sight-seers with babies in arms", it says (UGC: 1965: 91). From this it could be concluded that butterfly design, square design or circular design with massive ornamental stair cases occupying the most accessible part of the building fails to make the library building functional. However, the turrets, towers and domes above the roof level are outside the functional part of the building and these can be given any treatment the architect likes to make the building beautiful, characteristic and dignified. These do not interfere with the functional part of the building. What is important is the inside of the building.

Modular System

Realizing the fact that the basic aim of the modern design of the building is flexibility, there has been a revolution in designing the library buildings after the Second World War. To achieve the maximum flexibility, modular system of construction is adopted which implies construction of a building in units or modules. Angus Snead, MacDonald, Ralph Ellsworth and Keyeo Metcalf have been the pioneers of this system.

Under the modular system, the building has very few permanent walls in the interior. It is mostly supported by pillars placed at regular intervals. The size of the modules is mostly identical but sometimes modules of different sizes are also used in different parts of a building. What is the best size of a module has not yet been answered or found out so far. Different libraries use different sizes of modules according to their needs depending on local conditions. The size sometimes varies even from 3 feet to 27 feet. The greater the size of the module, the better the flexibility in the building since the open space without columns will increase. The cost of the building, however, increases with larger modules and beyond 26 feet it becomes highly uneconomical.

The idea behind such a construction is to avoid the rigid dimensions to the maximum and keep the building as open as possible. All the internal walls serve merely as partitions. Metcalf describes, "under the modular system ... a building is supported by columns placed at regular intervals. Nothing within the building is weight-bearing except the columns, though the outside walls may be. It follows in theory, that nothing within the building is fixed and immovable except the columns, though in fact, it is generally impracticable, if not impossible to shift the location of stairways, elevators, heating facilities, ducts and plumbing" (Thompson: 1970: 106). The modular building is made up of identical bays; usually a rectangular or square type defined by four adjacent columns is a bay. These can be furnished according to the needs and the use of the space and is not limited to one function alone but is conveniently interchangeable. These may be used as reading areas filled with ranges of shelving or divided by partition into rooms. Thus, the reading-rooms can be converted into stacks or vice-versa or into an administrative block. Further, the surface and the area can suitably be increased by combining two or more bays. So, a much bigger room is possible, yet sub-division by partitions can also be done, if not at will, at least from pillar to pillar. The pillars are conveniently and easily adjustable. The system admits of easy changes. No difficult alterations are required if a bay serving a particular purpose is intended to be assigned for another job. The use of modular system has since replaced the old concept of 'room' into a new concept of 'space' or 'area'.

The stack room has changed to stack area and the reading room to reading area. The space enclosed by walls is generally used either as work-room, seminar room, or librarian's room. The partition of area is conveniently done either by dry construction or book racks. The dry construction proves to be comparatively inexpensive and can be very easily moved.

The inflexibility in the building was permitted in less expansionist time but today the situation demands that above all, the building should be flexible. Difining flexibility, E.R.S. Fifoot says, "in library terms it means the interchangeability not overnight but over the summer vacation, of all major stack areas, reading areas and staff areas". This implies a building which can bear stack loads throughout, which will light and ventilate a large number of readers anywhere, a building with no interior load bearing walls and a building whose services and other fixed elements are grouped so as to free the largest area on each floor for changing library use. I would go further and require the building and all its individual areas to be rectangular (*Ibid*: 106). Thus, the emphasis is laid now on the functional aspect of the building and this has been the reason why most of the modern library buildings bear ordinary external appearance. "We have jumped from neo-Gothic movements to glorified shoe-boxes", says James Thompson (*Ibid*: 106). He further mentions that due to emphasis on purely functional aspect of the construction and tight position of the building grant, which does not leave any money to be spent on expensive finishes and aesthetic additions, the architects have been left with desperate attempts to improve the exterior of the buildings (*Ibid*: 106).

The advantage and convenience of the modern system are many. Metcalf sums up: "a building consisting largely of space that can be used for almost any purpose without extensive and expensive alterations should, in the long run, save money and prevent complications which so often arise as space requirements change" (*Ibid*: 107). He, however, also comments that this system is not without faults, as no system is. The first such fault noticeable is that no one column spacing or bay size is ideal for all purposes. What is an ideal module for creating stack area for books will not be equally ideal in the functioning for other work. There are certain other obvious defects of this system. The columns are generally obtrusive and, standing just in the middle of the office, they offend both eye and convenience. The pillars are a nuisance. Actually they hinder the view and restrict the freedom to arrange layout and indirectly the space is wasted because one size of the module is suitable only for a particular function. For instance, the module meant for book storage is not found suitable for using it as reading area.

Beauty and symmetry of the structure are adversely affected by the rigorous application of the standard modules. This defect is distinctly visible when you compare the older structure possessing good proportions, with the modern modular designed buildings looking deficient in quality. Since sound-proof partitions are not available, the noise emanates from the staff work-rooms.

But these defects do not outweigh the most important merit and advantage of a modular system i.e., flexibility and this is why the application of this system to library building in developed countries has become almost standard.

The standards and specifications used in modular systems vary. K.A. Lodewycks says that although it depends upon the thickness of the column, usually if the column spacing between 22.5 feet and 23 feet from centre to centre is provided, it will not offer obstruction to the arrangement of book-shelves catalogue-cabinets, tables and other kinds of library equipment.

Metcalf recommends that the modules should be 22 feet 6 inches or 25 feet 6 inches and the columns should not be more than 14 inch diameter. He points out that the bigger the module, the wider the pillars, thicker the floor and more expensive the building. He cites that at Edinburgh there are modules of 27 feet × 27 feet. With a distance of 4 feet 6 inches from one book-case centre to another and gangways of 3 feet, book-cases have to be filled within this. The centre-distance between book-cases could, however, be at 3 feet 10 inches, 5 feet 5 inches or 6 feet 9 inches (In Neal: 1970: 121). Lodewycks further mentions that there is uniformity with regard to dimension of ceiling height. The height of the ceiling should be low enough to be economically employed for book storage at any point. If the ceiling height is kept at 8 feet, it will provide adequate clearance for light fittings above a standard 7 feet 6 inch tier of book shelving. It is comfortable for a reading or work area, in case the areas is limited in size and is broken up with shelving or screening in between. For example, the new building of Edinburgh University has been built up according to the modular system providing standard ceiling height of eight feet. Its major reading areas have to be divided and humanized by curtains and potted plants (*Ibid*: 108).

Further, to obtain complete flexibility in the library building, it requires, besides the application of uniform modules, use of uniform standards of ceiling, ventilation and flooring. This provides absolute interchangeability.

Monotony in appearance is another disadvantage which is the outcome of the building planned on modular system. Therefore, while making the layout, selecting the design, choosing the furniture and deciding upon the colours, this fact should be kept in mind. To overcome the situation and compensate for monotony, it would be advisable to have the entrance deliberately non-modular.

Neal observes that the requirement of flexibility is that the floors should be load-bearing. This means that they will take a minimum load of per square feet of 150 pounds and their book stacks should be free-standing (Neal: *op. cit.* 121).

Co-operative Enterprise

In fact, the planning of a university library building is a co-operative enterprise in which the architect, librarian and representatives of the library committee, representative of trustees (if any), the treasurer and the superintendent of buildings and grounds should participate. All these personnel should constitute the building committee. A librarian possessing considerable experience in building programme naturally plays an important role.

The fact, however, remains that the modular planning is neither the panacea nor the last word in designing the library building. Ralph E. Ellsworth comments, "he who is satisfied that the concept of modular planning is the ultimate and final basis for library planning is lacking in both hind-sight and foresight indeed because it should be obvious to all that the technology of building construction is still in its infancy in some respects" (Ellsworth: 1960: 60). He observes further that the construction of a building is still too costly, the material too heavy to be moved and the structure deficient in proper ventilation, lighting and sound proofing etc. Keyes D. Metcalf also warns, "like most innovations, however, the modular system is not panacea; it has its faults and pitfalls. The fundamental objection is that no one column spacing or bay size is ideal for all purposes; the module that is almost perfectly adapted to one function such as book storage, will not be equally well suited to another" (Metcalf: 1965: 49). He also mentions that some inflexible features like columns at regular intervals are the outcome of this system. He further points out, "modern buildings have sometimes encountered serious acoustical problems because the movable partitions and bookcases on which they depend to divide up each floor have not been adequate barriers to sound" (*Ibid*: 51).

This discussion leads us to conclude that the architects and librarians cannot rest on the 'modular oars'. They should continue to explore newer concepts in designing and planning the library buildings and develop new ideas in use of the building materials and execution of the construction.

Library Plan

Even the most liberal and sophisticated plan fail to fit into the changing academic programmes. In fact, a systematic and organized research is necessary to find out the exact inadequacy of the existing library building and the remedial plan embracing the growing needs and aspirations of the academic community.

Every plan of the library building should make provisions to extend facilities to undergraduate study as well as postgraduate and advanced research by the students and faculty members. Here the two important factors to be kept in mind are: (i) the problem of growth; and (ii) the problem of organization. The problem of growth refers to the estimated size of the collection (number of volumes) expected to be housed inside the building so that the size of the building may be proposed in conformity with the expected stock. Divergent views have been expressed by different experts regarding the rate of growth of libraries. Keyes D. Metcalf mentions that because of the lack of material to procure and purchase, due to reduction in the output of the reading material itself, and also in the grant of funds to purchase, the growth of the library is not likely to be steady all the time and there will come a period of recession. Viswanathan, however, does not subscribe to this view. He says, "change is inherent to society, a library plan must also be receptive of any ultimate change that may be required by varying and increasing demands made from it." He further quotes, "library plans have their evolution in history from the single hall originating in antiquity to the functional, often modular, building of today" (Viswanathan: 1972: 51).

The second factor viz. problem of organization tends to consider the fact that whether the library services are to be distributed and administered department wise or not, they are to be organized together centrally under one roof.

British Library Building

The library building at Oxford is a sort of compromise between the tradition of the Bodleian with its series of reading rooms as a future library centre and functional stack room for the gigantic collection in new Bodleian on Broad Street. Erected in the first half of the twentieth century, it is the architectural style of the smaller library buildings.

American Library Building

The architecture of these libraries is, however, different. The first library building of Harvard (Gore Hall) was designed after the model of the Kings Chapel in Cambridge. It was completed in 184!. After 30 years (1871) books overflowed the accommodation and, therefore, a bookwing was added to it. That formed the first stack in America. Further extension of wings was made till 1915. The libraries developed very quickly in America and, therefore, in almost all the important libraries expansion was carried out. It was realized that the collection increases faster and the accommodation falls short too quickly. The buildings should, therefore, be planned liberally enough to admit of future growth without much difficulty. The planning should envisage growth between five to ten decades ahead. The rigidity and fixity in the design should be avoided to make it flexible enough for the future development.

However, American contribution towards development of library architecture has been more in the interior design of the building than the exterior one. This development has been more in respect of the buildings of public library than those of the university libraries. The position of the stock in the whole architectural set up of the building is a difficult task. American libraries have thrown enough light on this issue and have provided a wealth of information and data with regard to ventilation, temperature control, illumination, etc., facilitating the huge stock of the books to better use and activising the functioning of the libraries.

Indian Library Building

In India, planning and designing of the buildings of academic libraries during the later 20th century need and suggest sweeping modifications over the earlier designs. Earlier, buildings of different sizes were constructed in a variety of architectural styles—Gothic, Rinaissance, Victorian in Europe, United States and also at a few universities in India like Bombay, Delhi, Madras, Benaras, Baroda and Waltair. Functioning of these library buildings have indicated various shortcomings and defects in selection of the building sites, estimation, and calculation of the floor and the stack areas, anticipated rate of growth of various subjects and departments and allocation of space to them, planning and placement of various departments, interconnection of the section and facility of readers' internal movement and inadequacy of light, air and ventilation etc. These have ultimately led to the conclusion that since the university library has now to play a definite role in the academic programme of the university, there should be a proper planning for its building before the programme is undertaken. Thus, the situation has changed since 20th century and the present view of complete planning on rational basis for the library building is a recent shift to avoid the pitfalls noticed in the earlier planning. Harry Fair-hurst states, "the librarian of a new university is of course, in one respect, placed at tremendous advantage when compared with his colleagues in the older universities. He is dealing with an open site and should be in a position to discuss the location of his library in relation to the whole campus" (Fairhurst: 1965: 108).

Dr. S.R. Ranganathan lays down that the following provisions are important in a library building. (Ranganathan: 1962: 230);

(a) A gangway down the wall should be provided. This should be atlest 1 m wide in the stack-room. Such a gangway will protect the book-racks from rain and sun.

(b) Taking into consideration the Indian conditions, the lengthwise walls, in which these stack-room windows occur, should run from east to west.

(c) The floor of the reading-rooms should preferably be

sound-proof and if it is financially not possible, it should at least be covered with coir matting.

Dry Construction

It is a corollary to the modular type of planning. In the modular type, wall-loss space is provided in the form of modules for use of varying purposes. But such areas have to be earmarked and partitioned. For this partitioning work, instead of using wet mortar, dry materials are used. Such materials are thin and easily removable temporary walls of prefabricated materials like pressed plywood, glass, aluminium etc. The materials used are joined together with nuts, bolts and wooden frames etc. In the library, the book racks of standard size are also used in place of the dry construction.

The chief advantage of dry construction is that it admits maximum flexibility. The flexibility of the building is fully retained because the partition is easily removable. The materials used are also not wasted because the same can be used time and again for other purposes. Additional advantages are that the construction is very easy as well as speedy.

Planning Procedure

Certain general principles should be borne in mind while Planning the building of the library. Charles C. Soule outlined set of principles which are still relevant. These are as follows :

(1) Library should be planned especially for the kind of the work to be done and the community to be served.

(2) The architectural effect of the building should not be superimposed over the convenience of arrangement.

(3) Before the exterior of the building is considered, the interior arrangement should be planned.

(4) Accommodation for readers near the books stacked in the library should be provided as far as possible.

(5) The arrangement of the rooms for readers' use should

be made in such a way as to allow complete supervision with the fewest possible staff and the attendants.

(6) The plan should be elastic enough to admit of and adopt to probabilities and possibilities of growth and development.

(7) Full economy in administration should be the objective to be achieved out of the plan of the building.

While planning the building, climatic conditions should be kept in view especially in tropical countries. The architect should keep in view the climate of the place while considering necessary suggestions with regard to selection and treatment of the building, site, exterior and interior design, building orientation, insect control and other related subjects.

Preliminary Plan

Preparation of the preliminary plan is the most important phase of the whole process of planning. Here the librarian examines critically the architect's first drawing to see whether the provision is adequate and in conformity with the objectives of the library. He also ensures that the building is flexible, economical, expandable to admit of the coming requirements. All that has to be ensured is that the building is free from defects.

The architect presents the sketch of the building plan for discussion. It begins with the main floor. The first and subsequent floors are discussed until an agreement is reached. The procedure is applied in respect of other floors. Now, the architect may draw plans and add stair-ways, shaft-ways for elevators, book lifts, windows and other internal features. The preliminary plan can also be referred to a consulting architect for advice. Detailed consideration of the furniture and equipment may arise by now. The furniture layout be made, equipment located and tentative provisions indicated for the electrical outlets and lighting needs. The cost of the building should also be estimated.

Final Plan and Specification

The final plan, termed as working drawing as well, consists of floor plans, elevations; sections and details of the structure. This provides graphic illustrations of the building from the several physical point of view. The general construction plan is supplemented by separate sets of drawings illustrating the designing of heating, ventilating and air-conditioning system; electrical work, plumbing etc. There are additional drawing illustrating the detailed design and location of many general and special features of the building like stacks, furniture and built-in shelving along the walls. The plan is supplemented by written specifications describing the type and quality of the workmanship. Additional information is also supplied to serve as guide for construction of the building.

By his active participation in the preliminary drawings, the librarians will be in a position to examine the final plans and specifications. It may be difficult for him to understand some of the technical details but certainly he can review the architectural floor plans, and thereby review his plans for operating the library. At this stage he should point out to the architect the important errors and oversights and seek the necessary changes, if required. The librarian should also examine closely the drawings giving details of furniture, layout, floor treatment and ceiling treatment etc. This is the last opportunity for the librarian to point out the defects and propose the desired change. Once the contract is awarded, the construction is under way, changes can rarely be made.

Spatial Relationship

Organization charts representing graphically the organization of library resources and function and services of the personnel performing their duties is helpful for planning. The flow charts indicating the process of work performed by different staff in each department of the library prove to be useful for the building committee and to the architect in visualizing the specific function of the departments and working out the future growth.

The most heavily used departments of the library should be located on the main floor at ground level or nearby.

Cost Calculation

The cost of the building varies amongst different countries and even within the country. It depends on the type of the building, its size in terms of the floor area and volumes in terms of cubic feet constructed. The cost figures are maintained by the architect and the building contractors. Frequently, these figures are contained in the architectural and library science journals.

Selection of the Site

This is an important task. It should be decided in the very beginning of planning the new physical plant. The condition of the site affects the design of the building materially. In fact, site is a determining factor for the features of the building. Metcalf says, "to compare the advantage of the two sites, on must compare the two somewhat different buildings that could be created on them" (Metcalf: *op.cit*: 183). Therefore, this task of selecting the site should be included in the matter plan of the university.

There are five major factors to be considered while selecting the site.

(i) Adequacy of the Size : The area of the site should be large enough to accommodate the present building as well as permit the future expansion in the campus.

(ii) Relation to the Neighbouring Buildings : As far as possible, the building should be placed in the centre of the campus and close to the departments and class-rooms, which use the library most. A survey of the flow of traffic should be done to determine the suitable location. From architectural as well as functional point of view also, the site should be centrally located. Care should be taken that it is not surrounded on all sides by other buildings, otherwise extension will not be possible.

(iii) Surroundings and the Physical Orientation for the Building : The surroundings should be quiet so that there may be good working conditions and reading environment.

(iv) The Slope of the Land : It should be examined as to whether the slope of the land is advantageous or disadvantageous.

(v) Nature of the Ground : It should, be ascertained as to what complications will arise due to the nature of the ground beneath the building.

Basic Elements

The library building constitutes of the following four basic element:

(a) entrance area;
(b) processing area;
(c) book shelving area; and
(d) reading area.

(a) Entrance Area : The entrance area is, in fact, introduction to the building and, therefore, it is vital part of the construction. Its chief components are as follows:

(i) vestibule;
(ii) cloak room and lavatories;
(iii) issue desk and counter;
(iv) reference service; and
(v) catalogues.

Generally, the doors of the main entrance lead into the vestibule. The one side of the vestibule is given over to the cloakroom accommodation with male lavatories on side and female lavatories on the other. Most of the cloakroom accommodation is staffed by an attendant. In certain libraries, the cloakroom libraries or part thereof is left unmanned. The cloakroom accommodation is essential not only for the convenience of readers, which obviously is, but also for the security of the library. To exercise strict control over the loss of books, it is necessary to oblige readers to deposit their cases, coats etc. outside the main library area. An attendant is posted in this area for security of the possessions of the readers. He issues tag for the items deposited with him and stays guard over them. Sometimes, the readers who are too much in a hurry to deposit their belongings with the attendant, obtain a tag and retrieve them from him subsequently. In such cases they prefer to keep their belongings at the. unmanned accommodation.

Thompson mentions, "on the whole, readers seem to prefer expediency to security and the amount of unmanned accommodation provided is now greater than the superintended area" (Thompson: *op.cit*: 108).

From the vestibule, the reader passes through the control wicket to the main hall of the library. The control point at the wicket gate is an important provision. It is the one and only exist from the main part of the library. One assistant is posted at the control point who checks up and ensures the authorized issue of the books to the readers. All books must be shown by readers, as they leave, to the assistant posted here.

The books which are to be borrowed from the library are stamped and issued by the assistants posted on duty at the counter. Therefore, provision of issue counter is a necessity in the library.

The areas of keeping catalogues and that of reference service are important provisions in the library building. These should be so accommodated that these are visible to the reader as soon as he enters the library. Immediately beyond the lobby, the readers should see the library catalogues and reference sources and the information desk which serve as key to the library. These, along with the vestibule and cloakroom accommodation, are essential ingredients of an entrance area.

(b) Processing Area : The processing department of the library should be placed at short walking distance. These may be grouped around the perimeter of the main hall. Ellsworth says, "the layout, design and placing of these functions continues a problem that is unique to libraries for the reason that not only must each function have the right space relationship to the other functions but also to the technical process" (*Ibid*: 110). Alongside. the cataloguing department, the acquisition department should also be on this perimeter, conveniently placed near at hand with an access to the public catalogues and the reference tools like printed catalogues and bibliographies. Here, the accommodation should also be provided for receipt and despatch of books, library materials and for the preparation of documents.

The periodical department should be placed near the place where the periodicals are displayed. It is not necessary to set up the library bindary in this perimeter. Suitable location for this is the basement.

(c) Book shelving Area : In fact, while making basic arrangement of space, efforts are made to group the entrance and processing area compact; to use basement for storage and non-public services and then use the remaining floors of the building to provide space for books and places for readers. The underlying principle is that if the library building is a multi-storey structure (as often it is) the central entrance and processing area should be provided at a middle level and not at the basement, or on the ground-floor. The idea is to reduce the distance the user has to travel to the book and reading floors. To be precise, it means that if a library building provides four storeys of books and reading materials, the entrance should be placed in the middle, as thereby the user will need to ascend only two storeys instead of all the four storeys. This will reduce the travel to the half.

(d) Reading Area : The amount of space required for stacking the books and for use by the readers should be calculated. Efforts should be made to integrate books and readers to the maximum. Provision should also be made for several years ahead i.e., for the future addition of books as well as increase in number of readers. Standard formula should be applied to convert these needs into square footage. The usual formula for a rough estimate is as follows: 25 square feet for each undergraduate, 35 square feet for each graduate student, 75 square feet for each faculty member (Gelfand: 1962:128). Space for other purposes: 60 square feet for each 1,000 volumes.100 square feet per person for added space for the future, additional 40 per cent of the total floor space for stairways, lobbies, corridors, duct work etc. Thus, if 100,000 square feet of space required for books, readers and staff, 40,000 square feet should be added for all other purposes. The approximate size of the building should be calculated and by applying the current UGC formula as to the price per square feet, the probable cost of the building can also be calculated.

The space for books and places for readers are provided in several manner. The traditional pattern is to segregate the two, confirming most of the library's stock to high-density book stack areas and most of its readers to large reading rooms. The students are expected to use large reading rooms sharing multi-seat tables. The only seating provided in the book-stack areas are the tables on its periphery. In the present days, this type of division is becoming infrequent. The modern aim is to integrate books and readers to a much greater extent. However, there are exceptions. The storage areas for less-used books are usually not provided with reader-places. Such areas are located in the basement of the library building.

The traditional pattern of providing seating on large library table has changed. Readers mostly prefer individual small tables. The seating is also provided in carrels in various parts of the building like typing carrels, study rooms and special collection rooms.

There are various ways of mixing up book-stacks and readers in the main reading areas. There is a 'Checkboard System' in which the books of the book-stacks are alternated with groups of tables for readers. There is also the Alcove System, whereby the reader's tables are divided into a series of small groups by book-stacks placed at rightangles to the walls of the room. The greatest disadvantage of this system is that it often makes the classification sequence of the books difficult to follow. It works well where such sequence is not vital. Considering all the systems, the best arrangement seems to be the simple one of placing the book-stacks in a block or blocks in the middle of a room and locating the readers' places around its perimeter.

Centralized versus Decentralized Storage

These two terms refer to the housing of book-collections or to the administering of them. There are two systems of storing books in the university. Either the collection may be housed in a single repository or in a number of separate repositories. Similarly, they may be administered either as a single unit or as number of separate units.

These systems of centralized or decentralized storage of books and services in university have been the debatable points in library administration. There have been long drawn discussions and arguments both for and against these systems. These systems have their own implications on planning the library building as well. If it is decided to centralize the entire collection in one building and provide services for it, the building of the library has to be planned accordingly as the library will then invite students and teachers of all the faculties (undergraduates, graduates and researchers) at one place. On the other hand, if the decision is in favour of providing the autonomous faculties with independent libraries comprising the stack of books, and journals and the staff of their own, the university library will be appropriately reduced in size, stock and staff to the extent the centralization of library books and services are approved.

The three British universities viz., Oxford, Cambridge and London have organized their book-collection in decentralized form. A sizeable collection of books in these universities is housed as well as administered in the libraries of colleges and other institutions which are separate from and independent of their parent university libraries. In other British libraries, the book-collections are decentralized in the sense of being housed in various separate depositories and centralized in the sense of being administered as a single unit by the university library.

The type of decentralization that characterized the organization of the collection in Oxford, Cambridge and London has not been deliberate but, in fact, it has sprung from the peculiar circumstances in which these universities have developed. In other British universities, "the varying degrees of decentralization in the housing of the book-collections have like wise been due to varying circumstances (Parry: 1968: 93). The circumstances are many. It happens sometime that a particular faculty or a department of the university moves at a distance away from the university and more particularly from the central library. This necessitates transfer of books from the central library to the faculty or the department. Sometimes, the department itself, having moved into the new building, establishes a library with the financial assistance of University Grants Commission especially sanctioned in connection with the new accommodation or sometimes the department sets up its small library with the help of the grant received for the departmental research and maintenance. In course of time, this small collection become" large and highly specialized. Again, occasionally, the department or faculty may receive some donation or fund as a private gift for purchase of books and journals or a large collection of books (by way of gift) to be housed in a particular department. These varying factors lead to creation of departmental libraries. And, the faculty members and the students favour the idea of making the collection of relevant books available in the department or the faculty itself to save their time.

United States of America

During the past fifty years, there has been a tendency of decrease in the number of independent book collections in the country. Majority of the university library collections have a single administration and the book-buying is preferred centrally. A few American university campuses have their independent libraries where the book-buying is not wholly centralized.

Soviet Union

There has been an increasing tendency of centralization of libraries at the large universities in this country. However, there are still certain universities where the departmental libraries exist quite independently of the main library. Such libraries also duplicate the reading materials. L.I. Vladimirov mentions,'it is clear that there is a general or at least an active opinion in university circles in favour of the centralization of acquisitions and processing, the creation of union catalogues of university book collections, the development of a unified system of service that is brought as closely as possible to the readers and the strengthening of the leading role of the main library, which becomes responsible for the university for all library work (In Parry : 1968: 97).

Germany

There has been a significant impact of the British system over the relationship of the main university library to other libraries in the university. The book collection in this country is decentralized and housed in a number of separate respositories. Also these are administered as separate units.

Scandinavia

The dual system of library provision in Germany has profound impact on the academic library service in Scandinavia. Here all the older universities have set up separate libraries for their department or institutes. Some of these are large and fully independent of the university library.

India

Varying standard practices are followed here. In certain universities, the departments have established their own independent libraries. And, in some universities, the departments are served by university central library alone. There are some universities where departments are provided with a small working collection by way of permanent loan. In certain cases the collection loaned to the department is renewed periodically once a year or in a term. Such varying practices arose casually at a time when the university libraries were neither properly established nor organized. The problem needs reconsideration and invite rethinking over the issue.

The resources and services of the libraries in Indian universities are meagre compared to those of the Great Britain, United States of America and other developed countries. Some of the libraries are in infant stage. Therefore, the issue confronting the university authorities in this country is to provide a main central library fully enriched with resources and capable of satisfying the needs of the whole academic community. The question of setting up departmental libraries and equipping them with resources comes next. It never means that the provision of the departmental libraries has secondary importance. But the fact is that the resources being limited, it has to be fully harnessed for enriching the central library. C.G. Viswanathan mentions the experience derived from a few Indian universities regarding concentrating attention and the available resources of setting up and feeding the departmental libraries, in preference to the university central library, has revealed that "far-reaching economies in book and periodical budgets of departments could have been effected and the poor reference collection in the main library could have been strengthened with perceptible advantage to the academic community as a whole. The misdirected competition for funds among departments and monopoly of the collection exercised by each department tended to increase, resulting in lack of co-ordination in the planning of the library services" (Viswanathan: *op. cit.* 56).

Thus, the university central libraries in India have mostly remained ill equipped and undeveloped due to inadequate attention paid to them and in consequence, there has been sheer lack of a model for academic library administration. The situation has resulted in growth of departmental libraries usually set up in small rooms with scanty reading accommodation and equipment and generally supervised by a junior teacher of the department who has hardly any idea of administering library services. Such a departmental library functions in complete isolation, unaware and unconcerned with other such departmental library functioning in the adjoining room of another department. Such neighbouring libraries, working in one and the same campus, do not try to know each other or maintain co-ordination between them. There have been persistent complaints of non-availability of books and inaccessibility of reading materials in such libraries by the students and teachers. The organizational problems have been varied. Loss of books has increased. So, the absence of a strong central library has rendered the problem of organizing the departmental libraries complicated and acute. As such, the recommendations of the University Grants Commission (Delhi) is that "every university develops a strong main library for the university as a whole and then establishes departmental libraries avoiding wasteful duplication of books and services" (Viswanathan: *op. cit*: 57).

This discussion leads us to the view that the pattern of

decentralization followed in the three older universities of Britain is peculiar in Britain to the circumstances obtaining there and its application will not be appropriate and helpful to the conditions prevalent in Indian universities today.

The above discussion has been related to the problem of organization Then, there is the problem of expansion of the library which has an important bearing on its building plan.

Expansion of Library

While planning for the library building, future expansion and changes, organisation must always be kept in view. The site should be such as may have enough scope for future expansion. The design of the building should provide for additional areas for book-stacks, reading purposes as well as for the working staff. It should be possible to incorporate new departments. The main library also expands quickly when one or more faculty library is integrated with it. The interior plan should be flexible enough to admit of the larger special collections which increase with the growing specialization of the library.

Library Furniture and Design

The Principles

The following factors constitute the principles of library furniture and designing. These have to be borne in mind while making selections.

(i) Material : The material used for the furniture should be selected on the basis of the following principles durability, resistance to wear and tear, adaptability to different finishing techniques, cost and the beauty.

(ii) Construction : The construction of the furniture should be such as can withstand abrasions and impact and the joints are fully tight.

(iii) Comfort : Besides durability, comforts should also be sought in the furniture.

(iv) Finish and Colouring : The finishes should be surface-coated, well protecting the surface of the material and enhancing the beauty and attraction of the articles. The colour and the material should be combined to give an attractive and inviting look to readers.

(v) Proportion : Proportion is an inherent quality in the designing of the furniture. Proper proportion allowed to different parts of the furniture adds to the symmetry and aesthetic beauty of the furniture.

(vi) Standardized Shelving : The book shelving should be standardized so that the parts are easily interchangeable. The tables, chairs, counters, and desks should be purchased in uniform groups.

(vii) Local Climate : Attention should be paid to factors like the local climatic effect on the furniture, when making the selection of the material. This is all the more so in tropical climatic regions.

(viii) Mobility : These should be easily and conveniently mobile.

(ix) Easy Maintenance : These should be easy to maintain.

(x) Economy : Last but not the least, the furniture should be economical, besides being durable and serviceable.

The Standards

The Indian Standards Institution has set up, at the instance of the Chairman, Library Committee, University Grants Commission, New Delhi, a sectional committee on library buildings, fittings and furniture. Certain standards finalized by the said committee and adopted by the UGC are as follows (UGC: *op. cit.*: 102) :

The above table indicates the different types of academic libraries in terms of the number of books to be stacked, the number of periodicals generally displayed, the number of readers' seats provided and the number of professional and skilled staff generally accommodated.

Table 1 : Size of Library*

	Kind of Library	*Number of*			
		Volumes	*Current Periodicals for Display*	*Readers' seats*	*Staff at Service Points*
1.	University Central Library	1,00,000 to 3,00,000	500 to 2,000	1/5th of the number of students and 1/10th of the number of teachers	20 to 100
2.	University Departmental Library	1,000 to 5,000	50 to 100	10 to 20	Nil
3.	College Library	5,000 to 50,000	20 to 100	1/5th of the number of students and 1/10th of the number of teachers	3 to 10
4.	Dormitory Library	1,00, 000 plus 50,000	Nil	Nil	1 to 4 Janitors

Where n is the number of transfers to Dormitory Library.

* See Report of the Library Committee of the University Grants Commission, Delhi, 1965, p. 104.

Table 2 : Rooms Required for Different Types of Libraries*

	Room Normally Separate	*University Library*	*Departmental Library*	*College Library*	*Dormitory Library*
1.	Stack Room	R	—	R	R
2.	Catalogue Room	R	—	R	—
3.	Central Reading Room	R	R	R	—
4.	Periodical Reading Room	R	—	R	—
5.	Special Reading Room	R	—	R	—
6.	Research Cubicle	R	—	—	—
7.	Group Study Room	R	—	R	—
8.	Seminar Room	R	—	R	—
9.	Exhibition Room	R	—	—	—
10.	Librarian's Room	R	—	R	—

	Room Normally Separate	University Library	Departmental Library	College Library	Dormitory Library
11.	Deputy Librarian's Room	R	—	—	—
12.	Technical Staff Room	R	—	R	—
13.	Administrative Staff Room	R	—	R	—
14.	Committee Room	R	—	—	—
15.	Display Space at Entrance	R	—	R	—
16.	Night Watchman's Room	R	—	—	R
17.	Department of Library Science	R	—	—	—
18.	Microfilm Reading Room	R	—	R	—
19.	Document Reproduction Room	R	—	—	—

R = Required

— = Not Required

* See Report of the Library Committee of the University Grants Commission, Delhi. 1965, p, 106.

The above table indicates the requirement of essential rooms which may be provided for the different types of academic libraries. The size of rooms depends upon the actual individual requirements. The normal requirement of size has been shown in the Table 1.

Relative Position of Rooms

The stack-room of the library should be placed, as far as practicable, to run from east to west to prevent the direct sun through the windows. In order to facilitate the movement of book-trolley from one corner of the library to another, the floor of the building should have a single level. Arrangement for electric lifts should be made in a multi-tier stack.

The entrance to and exit from the library building should be only through the gangway. Each room of the library should be provided with a cover passage on one side to enable the readers to walk along the passage without disturbing other readers.

The entrance of the library should be kept open to the general reading-room. The periodical reading-room as also the reading-room for serious readers should be far from general reading-room. The text-book reading should be provided in a separate room. It should have stacking capacity for about 5,000 books. The stack-room should be centrally located facilitating access to it, from all parts of the library. The technical room should be like an ante-room to the stack and placed in close proximity to the rooms of the Deputy Librarian and the Librarian.

The room for exhibiting the books and other reading materials may be combined with the entrance lobby. The research cubicles, rooms for group study and the committee room should be placed in a separate wing or separate floor.

The UGC Committee in its report has specified the following dimensions of rooms, gangways, furniture and fittings. The report prescribes the following dimensions (UGC: 1965: 110).

Stack Room

(a) Clear Length : 1.80 n plus 3.15 metres where n is the number of rows of book racks.

(i) The centre to centre distance between consecutive racks should be 1.80 m (on the basis of 0.45 m of rack-depth plus 1.35 m of cross gangway width).

(ii) The distance from an end wall of the stack-room to the centre of the nearest row of racks should be 1.575 m (on the basis of 1.35 m of the end cross gangway width plus 0.225 m of half the rack-depth).

(b) Clear Width : 3 m (on the basis of one book-rack of 2 m long plus one side gangway of one metre) close to a longitudinal wall; or 5 m (on the basis of 2 book-racks each 2 m long plus one side gangway of one metre width) close to a longitudinal wall; or 8 m (on the basis of 3 book-racks each 2 m long plus two side gangways of one metre width) close to each of the longitudinal walls; or 10 m (on the basis of 4 book-racks each 2 m long plus two side gangways of one metre width) close to each of the longitudinal walls.

Three metres and five metres width should be generally in the case of stack space, as the stack-room and the reading-room may be combined into a single room in such cases. (See note on page 110 of the report of University Grants Commission, Delhi, 1965.)

(c) Clear Height : Floor to ceiling 2.35 m.

(i) The height of the book-rack should be 2.20 m and allowance for bay guides be 0.15 m.

(ii) Each unit book-rack of 2 m long may be assumed to house 700 to 750 volumes and one square metre of stack-room area may be assumed to house 150 volumes.

(iii) In a university library the number of tiers may be four and in a college library, it may be two.

Reading Room

The size of the reading-room should be as follows:

(a) Length : 1.5 n (excluding the central region, where n is the number of rows of reading tables).

(b) Width : 5 m (on the basis of two tables each 2 m long plus central gangway 1 m wide); or 7.5 m (on the basis of three tables each 2 m long plus central gangway 1.5 m wide); or 10 m (on the basis of four tables each 2 m long plus central gangway 2 m wide).

The size of the reading table is 2 x 0.70 m. The centre to centre distance between two consecutive rows of reading-room tables is 1.5 m with seating arrangement on one side of the table only.

Other Rooms

The sizes of the other rooms should usually be as follows:

	For use of	*Area in Sq M*
1.	Librarian and Deputy Librarian	30 per person
2.	Professor and other teachers	15 per person
3.	Classifier, Cataloguer, Accession Librarian and Maintenance Librarian	9 per person
4.	Secretary to the Librarian	9
5.	Secretariat of the Library School	30
6.	Visitors' Room	15
7.	Administrative and Professional Staff not at Service points and other than those mentioned in (3)	1.5 per student
8.	Class Room	1.5 per student
9.	Practical Room	3 per student
10.	Group Discussion Room	15
11.	Seminar Room	20
12.	Cubicle	7
13.	Committee Room	20
14.	Other Rooms	As per local needs

The above table indicates the size of the office-rooms required by the various administrative and professional staff of the Library.

Physical Services

	For public library readers		*For staff*	
	Male	*Female*	*Male*	*Female*
Water Closets	1 per 200 upto 400 persons For over 400 at 1 per 250 or part thereof	1 per 100 upto 200 persons For over 200 at 1 per 150 or part thereof	1 for 1 to 15 persons 2 for 16 to 35 3 for 36 to 40 4 for 41 to 100	1 for 1 to 12 persons 2 for 13 to 25 3 for 26 to 40 4 for 41 to 57
Ablution Taps	1 in each water closet	1 in each water closet	1 in each water closet	1 in each water closet
Urinals	1 per 50		Nil upto 6 persons 1 for 7 to 20 2 for 21to 45 3 for 46 to 70 3 for 71 to 100	1 in each water closet

	For public library readers		For staff	
	Male	*Female*	*Male*	*Female*
Water Basins	1 for every 200 persons or part thereof. For over 400 persons add at 1 per 250 or part thereof	1 for every 200 persons or part thereof. For over 200 add at 1 per 150 or part	1 for 1 to 15 persons 2 for 16 to 35 3 for 36 to 65 4 for 66 to 100	1 for 1 to 12 persons 2 for 13 to 25
Water Tap	1 for every 50 persons or part thereof in the vicinity of water closets and urinals, with draining arrangements.			
Fitment Cleaner's Sink	1 per floor minimum			

Provision for the rest-room of the readers and the staff, first aid room, canteen and parking areas should also be made.

Note : The tables and the standard dimensions in this chapter have been extracted, with acknowledgement, from the report of the Library Committee of the University Grants Commission, India, 1965, pp. 102—127.

Library Furniture

Bare physical plant of the library building will look naked unless provided and equipped with adequate furniture, fittings and furnishing. These not only add to the beauty of the building but also increase its functioning on the whole and convenience to the readers. Much of the efficiency of the library depends on the kind of the furniture and fittings placed in the library. Van Buren states, "the physical environment of a library depends on two factors; the architectural quality of the building and the design of its furniture. These closely related elements must be harmonious if a successful aesthetic result is to be achieved" (Van Buren: *op. cit*: 388-395).

The following items are included in the category of furniture and equipment in the library.

(a) Book Rack

(b) Catalogue-Card Cabinet

(c) Catalogue-Card Tray

(d) Periodical Display Rack and Newspaper Rack
(e) Reading Tables and Chairs
(f) Charging Desk (Issue Counter)
(g) Book Display Rack
(h) Dictionary and Encyclopaedia Stand
(i) Atlas Stand
(j) Exhibition Cases
(k) Photo-stating Apparatus
(1) Microfilm Reader
(m) Audio-visual Aids.

Provision of fittings and furniture should be made at the very outset of preparing the plan for the library building. In American libraries, the expenditure on this account is estimated at 8 to 14 per cent of the building. At least 8 per cent of the cost of the new building of the library should be allocated for its furniture and equipment. This provision may be adequate for the first few years. Additional equipment may be added later on as and when required.

The library furniture have been mostly standardized. The Sectional Committee of Indian Standards Institution on Library Buildings, Fittings and Furniture has finalized the standards published as IS: 1829 (Part I) 1961. The UGC Committee on Library Science, Delhi, has also discussed the issue and adopted the relevant extracts (UGC: *op. cit.* 118). Some of the standards are reproduced as under:

(a) Book Rack : This is one of the most important furniture in the library. Once purchased, it is a permanent item for the library and, therefore, it needs careful selection. Today, steel racks have replaced the wooden racks almost completely as the latter ones prove to be too heavy. These racks are available in different sizes. The most common size is 3 feet wide, 7.5 feet high and 0.75 feet deep (double side rack may be 1.5 feet deep). The dimension of a unit wooden book-rack, as prescribed by the Indian Standards Institution (ISI) are: height 2.20 m, width 2.00 m and depth 0.45 m. It consists of seven adjustable shelves. Dr. S.R. Ranganathan has laid down the following specifications for a unit book-rack in the library (Ranganathan: 1962: 230).

(i) Height of the book racks should be 7 ft. with the following dimensions and specifications; external dimensions 6'6" × 1'6" × 7', three uprights, each 2" × 1'6" × 7'. Seven shelf planks, each 3'× 81/2" × 1". While two of the shelf-planks should be fixed ones (one at the top and the other at the bottom), the other five should be movable ones, supported by Tonk's fittings, to be adjusted to an inch.

(ii) To facilitate cleaning of the floor beneath the rack, the book-rack should be allowed the sanitary bottom i.e. the lowest shelve should be fixed at a height of 6" from the floor. Similarly, the topmost-shelf should be fixed 6" below the top of the upright. This will provide easy vigilance also.

(iii) An expanded metal or weld-mesh partition should be provided to separate the two faces of the racks so that books on the shelves in one face do not get mixed up with the books on the corresponding shelves on the other. To admit of this frame, the planks should be made only 8½ inches broad, allowing a gap of 1 inch in the centre of the rack. The partition should start only from a height of 6 inches from the lowest fixed shelf and go right up to the lower side of the uppermost fixed shelf. This will make the giant-folios, which are more than a foot broad, lie flat on the bottom-most fixed shelves, extending from one face to the other.

(iv) To hold the shelf-cards properly, the front-edge of each shelf should have a wedge-shaped groove cut in it so that the shelf-cards could be easily slided from end to end.

(v) The three uprights should be bound together by the four

pairs of fixed shelves. This should be reinforced by means of two steel tie-rods binding them together, one at a height of 21/2 ft. from the bottom and the other at a depth of 21/2 ft. from the top. To admit of these rods, the portions should be made in three parts, allowing the rods to run between the frames of the parts.

(vi) All the shelf-planks should be of accurate length to allow interchange of them without any difficulty.

(b) Catalogue-Card Cabinet : The cabinet consists of two parts—the cabinet and the table-stand on which it rests. Generally, the cabinet consists of 24 trays in 4 columns of 6 trays each. It can be of 30 drawers also. The height of the stand should be 24 inches from the ground. The height of the cabinet should be not exceeding 5 feet from the ground.

(c) Catalogue-Card Tray : The size of the tray of the catalogue-card is based on the size of the card viz. 125mm × 75mm and of 5 inches × 3 inches. The internal dimension of the tray should be 130 mm wide, 10 mm high and 500 mm long. The side and the back planks should be 10 mm thick and 55 mm high.

(d) Periodical Display Rack : Three types of periodical racks are required in the library viz. (i) current issues display rack; (ii) recent unbound issues storing rack; and (iii) bound volumes shelving racks.

For display of current and unbound issues, racks of several designs are used. Common dimensions are: height 66", width 48" and depth 22". It consists of 5 shelves to accommodate nearing 35 magazines.

Another type of 'built-in-stairs' rack are also used. Usually these are 3' to 4'high and 3' wide on which the periodicals remain standing. Ordinary book-racks are used for storing the bound volumes.

(e) Newspaper Rack : Being unwieldy in size, these are difficult to handle and store. These racks are of various types. The problem of storage of the newspapers has however been solved during the modern days by introduction of microfilms.

(f) Reading Tables : Different types of reading tables and chairs are available in the market, which should be used in the library to break the dullness and monotony. These, however, should conform to standard sizes. The standard size recommended by the ISI is 2m × 0.7 m. These should be so arranged that the readers face the same side and not each other to prevent diversion of attention of the readers.

(g) Readers' Chairs : The chairs should be fitted with noise prevention pad in the legs. The height of the arm should be 215 mm and seat back from the frontage of seat 75 mm.

The chair used at the counter should be armless with its seat 760 mm high from the floor level. A foot-rest should be provided at the height of 300 mm from the floor level.

(h) Charging Desk. (Issue Counter) : Registration of the new readers, issue and return of books and their registration are done at this counter. It should have adequate shelving space to arrange the discharged books. The counter should also have enough drawer to file the book cards. Its height (facing the readers) should be 40 inches and width 26 inches to 28 inches, with provision of knee space and foot-rest.

(i) Issue Trays : Primary issue tray should provide space for book-jackets and readers' tickets. Its internal dimensions should be 200 mm long and 55 mm wide and 55 mm high.

Secondly, issue tray should possess the same internal dimensions as primary tray except that it should be 400 mm long with three channels. Charging tray should conform to the same internal dimensions as for the secondary issue tray except that it should have nine channels with 10° slope.

(j) Book Display Rack : Different types of display racks are used in the library. The commonly used ones are: Rackcum-Bulletin Board Type and Display Troughs used for books and Portable Troughs for books which are kept on a table.

The height of the book troughs should be about 3 feet from the floor.

(k) Dictionary and Encyclopaedia Stand : Multi-volume dictionary, encyclopaedia and other such volumenous books add to the beauty of the library if arranged separately on small racks. Besides it proves convenient as well for the readers to handle them.

(l) Atlas Stand : Atlases are oversized publications. They are, therefore, unwieldy to handle and inconvenient to be shelved on the ordinary racks. These should be arranged on specially designed racks of 3 feet to 5 feet height, 2.5 feet depth and 2 feet width.

(m) Book Trolley : Books have to be generally transported from one section to another viz. from acquisition section to the technical section and then to the stack-room and to the binding section etc. In a big library of a university and college movement of books is more frequent and the volumes are also greater in number. As such, it is economical and convenient to move books through trolley from one corner to another in the library.

Thus, the furniture in the library should be durable, functional, utilitarian as well as aesthetically pleasing to the eye, so that they present an attractive and inviting environment for the readers. Also, the floors of the library should be covered.

Lighting

As an important provision in the functioning of the library, this has all along been a matter of concern for the librarians to choose the best lighting for a library. Advice of illumination experts has often been sought and the experiments in this area still continue. It is a complex problem because lighting is concerned with several entirely different aspects like adding to internal attraction of the construction as also to external impact of the building and above all to allow reading to take place in comfortable position.

The following factors are the determinants of a proper lighting system: (i) effects of ceiling heights; (ii) nature of the fixture; (iii) relative advantages and costs of incandescent and fluorescent lighting; and (iv) kind of lighting needed for specific area in the building. These factors are related to the economics of an illumination system which is an important consideration for university administration. Therefore, the librarian strives to make every effort to obtain the best possible illumination for his building. It is still a matter of controversy as to how much lighting is necessary. Wilson and Tauber mention, "a uniformly illuminated field of view is the goal of good lighting. They also quote the suggestion that the library lighting might be equivalent to the light from a 30-foot candle. Some recommended 40 to 50 foot candles for library reading. A table of recommended foot candles for various parts of the library building has been worked out by Krachenbuchl to be from 5-foot candles for hallways and corridors to 25-foot candles for all reading species" (Wilson and Tauber: 1958: 515).

Natural light should be used as much as possible but sometime such a light also is found to be too extreme requiring proper shades and blinds to check the glare. The natural light is much less controllable while the artificial one is entirely controllable. Further, it is not only the lighting system but the illumination and reflection from the surfaces of ceilings, walls, windows, tables and books that need careful consideration.

Effects of lighting upon the reading materials in the library are varied. The words and other marks (on the paper) as well as the paper, vellum and parchment and other sensitive materials kept in the library can be damaged by light. The papers of the mechanical wood period of late nineteenth century are particularly vulnerable. The damage is caused by ultra-violet radiation emitting from all white light sources and the day light is most dangerous. The higher the intensity, the greater the damage; the longer the exposure the greater the damage.

The glare and excessive contrast cause fatigue to the eye. A reader in a dark-room working with a pool of light on his book is not a healthy arrangement. Efforts should be made to provide smooth graduation in brightness for the book itself to the immediate surrounding and finally to the general background. A ratio of luminance of about 3 : 1 between page and table top is good and more than 5 : 1 is bad for continuous reading, If the page of the book becomes white, the table top should not remain too dark and certainly it should not be black. The general background should be less.bright than the table top but not excessively so.

The librarian should endeavour to obtain the best illumination possible for his building, although this problem has never been satisfactorily solved as yet. The standards differ widely and wildly. It is difficult for the librarian to present the problem and for the architect to provide solution. At the best of it, the architect can be master of aesthetics and the means of providing light but to measure its adequacy for the readers' need, there is no authoritative technical solution; only there are numerous opinions.

Air-Conditioning

Air-conditioning will keep the library cool during the heat waves of summer. The American Society of Heating and Ventilating Engineers defines the air-conditioning as, "simultaneous control of all or at least the first three of these factors affecting both the physical and chemical conditions of the atmosphere within any structure. The factors include: temperature, humidity, motion, distribution, dust, bacteria, odours, toxic gases and ionization, most of which affect in greater or lesser degree human health and comfort" (*Ibid*: 516). The engineer makes a distinction between air-conditioning installation meant for winter, summer and all the year round. Comparison of suggestions from various sources suggests a temperature range of 65 to 75 degrees F. combined with about 50 per cent relative humidity as a desirable indoor climate for libraries (Gelfand *op. cit.,* 129).

The object is to keep the library reasonably cool in summer and comfortably warm in winter. In a poor country like India, air conditioning is considered a luxury. But the results of certain recent researches show that comfortable place of work increases the efficiency of the staff and, as such, the surrounding helps concentration of the readers beyond expectations. Report of the Summer School office of Harvard University brought forth that the air-conditioning of the Layout Library used by the undergraduate students "resulted in fourfold increase in book used and that there was significant decline in the number of failures and unsatisfactory work of students" (Sharma: 1970: 79). It is significant to note here that summer is much more intense in India as compared to that in Boston and, therefore, it would be a bad economy to drop the proposal of air-conditioning the library on monetary considerations; especially when we spend lacs of rupee on construction of library building, its furnishing, equipment, books, journals and other such materials. The proposal will actually help increase the use of the library as well as efficiency of the staff.

The Parry Committee notices the seriously deleterious effect on books and manuscripts caused by the solid particle of dirt and liquid and gaseous forms of acid suspended in the atmosphere. Further, the excessive change of temperature and humidity accentuate this deterioration due to growth of moulds, fungi and bacteria etc. Therefore, it is essential that to provide the best conditions for the preservation of books, the atmosphere should be free from dirt and acidity in gas or liquid form and also temperature and humidity should be controlled. In fact, "these conditions are obtained only by the installation of full air-conditioning plant." In areas of highly polluted air, the committee views that library stocks, housed both in reading-rooms and stacks can be preserved only in a fully air-conditioned atmosphere (Parry: *op. cit*: 92).

The committee further mentions that in the cleaner areas, however, the need will be reduced. But all results at least show that materials of lasting values should be stored in conditioned air.

The Library Committee of the UGC (India) in its report (on University and College Library) has highlighted this point saying that air-conditioning is, for the time being, beyond our means due to economic and foreign exchange difficulties. However, many of the benefits of air conditioning can be had by cheaper indigenous methods. Therefore, air-conditioning may have to be confined to the small area containing the rare books and manuscripts (UGC: *op. cit*: 98).

Safety of the Library Building

The library is an important institution housing the precious materials in the form of books, journals, manuscripts, microfilms and other documents. The destruction of these documents would be an irreparable loss and, therefore, all care and precaution should be taken for their protection. The following safety measures should be taken for protection of the materials:

(a) Protection from Fire : Fire hazard in a library would be a great loss to the nation, as the whole knowledge preserved for generations would be lost. All precautions should, therefore, be taken against fire hazard in the library premises and nearby building. Smoking in the library should be strictly prohibited. The staff of the library should exercise strict control through notices and personal supervision not only over the readers and visitors but also over their colleagues against prohibition. A separate lounge may be provided in the premises for smoking. As a preventive measure, fire extinguishers should be provided in every section of the building. The stock of the library should have more fire-points.

(b) Protection from Dust : The pages of books are damaged by the dust. This should be properly protected. The central vacuum system served by a central compressed air suction plant, is a good preventive measure. In the library, portable Electric Vacuum Cleaner is generally used as its cost is less. The central vacuum cleaning system proves costly.

(c) Protection from Sun : Precaution should be taken to avoid solar heat affecting the readers so that they may perform the intellectual work continuously. This needs provision of sun breakers to all the windows. In some areas, sun-shades also help. Direct sun falling on the books should also be prevented.

(d) Protection from Rain : The rain-water should be fully prevented from falling on the books. Provision of gangways along the walls helps in the matter. But to save from storm and torrential rains, the protection should be reinforced by providing glass shutters for the windows turn on a horizontal axis which can be adjusted at a suitable slope during the rains. The architect may adopt other such techniques for protection during the rainy seasons.

(e) Protection against Book-Theft : *(i) Protection of doors and windows*: The modern system of keeping the library on open access has some dark sides as well. The freedom given to the readers may be abused unless adequate safeguards are provided in the design of the library building. The construction of the building should be such as to give no opportunity for unauthorized removal of books through windows, doors and other openings in the outer walls of the building. Therefore, all the windows and doors opening out should be properly fitted with locked or fixed shutters with meshes. The doors of the library should be on either side of the circulation counter which must be at the very entrance. No person should be able to enter the library or leave it except through the turn-stile controlled and operated by the library assistant inside the counter enclosure. This will also ensure the queue system automatically, besides proper control and supervision of receipt and issue of books.

(ii) Protection of no-man's zone : There may be subsidiary enclosures in the library on the outer side of the gangways for entrance and exit. These are generally used during the unusual rush hours. These enclosures, in fact, serve as no-man's zone preventing persons inside the library from passing on books to any person standing in the entrance or exit gangway. These should be carefully manned.

(iii) Provision of detection device : In the UK libraries, Diver Detection Device is used in which a magnetised metal strip is placed in the binding of each book. If any person tries to remove such a book from the library without the metal strip having been first demagnetised by counter staff, his exit is prevented by the automatic locking of the turnstile.

Such measures may be taken in our libraries as well since the book-theft in the libraries here are becoming a common feature now-a-days.

Control of Noise

There should be a quiet atmosphere in the library because it is a place of reading where even intellectuals do serious reading and work. Therefore, the reading areas and their surroundings should be fairly quiet places. The noise in the library should be properly controlled.

There are two sources of noise coming in the library viz. (i) outside source; and (ii) inside source.

To prevent outside noise, steps should be taken in the very beginning while selecting the site for the library building. Placing the library near a playground, music room or on the main road will mean greater disturbance to the reader. It should be situated in the most calm and quiet place. Once the building has already come up, the library can hardly exercise control over the outside noise coming in the library.

This, however, does not mean that the library should be situated at a place out of the way and beyond the reach of the reading community. Sound proof walls, windows and ceilings can reduce the amount of noise coming in the library. With the developed techniques now available the materials like Thermocole (foamed polystyrene) are available which possess excellent insulating qualities. Used on the ceilings and walls, it can check heat, noise and moisture.

(ii) Inside Noise : This noise is produced in the library by talking, walking and moving furniture and other such items inside the library. The administration of the library should take care to avoid the inside noise at the best. The lower ends of the legs of library chairs should be fitted with rubber cushions. The floor of the reading-rooms and surrounding areas should be covered with rubber or jute matting. Speaking loudly or talking in the library should be strictly prohibited. The staff of the library itself should set an example for this while talking to their colleagues and other readers. The echoing sound should be reduced to the minimum by adopting necessary techniques. The aim is to control the noise as much as possible.

Ancillary Public Amenities

(a) Lecture Room : Library needs rooms for holding meetings, lectures, discussions and debates, for play-readings and other such activities. These are the important extension activities of a modern library. The rooms may need separate approaches from outside the building with special arrangement made for security and public safety. Public lavatories need be attached to these rooms and in some cases cloakrooms are also needed.

(b) Theatre Hall : Modern libraries today are getting associated with theatres. This is natural because the libraries have to deal with the written and spoken words. In a large educational campus, the theatre is a companion to the library in it service to the academic community. For a public library, however, the theatre is often planned within the same building.

(c) Book Display Hall : This is an old system of inviting readers' attention to special, changeable groups of books. In the past, book-jackets were used to be displayed by pinning them on the boards. Now, these jackets are sealed into books, and, therefore, the books themselves are displayed. As such, provision for a display hall should be made in the building.

Exhibition Area

The exhibition area should be associated with decorative features in the building. The architect will be well advised to keep in mind the librarian's requirements and accordingly to provide the framework for changeable displays. For displays to be incorporated in the corridors and entrance halls, the architect should keep in mind the potential size of the displays to allow clear passages. In small libraries, open-backed display units may be provided to economise the space and make the best utility of it, as these serve as space dividers without drawing separate area.

Alternative to a New Library Building

Sometimes a situation arises when the existing building is almost full to overflowing but simultaneously it is also not possible to have a new building for the library. To meet such a situation, certain possible alternatives have to be adopted. These may be the following:

(a) Economical use of the existing space in the library :

To achieve this objective, the following steps should be taken:

(i) Layout of certain rooms should be changed.

(ii) Such rooms as are little or less-used, like exhibition rooms, staff reading room, display room etc. should be converted into reading-rooms.

(iii) Big and heavy furniture may be changed. Large study tables should be replaced by small ones. Mobile book cases should be adopted.

(iv) Microfilms of books and back volumes of journals and periodicals should be kept in the library as far as possible to save the storage space.

(b) Reducing the concentration on the library :

(i) Extended hours of the library : The opening hours of the library should be increased. This will spread the intensity of the concentration of the readers in the library. But at the same time, the total work-load on the library staff will also increase.

(ii) The non-members of the library may be discouraged to use it.

(c) Transferring of some of the library stock : The less-used, duplicate and unused material of the library should be transferred from the library to create space.

(d) Transferring of some of the library work :

(i) The work of the binding should be transferred to a commercial binder.

(ii) The processing, cataloguing and classification of books may be done at a centralized place.

(iii) Some of the library equipment may be transferred to the departments.

(iv) Selection of books, periodicals and other reading materials should be done quite carefully.

These factors are taken to be only the possibilities, depending upon the conditions obtaining in a particular situation.

These may have then disadvantages as well. This fact

should also be borne in mind while introducing the proposed changes.

References

1. Ellsworth, R.E., 1968, Planning the college and university library building: a book of campus planners and architecto. 2nd ed. Pruett Press, Boulder, Colorado.
2. Fairhurst, Harry, 1965, Accommodating the library in the new university, ASLIB Proceeding, V17, N4, April 1965. p. 108.
3. Gelfand, MA, 1962, University libraries for developing countries, UNESCO manual for libraries-14, UNESCO.
4. Indian Standards Institution, New Delhi, 1961. Code of practice relating to primary elements in the design of library buildings and specifications for library furniture and fittings, New Delhi.
5. Kaula, P.N., 1971, Library buildings: Planning and design. Vikas, New Delhi.
6. Metcalf, K.D., 1965, Planning academic and research library buildings, McGraw-Hill, New York.
7. Neal, K.W., 1971, British university library, published by author at 7 Church Road, Wilmslow, Cheshire.
8. Parry, Thomas (Chairman), 1967, Report of the committee on libraries, University Grants Commission, Her Majesty's Stationery Office, London.
9. Ranganathan, S.R., 1962, Library manual, Asia, Bombay.
10. Sharma, HD, 1972, Library building and furniture with special reference to college libraries, Indian Bibliographic Centre, Jullundur.
11. Thompson, Godfrey, 1977, Planning and design of library building, 2nd ed. Nicholas Publishing Company, New York.
12. Thompson, James, 1970. An introduction to university library administration, Clive Bingley, London.
13. University Grants Commission, New Delhi. 1965, University and college libraries, containing the report of the library committee of the University Grants Commission and the proceedings of the seminar from publisher to reader held on March 4-7, 1959, UGC, New Delhi.
14. Viswanathan, C.G., 1972. University libraries in India-principles and policy, published by the author, New Delhi.
15. Wilson, L.R. and Tauber, MF., 1958, The University library, 2nd ed. Columbia University Press, New York.

5

BUILDING UP LIBRARY COLLECTION

The Acquisition Policy

Academic libraries have a special responsibility to collect and disseminate reading materials appropriate for study and research. This implies that the library should have a well-defined policy and procedure of acquisition, the character of which may, however, differ from institution to institution. While the schools and colleges remain confined to their study programmes, the functions of the university include conservation of universe of knowledge, dissemination and imparting instructions and taking up research, publications and extension programmes. Of these functions, the first three are closely related to the university library. These influence the characteristics of the acquisition policy in building up the collection. The other contributory factors in this regard are : (i) size of the existing holding; (ii) nature of the collection; (iii) the curriculum; (iv) pedagogy; (v) nature and extent of the research programme; (vi) size of the student population; (vii) size and diversity of the facilities; and (viii) nature and physical organization of the library-working in the centralized or decentralized form. These are the elements for designing and planning the library's acquisition policy. The aspect, kinds and diversity of the educational programmes pursued at a particular university are the determinants of use to which its books and other reading materials will be put to and, accordingly, such kinds and types of the materials have to be acquired in the library. Fusser observes, "a library's acquisition policy may represent anything .... from the purely fortuitous to the most rigorous selection, but these practices in themselves constituted a policy of sorts. The extent to which a library fails to recognize the kinds of policies which it is following may possibly be a measure of the potential inadequacies of its collection over a long period of time" (Fussler: 1953: 363).

Book Selection Policy

Dr. S. R. Ranganathan mentions that there are various sources for selecting books in the library. Some of these may be enumerated as follows (Ranganathan: 1952: 93)

(a) Trade list, State and National bibliographies.

(b) Bibliographies and Reviews published in books and periodicals and Sunday Magazines of newspapers.

(c) Suggestions from the readers.

(d) Reference Section, Circulation Section and the Shelf-Section of the library.

(e) Experts and Specialists of the subject concerned.

The library staff should not take upon themselves the entire book-selection. It would be a good policy to involve experts and specialists of different subjects in making the selections and finalizing the list. But they should be burdened with the minimum load of work.

Funds are always limited. Therefore, it is for the library staff to ensure that the book-grant is utilized for the maximum benefit of the library clientle. The Book-Selection Section should ensure that the book-grant is distributed in proper proportion among the different subjects in the light of their legitimate needs and demands and that "no particular subject usurps for more than what should be the proper share, simply because it happens to be sponsored, for the time being, by an influential person or clique" (*Ibid*: 92). The Book Selection section should work in close co-ordination with Book Order Section, Periodical Section and the Accounts Section of the library. The acquisition programme should be evenly distributed the whole year. "The book resources to be added to the library in various subjects should be taken up for treatment in systematic cycles, the periodicity for each subject being adjusted from time to time in the light of supply and demand" (*Ibid* : 92). All this will help systematic building up of the stock in the library.

Ranganathan further mentions that the work of the Book Selection Section should be planned with reference to the following factors (a) Sources; (b) Selections; (c) Indent; and (d) Finance.

(a) Sources : The names of all useful sources for book-selection should be noted along with particulars. Similarly, particulars of the book of the interest to the library should also be noted down.

(b) Selections : Such titles, as may be of probable interest to the different departments, should be selected from the various sources in the library. Book selection card for each title should be prepared. These cards and other references should be sent to the experts soliciting their opinion regarding utility of the books for the library and then a list of the approved items be prepared.

(c) Indents : Indent prepared for all the books should be thoroughly checked with the stock, order tray and the bills on hands. The final indent should be forwarded to the sanctioning authority.

(d) Finance : Annual allotment of funds for books for different departments should be fixed. The departments and the experts responsible should be informed from time to time about the financial position of the grant for different subjects.

Book Ordering

In India, book ordering is a difficult job. It is European and particularly English books that are more prevalent in India. So the main book markets for the country are very far off—in London, New York or other European centres. So our libraries are not able to get the books on approval. It is not possible for them to assess and scrutinize the books of different editions.

The situation is even worse in respect of Indian publications. The publishing trade is not fully developed and properly organized. Several authors in this country are themselves publishers-cum-booksellers. They remain scattered far and wide and their response is poor.

Further, there is no conformity to the bibliographical standards either in respect of the make-up of the title-pages of the books or in preparation of the indents of the titles needed in the libraries. Specialists of the various fields still continue to refer the books only by the titles. The variations in the rate of discount prevalent in the country is yet another problem. The multivolume books and prepaid books pose another problem.

To obtain the out-of-print books, it is better to obtain quotations from different second-hand booksellers and then decide the vender in each case, on its merits.

Accession work

Every volume to be included in the stock of the library should be given a serial number called Accession Number. The Gift Books should be given Donation Number, in addition to the Accession Number.

Dealing with 'Work with Book Stock,' D.N. Datta mentions that the essential task of every library is to provide the books and information sought for by its clientele. To fulfil this objective, the library should plan to acquire all such reading materials as would meet both the implicit (unexpressed) as well as explicit (expressed) demands of the readers. For this purpose, the library should not wait for the receipt of the precise requirement from the readers. In fact, it is for the library itself to anticipate the demand and accordingly plan and execute the acquisition programme to fulfil all the reading needs of readers. Selection of books in the academic libraries is largely dependent on the suggestions of the faculty members. The most useful aid for selection of British books is *British National Bibliography, for U.S. books it is Cumulative Book Index and for Indian books, it is the Indian National Bibliography* (Datta: 1978: 125) :

B. Sengupta says that prime responsibility of the college libraries is to provide resources to meet the curriculum demands of the college. The library has, therefore, to equip itself with current books and journals to feed the students and faculty members. It has to help the faculty to keep abreast of the growing knowledge. It should "introduce students to the national heritage." The library should possess basic general collection of classics to arouse and instill in the students enthusiam for great books, which will generate good reading habit. An ill-equipped or poorly stacked library will just affect the students very adversely. The collection of the college library should, therefore, consist of books including reference books, popular and current journals, archival materials and the audio-visual aids. Linguaphones prove very useful for teaching languages. The holding should be carefully chosen. While the browsing room of the library should provide recreational reading, the general reading room should provide "works which will arouse intellectual curiosity, counteract parochialism, foster national integrity and help to develop critical thinking" among the students. (Sengupta: 1974: 71).

In institutions where funds are limited, the acquisition policy of the library may be precise and streamlined. But in case of universities where grants are not restrictive and practically all demands of the members for reading materials have to be met, a definite policy has to be followed to ensure bright results. Donton says, "the university administration, following consultations with, and advice from, appropriate academic groups, should provide the library with an official statement of policy in some detail, as to the institutions' present and probable future programme of teaching and research" (Donton: 1963: 188).

The university librarian and his professional staff are responsible to execute the programme. Besides the other responsibilities in the functioning of the library the important one is to see that right books and journals are added to the library. The acquisition policy should, therefore, clearly mention : (i) the authority responsible for framing a definite acquisition policy; (ii) authority responsible for executing it; (iii) authority vested with final powers for directing and controlling the book grant; and (iv) participation and role of the faculties in the selection of books.

Executing the Policy

Step 1: In a university library, the librarian is responsible for formulating and implementing systematic and well-co-ordinated book acquisition policy. Then, the responsibility for actual selection of the reading material is, however, divided among the library staff, the faculty members and him. The library committee also shares the responsibility partly in-as-much as it distributes funds for books, periodicals and other materials and outlines the general policies of acquisition.

The library develops a close working relationship with the teaching staff which is its nature. The members of the faculty select the materials in support of the courses and the research programmes pursued by them. They are in a position to discover the deficiency of the material while looking at the shelves, which they should point out to the librarian. The librarian and the library staff mostly select general reference books, bibliographical tools and aids, non-curriculum books, periodicals of general interest and recreational reading literature.

Step 2 : It includes the following measures : (i) constituting a departmental committee to initiate and supervise the selection of reading material for the department. This committee is constituted by each department separately; (ii) notification regarding the position of the grant of the department periodically; (iii) notification of availability of the material to the interest of the departments and the faculty members; and (iv) assigning the responsibility to particular acquisition staff of the library to provide with actual position of the acquisition orders outstanding and the funds available under the budget heads. This responsibility to the staff is assigned by the librarian. A list of new acquisitions made in the library is circulated amongst the departments and the faculty members.

After having taken these steps the policy is put into operation by the librarian. An important assumption here is that, in certain cases, the faculty members are considered more competent as subject experts in selection of reading materials. This is true; the faculty members are more familiar with their subject-fields, as compared to the library staff but the fact remains that usually they do not (or cannot) devote sufficient time for this work. Wilson and Tauber say, "it is altogether possible that a library staff which includes members who are expert librarians as well as experts in special subject-fields, whose task it is to review current publications and second hand catalogues as a part of their regular duties, will be more successful than the faculty members, whose time, with few exceptions, is occupied in other ways. A few university librarians have appointed staff bibliographers to select materials in special fields" (Wilson and Tauber: 1958: 352).

In fact, the observance of the acquisition policy is not the single responsibility of either the library staff or the faculty. To achieve better results, the programme should be well conceived and co-ordinated. All the members interested in the successful functioning of the library should actively participate in seeing it through. In the selection of reading materials even of a general nature, the collaboration of the faculty members is valuable, as the reading materials form the base for development of reading habit. To this end, not only the librarian and his staff but also the faculty members, special bibliographers, departmental staff, students as well as the friends-of-the-library groups (benefactors and donors), the societies and organizations all should contribute.

Wilson and Tauber suggest the following five steps in building up the collection of reading materials. These are: (i) survey of the literature-field including the university, department, collection and the entire region; (ii) core selection which includes texts and major critical works; (iii) expanded selection based on authors, subjects, periods and the material relevant to the institution's needs; (iv) selection of micro-documents like journals, abstracts and publications of the learned societies and institutions; and (v) acquiring the en-block collections of renowned authors, book-collectors and libraries, relevant to the subject of study in the institution. These steps are applicable for acquiring the reading materials in all branches of knowledge (*Ibid*: 362).

For a progressive book acquisition policy, it is necessary that provision of adequate funds is made, restriction on import and currency is removed and the cumbersome procedures are modified. These are serious impediments to library development and have been often discussed. The South Asia Regional Seminar on Library Development (Acquisition of Foreign Materials) held in October 1960 discussed closely the obstacles in importing foreign books and journals. The following were noticed at important impediments: (i) lack of sufficient funds in the library; (ii) non-availability of the bibliographies and library's failure to use them; (iii) procedural difficulties involved in import licences, customs clearance and remittance of payment for the material received; and (iv) restrictions of foreign exchange preventing the libraries from ordering books from the suppliers of foreign countries.

To overcome these impediments and remedy the situation, the acquisition procedures should be simplified and the customs regulations modified to make the remittance of the cost conveniently easier. The amount of exchange should be enhanced in relation to the book-budget of the college or university and open general licences be granted to the educational institutions and the library. The library should also develop close understanding and co-ordination with the teaching departments and the staff, to make use of their specialized subject knowledge. During the course of their search for literature, the readers notice the deficiency of the collection. They should be encouraged to bring such deficiencies to the knowledge of the library staff for acquiring that material. A committee constituted at the level of department or the faculty proves quite helpful and useful in executing the library policy provided the members have open and comprehensive, not sectional or narrow, interest in the development of the library

After the policy has been formulated and the programme initiated, the university librarian is there to control the acquisition work. The librarian should be vested with full authority to control and direct all the activities of the acquisition work. While the accounts should be audited periodically, it should not be necessary for the librarian to obtain approval and sanction for each routine item of work. Gelfand recommend, "adequate financial controls can easily be established in the university business office and the librarian can be relieved of personal financial liability except clear cases of deliberate malfeasance. The university should do everything possible to expedite efficient and economical book selection and acquisition" (Gelfand: 1962: 76).

The Government should take steps to exempt library reading materials from internal taxes. The import duties should be removed and the customs and postal restrictions should be simplified for books and journals. The procedure for keeping accounts in the library as well as those relating to the budget should also be made simple. R.E. Barker says by removing import restrictions and internal taxes, the government loses very little. He cites, "national expenditure on book imports is always a minute proportion of total expenditure, and that those countries which need most to import books appear to import them least.....The revenue from taxes on books fails to justify the imposition of these taxes" (Barker: 1956: 102). Gelfand mentions that to facilitate the import of educational, scientific and cultural material, the Government should revise the existing agreement. He suggests, "it (Government) can reduce a shortage of foreign exchange—to a degree— by encouraging the use of UNESCO Book Coupons and participation in programmes like the United States International Media Guarantee Programme where applicable. It can encourage co-operative acquisition programmes" (*Ibid*). Removal of these barriers will go a long way to improve the condition of acquisitions in the academic libraries.

Selection of books, especially in a scholarly library, is most important and is a highly professional job. It determines the quality of collection. The prerequisite for book selection is knowledge of the subject, syllabuses, the readers for whom selection is to be made and the collection already made in stock of the library. It demands, therefore, that adequate attention may be paid to the basic problems and policies of book selection by the academic libraries. The book selection is the most important and highly professional task of the librarian. But the library staff, remaining otherwise busy, do not give adequate time for this work. This is one of the reasons that in most of the university libraries, major part of the book selection is done by the academic staff. This leads to improper selection of books in different departments.

The bibliographical details of the books have to be collected out of the National Bibliographies, Book Indexes, Review Periodicals and the Newspapers Columns. The selection of books for undergraduate courses is not difficult. Most of the books are popularly known titles. But at the postgraduate and research levels, the problems are complex because the titles have to be selected out of the enormous range of the materials available in so many languages. Acquisition, of foreign language titles is all the more time consuming, complex and frustrating too.

The selection of books and other reading materials in the library should conform to the academic needs and functions of the institution, the library belongs to. The academic programme of the university generally covers four major areas viz. (i) Humanities ; (ii) Social Sciences; (iii) Pure Sciences; and (iv) Applied Sciences (Technology). These are related to the following standards: (a) Under-graduate; (b) Postgraduate ; (c) Research; (d) Post-doctoral works; (e) Teaching-level; and (f) Extension Programmes. The reading material should be acquired in the library keeping in view the needs of these classes of readers. The materials should be varying in nature and comprehensive enough to meet the needs.

Undergraduate Collection

This collection includes text-books, supplementary readings and reference books. More precisely these may be classified as follows: (i) Text-books; (ii) Books of supplementary reading; (iii) Reference Books; (iv) Browsing collection of fiction and non-fiction; (v) Union catalogues; and (vi) Periodicals. It is necessary to distinguish between text-books and non-text-books with a view to utilising the book-grant separately, A book is categorized as text-book generally when it treats the basic and fundamental part of the subject in introductory manner and according to the curriculum. It is also termed course book. Text-book is essential for every undergraduate student to possess as his own copy.

In case of certain overlapping fields of knowledge, it becomes difficult to distinguish text-book and non-text-books.

When the thought-content of a particular book deals with two or more subjects together, like geophysics, biochemistry, geochemistry etc., it becomes text-book for one student and serves as reference book for students of another related subject. In preparation of list of such titles, the advice from the faculty proves useful. All standard text-books get revised from time to time. As such, adequate care, should be taken in acquiring multiple copies of such books in relation to the prevailing demands from them.

The courses of studies and the books prescribed and recommended in various disciplines are generally the guidelines to indicate what books are considered text-books on the subject. Majority of the undergraduate students look for relatively small proportion of book-stock. Consequently, text-books are required to be purchased in multiple copies. In fact, it is an obligation on the part of the library to make available adequate number of copies of such titles as are constantly in heavy demand.

Whenever a number of copies of a text-book are purchased in the library, all the copies are not meant for circulation. A certain number of copies (depending upon the popularity of the subject) in various subjects are kept separately and maintained as a separate unit called Text-Book Library. This unit is maintained as a separate reading section which functions ten to fourteen hours every day to enable the students to derive maximum benefit in preparation of their courses. Availability of every text-book prescribed for the different courses of studies, should be insured in this section by the library. The Parry Committee has also emphasized upon the needs of the undergraduates saying, "we recognize that the needs of undergraduates demand special attention and that their work is certain to suffer if library facilities are inadequate" (Parry: 1968: 46). The Association of University Teachers also highlights necessity to provide supplementary collection of additional copies of essential text-books, in view of the change from public lecture to the more intimate seminar (In Thompson: 1970: 50).

The text-books get revised from time to time. It happens more frequently in the subjects of science and technology than to those of arts and humanities. The previous editions become old and less useful or even of little use. It is, therefore, essential that adequate care is taken to acquire the minimum number of copies of the actually needed titles for the readers and that book-fund is conserved for continuous replacement with the latest editions and with coming new titles. Buck also stressed upon the needs of the undergraduates saying, "in teaching, to be sure, there has been a movement away from the text-book; but it is a movement away from the use of a single book, which the student owned, to a variety of books supplied, for the most part, by the college library. Despite the development of important audio-visual aids to learning, and despite increased emphasis on the laboratory sciences, there can be no doubt that the college student of this generation uses more books than any of his predecessors" (*Ibid* : 50). These discussions lead us to conclude that the need for multiple copies of text-books for undergraduates is no more a debatable point.

Separate Text-Book Library

The idea behind providing a Text-Book Library (separately as a unit of university central library) only for reference and consultation is that every student of undergraduate class buys almost all the text-books which he needs to use them regularly throughout the academic session and that only for highly expensive text-books he should depend on the library. The student editions of the text-books at a low price have been recently brought out by several publishers and organizations like East West Press, ELBS and US Education Foundation etc. to suit the pocket of the students. Yet there are some other measures through which the students may be induced to purchase text-books and a few other reference books on their own which, in course of time, would become a working library and personal book collection for the rest of his life. In

England, local educational authorities are required under the Education Act, 1962 (Section 1) to pay the maintenance grant to students to cover their expenses during the academic terms. This grant includes £35 (1965) as annual allowance for books, instruments and other educational materials. The staff of the college, university and other academic libraries advise the students on the kind of the books and the particular titles and the editions which they should essentially buy for preparation of courses of studies. Several safeguards have been suggested to ensure that the amount paid to the student is well utilized for the purpose of books. At the very beginning of the academic session, vouchers covering a major portion of the book grant are issued to the students and part of the amount is paid in cash to enable them to buy necessary second-hand books and some stationery.

In India, no such book allowance is paid to the undergraduates either by the State Government or the University Grants Commission. Even the poorest student has to depend on his own resources. Since a large number of students cannot afford to buy all the text-books or even a few essential ones, they largely depend on the text-book collection in the university library. There are certain university libraries like Allahábad, Banaras and Lucknow etc. which maintain their separate Text-Book Library. They purchase multiple copies of the text-book to enable the large number of students to read extensively. As a help to the needy and poor students, some of the colleges and universities are loaning text-books for the full term of the academic year under the book-bank scheme for which special budget has been provided by the State Governments.

Viswanathan mentions a scheme introduced in the first Agriculture University of India at Pantnagar (Uttar Pradesh). The university created a collection of multiple copies of text-books, specially the costly ones, and loaned them to the students for a full term on payment of 5 per cent of the cost of the books. The scheme became quite popular with the students. Due to rotation of subjects from one term to another, different batches of students could make use of the same text-books. The fee realized was used to buy the new titles and more copies. Yet, another scheme introduced in the same university was to provide subsidy of 50 per cent to such students as were willing to meet the remaining 50 per cent of the cost of their text-books. The students being keen to create their own collections took advantage of this scheme. These schemes intended to cultivate the book-buying habit among the students were emulated by other universities too. (Viswanathan: 1972: 33).

The British university libraries generally do not favour an entirely separate building for undergraduate library facilities. Majority of them, however, feel inclined to have a separate area within the main building. The main reason is the feeling that an undergraduate, though basically needed to use only a limited number of text-books, should be exposed to the larger collection and granted access to all other collections the library maintains. The Parry Committee strengthens this point saying that "undergraduate collections actually stimulate rather than discharge use by students of the main collection" (In Thompson: *op. cit*: 50). As such, a compromise situation is that if the undergraduate collection is provided separately but within the main building, these students will be saved from premature confrontation with a very vast, research-oriented library. Thompson sums up : "A final point is that the actual administration of providing extra copies of students' texts is made very much simpler if such collections are annexed from the rest of the library's stock" (*Ibid*: 51).

Non-Text-Book Collection

Besides the text-books, the students need other reading materials like government reports, statistics and pamphlets etc. These are more frequently needed in the discipline of social sciences and humanities. It is the responsibility of the library to provide all such reading materials in the library. Further, a good number of references are cited in the text-book by the authors and students are required to look for these references and consult them as original source of information to enrich their knowledge on the subject. All these references should be made conveniently available in the library. The number of such references in Arts, Social Sciences and Humanities are more as compared to the Pure Sciences and Technology. But the price ratio of books between the above two areas is roughly in order of 2 : 3 and, therefore, the amount required for books on science and technology is usually more than the sum spent in the arts and social sciences. Besides the text-books, general books and the supplementary reading materials, the library has to provide for recreational reading material as well for the readers for light reading.

With the increasing number of enrolment in the various courses of universities, the pressure on the accommodation and demand for books have been increasing. Viswanathan mentions, "the larger and better the undergraduate library, the finer is the quality of the postgraduates of the university" (Viswanathan: *op. cit*: 35). The undergraduate libraries should, therefore, be developed as an integral part of the university library.

Postgraduate and Research Collection

An important function of the university library is to cater to the needs of the postgraduate students, research scholars and the teaching members of the university. This class of readers need highly specialized and advanced material on the subject of their specialization. These consist of systematic treatises, special monographs, reports of the professional conferences and symposia, proceedings, transactions of societies and abstracts, authoritative reference books, periodicals and back volumes of journals, indexes, manuscripts and archival materials. A very huge amount of literature in the form of the above documents are coming up every day and it is difficult for the library to keep pace with them. The problem assumes greater proportion and gravity with the increasing number of the postgraduate students and the research scholars, coming up with their varying needs. On the other hand, constraints like limitation of book-grant and staff expenditure are there. These make the preservation of reading material difficult. However, pressure of demand on the library by the readers is already there. To meet this contingency, certain steps like strict choice of material, discreet selection and subject specialization of individual libraries etc. need be adopted. The system like voluntary co-operation amongst the various libraries regarding use of the reading material also helps.

Qualitative Acquisition

The reading material needed by the postgraduate students and research scholars are mostly advanced and for depth studies. The collection should also contain current and contemporary literature as well as those providing the historical and bibliographical background to the subject of research. There are certain core and basic books in each areas of knowledge which are found necessary for research scholars. These should be included in the basic stock of the library.

The archival materials like manuscripts, inscription report, proceedings and investigations are generally needed in humanities. In science, current publications embodying the results of present day investigations and day-to-day findings of the laboratories and workshops are sought for. Abstracting and indexing journals are also important. Recently, certain periodicals have started listing the titles of scientific papers and research reports in the specific fields of studies to reduce the time taken in publication of the full investigation report. Complete set of these periodicals should be procured to provide current information to researchers.

Libraries in Students' Hostels and Halls

Setting up of libraries in the halls of residence or the hostels of students is influenced by the following four factors : (i) distance of the hostel from the central library of the university; (ii) number of students living in the hostel; (iii) kind of courses of studies the hostel students are pursuing; and (iv) availability of funds for the library.

(i) Distance : Some of the universities possess very large campus. Hostels are situated very far from the central library of the university and the students feel inconvenience in attending this library as they have to travel long distances. Such a situation justifies the location of a library in the hostel itself. If, however, the hostel is situated in close proximity of the central library, the need will not be much.

(ii) Number of Students : If the inmates of the hostel are sufficiently large in number, they would need a library.

(iii) Kinds of Courses : The necessity of a library depends on the kind of courses the students of the hostel are pursuing.

(iv) Finance : In certain cases, finances for these libraries are voluntary contributions by students themselves. In other libraries, fund is made available out of the general book-grant of the university.

All these factors decide the nature and contents of the library to be set up in the hostels or the halls where the students reside. The reference books are not generally duplicated. The collections here should consist of text-books mostly and recreational literature to provide pastime reading material to the students during leisure hours.

The Parry Committee has characterised the following functions of the libraries in the halls of residence: (i) duplication of some of the service of the library like providing the textbooks, provision of some new services like making the recreational and general reading literature available to the students viz. books dealing with humour, art, satire and sports etc.

Departmental Library

There is another source of getting books for students. The prime objective of creation of libraries in the department was to make the research material available conveniently at hand for senior academic staff without necessitating them to go to the central library of the university. Making this collection open to the students is a later development. The Cambridge Report recommended that the departmental libraries should bear the major responsibility of catering to the needs of the undergraduate students leaving the university library for the research scholars alone. The British university libraries, on the whole, do not favour the creation of departmental libraries for the following reasons:

(i) The university should aim at providing a main central library possessing a very comprehensive collection of books and journals, manuscripts and other audio-visual materials to the university community as a whole.

(ii) Such a central collection so established can be organized and administered more conveniently than a departmental collection.

(iii) Most of the titles and subjects are interdisciplinary in nature and hence they overlap. There are very few subjects which do not interest the readers of other departments. Therefore, it is not feasible to limit and confine the popular collections only to a specific class of readers.

(iv) It leads to wasteful duplication in respect of acquisition, processing, organization, staffing, administration and accommodation of the collection.

There are two exceptions where the librarians are agreeable to the creation of departmental libraries. First is that they agree the departments should possess a small collection of basic and core books called 'bench-books' which the departments need to refer essentially and most frequently for reference. The second exception is related to the geographical location of the department. If the department is situated at a far distant place from the main central library, the convenience of the readers demands a separate library near the department. From the above it may be concluded that the fundamental reason for the setting up of departmental libraries is the convenience of the readers (academic staff more than the students) both from viewpoints of geographical location as well as the size of the library. It is a small library (easy to locate the material) situated at a small distance to help the rapid consultation.

The Parry Committee has discussed this point in detail. It says, "the committee is aware of the necessity for conserving the time and energies of both staff and students. Departmental libraries are an effective method of meeting that need has been sufficiently proved by the long experience of universities generally. The committee is, therefore, in agreement with the views put forward for the maintenance or establishment of libraries in departments and regard such libraries as recognized features of the academic library system" (Parry: *op. cit*: 103). Characterising the above arguments as valid one, Thompson also agrees when he says that "the departmental libraries have amenity value, because of their very proximity to those who teach and study in a particular subject-field and they can be more effective to readers because they do present a limited, compact and specialized collection as approved to a large and difficult one" (Thompson: *op. cit*: 54).

Thompson further emphasizes on the point that the central collection "must always be regarded as having first priority; it must never be weakened or deprived by irresponsible investment in departmental collection. He, however, argues that once that priority is met, the departmental library may be regarded more positively than Weledge and Page's dismissal of them as 'at best but a necessary evil'" (*Ibid*: 54).

The departmental libraries are characterised by the university teachers as an essential ingredient to the process of encouraging the undergraduates to make intensive reading of their subject. As such, these libraries should develop their collections in the following manner:

(i) Only essential text-books, reference books frequently needed for preparation of the course of study should be provided here.

(ii) This collection should be integrated with the main university collection and it should be catalogued by the central library. Union catalogue of the holdings of all the libraries in a particular university is necessary. In case it does not exist, it should be compiled as early as possible.

(iii) The special items available in the university library should not be duplicated in the departmental libraries unless the latter is large enough to justify that acquisition and also possess the necessary resources of staff, space and time to offer services of that standard. Ordinarily these libraries should confine to books and journals alone.

(iv) No library should be created outside the university central library unless it possesses sufficient funds to support the initial purchase as well as its continued maintenance.

(v) The acquisition policy of the departmental library should not came in the way of the acquisition policy of the university library.

(vi) These libraries should be under the jurisdiction of the university library committee or the similar authority constituted at the university level.

(vii) The organization and function of these libraries should be supervised by the staff of the university central library.

(viii) It should be open to all readers of the departmental or faculty library.

From the above it may be concluded that the organizational set-up of the departmental library should be such as it functions within a given framework and that the university central library exercises a degree of control over it.

Special Collection

Most of the university libraries possess some such collections as are termed special collection. It is special because of its nature and content. It is self-contained collection quite separate from the rest of the stock of the library. Usually such a collection is received in the library by way of gift or bequest. It is mostly related to a particular subject of the interest of the person, it originally belonged to. The collection continues in his name in the library also. The authorities of the university library tend to be proud of such a special publication. "They add a distinctive flavour to what would otherwise be a very work-a-day book stock. Woledge and Page point out other merits: "that such collections act as magnets for other gifts and bequests; that they are of great value to scholárs in the particular subject-field; that they appeal to the collecting instinct of the library staff, and that they encourage the staff to pursue bibliographical studies based on them" (Thompson: *op. cit*: 58).

The justification for accepting the special collection is that the library has a repository function. It bears the responsibility to act as keeper of 'the records of human spirit'. All libraries are the custodians, so whenever an offer comes to the library, the library has to accept it, although in certain cases the collection may not be of immediate relevance to the library—its teaching courses and the research programmes. What is relevant is that the library has to assess its shelving capacity to see whether it can accommodate the collection without causing any serious dislocation or adjustments to its existing storage; measure its intrinsic value against the cataloguing and processing labour involved and calculate whether the library has adequate funds to maintain it. In case of purchase of special collection by the library, however, strict scrutiny is necessary to examine and ensure that the allocation has specific relevance to the university teaching and research needs.

Reference Collection

The books which constitute the reference collection are: Encyclopaedia, Dictionary, Bibliography, Biography, Index, Abstracts, Atlas, Concordance, Almanac, Statistical compilations, Book catalogues and Translation lists etc. These are the sources of basic information and, therefore, form part of the university collection. Important outlines of specific subjects and standard treatises which are not studied as course books are also included in the reference collection.

Rare Book Collection

Preservation and retention of the important human records and cultural documents in printed form are the responsibility which the library should carry. Such documents represent national heritage. It should be the primary responsibility of the National Library to collect these documents. Their purchase in the academic library is, however, a debatable point. The Parry Committee comments, "it is not proper to subsidize from public funds a desire to acquire items simply because they are bibliographical curiosities." Thompson adds, "this cannot really be contested, and there was certainly an unfortunate tendency in university libraries during their 'store house' period of development to indulge in this type of acquisition, which in merit ranks no higher than collecting postage stamps" (*Ibid* : 59). But the fact remains that in the absence of such a National Library, the university library should assume this responsibility. The rare books are necessary for research especially in areas of history and politics. Further, rare books stimulate and develop the interest amongst the students and usefully help the library publicize its collection and exhibit it on occasions. The building up of rare collections should be done with purpose. The material should be related to the findings of the university; may be the instructional programme, research or the service to the public.

Serials

It is a publication which is intended to be continued indefinitely. The issue bears consecutive numbering. It is published at a regular or irregular intervals. As such, periodicals and continuations both come under this definition. The continuations include annuals, year books, reports, memoirs, proceedings, transactions, college and university catalogues and similar publications. Many government publications are issued as serials.

Since serials are so many dealing with different subjects, their acquisition is a complex problem in university library. It is difficult to distribute funds also for serial publications. The serial programme of university library is generally found to be weak in acquisition, organization and service. But these are important for purposes of research.

The titles not related to the institution's programme should be eliminated. A basically sound acquisition policy for serials is to systematically link the materials with the course of work and research policy of the institution. The needs of the institution should be assessed and then selection be made on that basis from the union list. Also, co-operative arrangement should be made from other libraries in the region.

Serials present problems of not only acquisition but their organization and storage as well. They involve extra difficulties in cataloguing and indexing and absorb the shelf-space very quickly. To have a centralized control and effective service to the members, a separate division of serials may be created in the library.

Government Publication

The documents issued by the various Governments—

Central, State, Local and Foreign—contain useful material and they are important sources of information on a variety of social, scientific and technological problems. Therefore, their acquisition in the university library is important. The United Nations publications are also acquired. These documents are used constantly by post graduate students, research scholars and the teaching members of the society.

These publications present serious problems of their acquisition, organization, care and shelving. A carefully planned programme should be drawn to acquire and organize these documents in the library.

Foreign Books

In course of acquisition, transmission and advancement of knowledge, the university library has to acquire major works in one or more principal modern languages to keep abreast of the modern learning, progress and research on the subject. The library has, therefore, to cross the language barriers and acquire the document. It has to include the documents on the subjects published in other foreign languages popularly known in the country. As such, the university library should frame a well-defined policy with regard to acquisition of documents in foreign languages as per local needs.

Periodicals

It is a publication with distinctive title which appears in successive members for an indefinite time. Periodicals are the staple food for research workers and form the backbone of the university library collection. They are indispensable sources of information in all fields especially the science and technology. Thousands of titles are being published and a large number of new ones also appear every year.

The selection of periodicals for subscription to university library depends largely upon the instructional and research programmes being pursued in the university. Generally, the selection is done by the faculty members in their respective subject-fields. This needs continuous and recurring budgetary provisions to meet the cost of the periodicals as well as that of its binding. A separate budget for this item is maintained the library. Periodicals may often change in their importance and need reappraisal. This should be done in consultation with the subject-experts of the faculty.

Newspapers

Newspapers are considered to be the primary source of information. They are particularly important in certain subject-fields of reference. Winchel observes, "current issues are helpful on the question of the day, events, policies, opinion, personalities and many others. Back volumes serve the same purpose for the contemporary history of an earlier period and often record details of a situation local in its application that are not found in general reference works" (Tauber and Wilson: 1958: 387).

The newspapers are used for research work in the areas of sociology, political science, history, philosophy, economics and education. The collection of the newspapers have to be representative. It should include at least the best and most important papers of each region in the country. Proper selection of newspapers is an important element in its acquisition programme and this should be done quite intelligently and purposefully.

Lost or damaged copies, irregularity of delivery, non availability of the duplicate copies are some of the problems the newspapers present to the librarians. The shelving and presentation of the newspapers in the library is really a tedius problem. Through the improvement in microfilming techniques, new possibilities in acquiring and preserving newspapers have been opened up. The microfilm copies are easy to handle and their accessibility is increased. Pressure on the storage is considerably decreased.

To sum up, the collection of university library should consist of well selected stock of books, journals, serials, government records and its reports, pamphlets, newspapers and special materials like microfilms, manuscripts, theses and dissertations, maps, gramophone records, tapes, photographs and charts etc.

Special Materials

Since World War II, the acquisition of special materials in the libraries has greatly increased.

Theses and Dissertations

A large number of theses and dissertations are provided every year in different areas of knowledge at various universities. These enhance knowledge. The university library is the prime collector of such theses submitted at various universities. The students and teachers look for these documents to use as reference in their fields of investigation.

Manuscripts and Archives

These are primary sources of materials needed for basic studies and research. During the recent years much attention has been paid to problems of acquisition, organization, preservation and indexing of the manuscripts. The manuscripts are preserved in the rare collection section or the archives room of the university library.

Archival Collection

These are mostly records of government agencies, societies, semi-government organizations, churches, business firms, institutions and universities. Acquisition of the archives is a special task for the librarians. Following are some of the suggestions advanced by Tauber and Wilson for acquiring the manuscripts and archives in the library :

(i) the material should be in respect of a well-defined geographical area or the cultural region;

(ii) they should reflect the political, social, economic, cultural, spiritual and scientific interests and viewpoints in the area;

(iii) they should be relevant to the topic of interest and programme of research being pursued in the university; and

(iv) they should prove to be of interest to the scholars beyond their area of research.

Acquisition and preservation of the manuscripts and the archival materials is a costly operation. It is worthwhile that the university and the State Historical Societies work in close co-operation and formulate a co-operative programme of acquisition.

Incunabula

This is a prime source material for the scholars of the subjects like art and painting etc. Libraries of American universities have been adding incunabula more to their collections. Most of the libraries there obtain them through the benefactions of collectors and donors.

Maps

In recent years, use of maps has become increasingly more important. It has gained importance more since World War II when the libraries realized the need for making the maps available to the students, research scholars and the faculty members.

Most of the libraries have confined their collection of maps only to those of geographical nature. In USA, the university library of Chicago started very early to collect maps dealing with political, social, historical, military, geological and meteorological subjects. The other universities have also now started map collections.

Maps are extensively used by research scholars for quick reference and furnishing the datas in their dissertations and theses. They present problems of organization, storage and maintenance. Their acquisition is also difficult because of the methods of publication. It is very difficult to obtain foreign maps. A well thought-out policy should be formulated for collection of maps. It should define the geographical area to be covered, types of maps to be collected and the time and period to which it belongs.

Microfilms, Microprints and Microcards

By the passage of time, the micro productions have come to be standard materials for the research libraries. The micro-production source includes Microfiches (microfilm in sheet form), Microfilms (including filmstrips), Microprints, Micro-cards, Microlex (raw materials in microprint form) of materials in books, periodicals, newspapers, pamphlets, manuscripts, documents and archival records.

The microfilms acquired in a library especially a research library cover almost all the fields of knowledge in several languages. Microfilms have now come to occupy an important place in the library documents. Fusser observes, "there are certain items that in their original forms will probably tend to disappear or at least diminish in the future library. The most conspicuous and bulky are the newspapers. Microfilming of newspapers has been applied broadly and has, in general, proved successful" (In Wilson and Tauber: *op. cit*: 416). The forms of micro production are also becoming popular in the library.

Slides

These are important media of teaching and instructions, especially in biological and medical sciences. In the field of art, architecture and archaeology also, these have become popular. These are usually purchased by the library for teaching. These are arranged in specially built files containing drawers and trays having individual slots permitting the slides to stand on their narrow ends. These are used with the help of projectors. Broad subject arrangement is done to facilitate their use conveniently.

Standards for Collection

The academic library is meant to cater to the needs of the undergraduate, postgraduate, research and the teaching community of the institution. Its scope is, therefore, fairly wide and comprehensive. But the resources being limited, one cannot buy one and all; whatever comes in the publishing market. Therefore, it fails to maintain an open acquisition policy and has to take recourse to the selective acquisition programme in conformity with the availability of funds. This is a difficult task. The pressure over the academic libraries has been changing during the course of time. Earlier, the undergraduates were instructed through certain prescribed text-books which they used to buy for themselves. They supplemented their studies by consulting the reference works available for them in their libraries. Today, teaching is not limited to prescribed textbooks. Reading lists are issued instead. The students need to read them making use of the library facilities. Also, the titles published on the subjects have immensely increased now in comparison to earlier times making it difficult to build up personal collections. The situation has led to increase awfully the demand on the library. Further, interdisciplinary and multi-disciplinary research studies pursued these days add to the problem all the more. This demands that libraries should be well-equipped with standard books, reference works and journals.

It is also necessary that the collection should be kept up-to-date. The additions should be made on the basis of students' enrolment and the research programme pursued in various disciplines at the institution. M.A. Gopinath has mentioned that a college should possess 5,000 to 50,000 volumes and university up to 3,00,000 volumes. The desirable ceiling, he says, for a university library is 4,00,000 volumes. N.K. Goel recommends that provision of textbooks should be made in the college library at the rate of 1 copy for every 10 students. At least one dozen periodicals for each of the subjects taught should be subscribed.

Co-operative Acquisition

The heavily-used materials—those of frequent and daily use by the students and teachers of colleges and universities should be acquired by all the libraries. In this type of reading material, the library should be self-dependent, otherwise its dependence upon other university or library for this type of material will come in the way of its providing efficient service to the members. The rare, costly, out-of-print and advanced treatises pertaining to specialised treatment of subjects are, however, used by only special types of readers, the demand of which cannot be anticipated. Further, every university library cannot financially afford to buy all such reading materials which prove uneconomical too. The various university libraries in the country should, therefore, come closer and join hands to support each other by lending the reading materials to another library on demand. The collection of all the libraries should form part of a common pool of resources for legitimate use by any student or teacher from any university centre.

Farmington Plan

Preliminary discussion for formulating a plan for acquisition of foreign literature on a national basis was held in the town of Farmington, Connecticut (United States). The plan took the name of its place of origin and is known as Farmington Plan. It was sponsored by the Association of Research Libraries and came into operation in 1948. The objective of the plan was to increase the nation's total resources for research provided to ensure that at least one copy of every new publication deemed to be of interest to research workers in the United States would be acquired by one or the other of the research libraries taking part in the plan. The number of the participating libraries were more than 70 and they were all university libraries. The publications acquired under the plan were listed in the National Union Catalogue. The material was available for loan or photographic reproduction. To cover the European countries (excluding Britain) the plan included 150 countries in Africa, South America and Asia. An agent, appointed for the purpose, mostly purchased a copy of every suitable publication and sent it to the library of the respective subject. The periodicals and official publications were not covered under the plan. The plan helped acquire a large number of unique books which, under the normal procurement programme of the library, might have been missed.

Exchange

Exchange of documents is a significant source of building up the library collection, provided the library is in possession of the material to be offered in exchange. If the university has some publication programme, the library should obtain copies of each publication for this purpose. The library should also explore the possibility of acquiring the multiple copies of its Government publications as also those of the educational and research organizations for its exchange stock. The handbook on the International Exchange of Publications is a valuable guide to exchange activities.

References

1. Barker, R.E., 1956, Books for all—a study of international book trade, UNESCO, Paris.
2. Donton, J.P., 1953, Book selection and collections—a comparison of German and American university libraries. New York, Columbia University Press.
3. Fussier, 1953, Acquisition policy, College and Research Libraries V. 14, pp. 363-67.
4. Gelfand, M.A., 1962, University libraries for developing countries, UNESCO manual for libraries-14, UNESCO, Paris.
5. Parry, Thomas (Chairman), 1967, Report of the committee on libraries,

University Grants Commission, Her Majesty's Stationery Office, London.

6. Ranganathan, S.R. 1959, Library administration, Asia, Bombay.
7. Sengupta, B. 1974, Book Selection, World Press, Culcutta.
8. Thompson, James 1970. An introduction to university library administration, Clive Bingley, London.
9. Viswanathan, C.G., 1972, University libraries of India: principles and policies, published by the author, New Delhi.
10. Wilson, L.R. and Tauber, M.F., 1958, The university library, 2nd ed., Columbia University Press, New York.

6
Library Organization and Administration

In the last chapter, we discussed the financial aspect of the library administration. Here we consider such aspects of library organization and administration as would help the library perform and carry out its functions effectively and execute the programmes of academic pursuits and research in the institution expeditiously; be that a school, college or university; regardless of size or staff whether manned by one librarian or by a large number of library personnel.

The administration is actually concerned with the translation of the policies of the institution into action. It involves forecasting and planning in relation to the library's objectives. As the institution of the library expands and its function gets diversified, the need for proper and efficient organization and administration becomes imperative.

Lyndall Urwick worked out the principles of administration, developed the relevant theory and systematised it. First, the general objectives of the library are determined by the authorities and government of the institutions like the governing body, board of trustees or control, executive council or the committee or the local body constituted for the institution. In the interest of efficient administration it is necessary to delineate and forecast the plan in relation to library's objectives. The objectives and the plan so determined and delineated by the board of control of the institution are clarified in detail by the Chief Librarian who formulates the policies and the service regulations to put them to practice. For this purpose, the librarian designs an internal organizational plan which is followed by the actual operation of the services and the functioning of the institution. The different constituent parts and the elements of the whole organizational work are divided in different units and divisions and each of them is recognized as a separate entity to be tackled and attended to. But at the same time, the element of coordination and integration between the various divisions are also maintained to ensure a coordinated and wholesome result. To this end, as we have said earlier, designing of an internal organizational plan with its structure is the first step. The plan consists of the following important parts :

1. Theory of Administrative Organization;
2. Library Administration;
3. Functionaries of Administration;
4. Responsibilities and Duties of the Functionaries;
5. Authority and its Area of Functioning;
6. Structural Organization of the Library; and
7. Departmental Library System.

Administration has become an important subject of study in the present-day education. This subject has developed and come to occupy a place in studies to be looked at scientifically. The science of administration has since gained so much prominence that hardly any administrator, in whatever field, can afford to overlook its basic elements—rather it is applied in all the fields with profit. The theory has been expressed in generalization concerning the elements of the administrative function and the principles commonly associated with it. It serves as a frame of reference for the functionaries; helping them perform their duties and achieve the objectives and most significantly it enables them to distinguish clearly between the administrator and his operation—a fine difference that mostly confuses the functioning and leads to consequent inefficiency.

Elements of Administration

The function of administration consists of various elements like (i) planning; (ii) organization; (iii) staffing; (iv) direction; (v) co-ordination; (vi) reporting; and (vii) budgeting etc.

Planning is a method which broadly indicates and outlines the objectives and needs to be achieved as well as the ways and means to be adopted to gain the determined purpose. It is an essential part of the university administration to enable the librarian to foresee the future and act accordingly. An effective planning needs awareness and wide knowledge of the varying programmes of the university and recognition of the philosophical elements and the practical aspects of university librarianship. The organization, in a university library, establishes precisely a relationship which facilitates management and the operation.

The staffing is concerned with the personnel in relation to their appointment, training and upkeep to help create a favourable working condition. To ensure proper and adequate service to the library, it is necessary to formulate a definite personnel policy. The personnel problems occupy a very significant place in the library and needs the constant attention of an able administrator.

Direction means taking decisions and incorporating them in the form of general or specific orders. The chief librarian, deputy librarian or other administrative staff of the library have to issue more frequently orders which define and determine the present as well as the future policies of service. The factors of coordination interrelate the various aspects of the work of organization. It may be concerned with one part or the unit of the organizational work or the organization as a whole. The element of coordination in the various works of library's operation is very important. Otherwise there is danger of the different technical and readers service operations drifting in the ways inconsistent with the objectives of the institution.

Reporting is a process through which the administrator keeps his superiors informed of the organizational development, progress and the performance as well as the future needs of the organization. It presents the factual state of the functioning through the actual records, research and the accumulated datas and depicts the real condition of the library. It also helps determine the efficiency of the organization.

Budgeting is an essential element of the organizational work. In an earlier chapter, we discussed this process. Successful administration needs careful planning, accounting and control. A well-designed budget helps him foresee the actual needs and requirements of the organization and make the economic provisions accordingly. Scientific management is an essential basis for proper budgeting.

Authority and Responsibilities

There are two sectors of authorities—(a) statutory and (b) personnel. The statutory authority is related to an established authority belonging to a given position. The personnel authority is the outcome of the possession of leadership. In certain cases, the head of the department delegates his authority of powers to pass orders and for the execution to his subordinate. The executive, getting such a delegation of powers, owns up responsibility for proper action. Once the power is delegated, the delegating authority no longer possesses that particular power, unless it is recalled in case of its misuse etc. However, even after his delegating the power, the authority does not absolve himself from the responsibility; he continues to share the responsibility still and is answerable to his chief for the performance of his subordinate. In this manner for all the accomplishments and performances by his subordinates, the chief librarian is responsible "for all that goes in a library, no matter by whom the actual work is done" say Wilson and Tauber (Wilson and Tauber: 1958: 118).

Unity of Management and Unity of Command

These are the two separate terms in the area of administration. Their objectives and aims should not be confused. The unity of management demands that for all the operations having same objectives in view, there should be one manager and one plan. It aims at the arrangement for providing proper organization. For example, in the technical section of the library there should be one manager of the executive and one plan of operation for the classification work. Similarly, in the cataloguing section, there should be one person incharge and one plan of cataloguing books. This system will ensure correct processing of the books as well as accelerate the speed and facilitate the readers.

The unity of command suggests that one person should be responsible to and receive orders from only one superior. This principle should not be violated. In case, it becomes necessary for a service-incharge of one section of the university library to order an official of the other section in a particular case, such an order be transmitted to that official through the chief of that division and not direct.

Discipline is a pre-requisite for successful operation. It should not be an imposed one but actually the staff itself should have respect for obedience. It should apply equally to those in the highest position as well to the lowest one. To enforce effective discipline, it is necessary to provide good leadership throughout the staff. The disputes between the staff should be settled fairly and amicably and those found guilty should be awarded punishment judiciously.

The administrative efficiency is also affected adversely if the individual interest is not subordinated to the common good. For example, the library staff posted at the issue counter or at the reference desk should not be permitted to join any other course or take up any other business during the period they are on duty. The salary-structure of the staff of the library should be comparable to that of the teaching staff. To promote the professional growth and increase efficiency, incentive should be provided in the form of rewards and enhanced pay to the deserving individuals.

The centralization of administration should be used with caution and depending upon the situation. For example, if the individual departments are permitted to make their purchase of books separately, independent of each other, such a decentralization will result in duplication of the purchase; including the bibliographical tools, records and other acquisition materials. On the other hand, the process of selecting books should be decentralized because the respective heads of the departments know their subject-field and the specialized production of literature better than the one individual librarian. As such, in certain areas of library administration, the restricted decentralization creates a healthy and helpful atmosphere for work and improves the functioning of the library. The hierarchy is also necessary to a certain extent. It is termed as 'Scalar Principle', as it involves the various steps in a series according to the degree of authority at each level. The chain of hierarchy extends in an unbroken line beginning from the top executive to the lowest point of the staff-level. The official communication travels through this line uninterrupted from the top to the bottom and vice-versa. In the administration of the university library, the top highest official is the university librarian.

The items of work in the library should be grouped together on the basis of nature of the work and the homogeneity. Similar types of works, classed in one group, should be placed under the charge of one sectional head or the administrative officer. This should be the basis for creating different departments in the library like classification section, cataloguing section, circulation section, documentation and reference sections etc.

The other factors which influence the formation and characteristics of the university library are (i) the nature of the reading material which creates book-division or the journal section; (ii) standards of the readers which create undergraduate and postgraduate sections; and (iii) the geographical factors which create departmental libraries for the different departments. The span of control is also an important element in the administrative set-up of the library. It refers to the number of persons with whom one sectional head should deal with. The specialization, knowledge of the particular technical work as well as the energy of an administrator is limited. Though, it will be impracticable to suggest a particular number of the staff who should be placed under the charge of one administrator as it would differ and vary with the situation, Wilson and Tauber mention that "the number recommended by various authorities ranges from not less than three to not more than ten to twelve" (*Ibid*: 120). These are certain factors which influence the situation. These are the nature and type of the work i.e. whether the work in question is a routine or complicated work. For instance, the work of cataloguing department in a library is homogeneous and of a routine type. All the persons engaged in this work can therefore be supervised by the chief of this section. The responsibility and burden of the chief may be shared by a few supervisors and assistant librarians in the department so that the chief has not to deal with the whole department directly.

Line and Staff

In the administrative organization of the library the line is synonymous with the authority and the command whereas the staff refers to the advice and the counsel. The staff officers are made responsible to the line officers and they possess no voice of their own except through the latter.

Order in the administrative set-up of the library means the arrangement which may be best for the most efficient operation. The different working sections of the library should be situated in a convenient state of relation with others to facilitate the operations. The related departments should be placed in close proximity of each other. For example, the sections of acquisition of books and the reading materials and the cataloguing should be placed nearer to each other to help facilitate work. Such an arrangement expedites the activities and conserves the materials used.

In addition, the order also suggests that a right person should be placed at the right job which is most suited to him. An expert in classification should not be put at the circulation counter and similarly, the cataloguer should not be asked to take up the reference desk. In a fewer case, the classifier and the cataloguer might be doing efficiently their changed jobs.

In the exercise of administration, equity is an essential element. There should be uniform treatment with every authority, be that the highest or the lowest one. The scales of pay and other service facility should be equal for the staff possessing equal qualification and responsibility. The preferential treatment given to particular employees mars incentive as well as efficiency of the other employees in the organization.

While an administrative climate should be created to respect the authority and the discipline of the organization, there should an element of incentive put into it to arouse as well as encourage it. It provides satisfaction to the staff. Attempts should also be made by the administration to foster harmony and unity in the library. These two elements strengthen the functioning of the library. Even the highest executive of the library should be available to the lowest ranked employee to help resolve disputes and doubts.

Administration of Library

We have discussed the philosophy and theory of administration. Now it has to be examined as to how far these theories have been applied actually in the operation of the library administration. For the last twenty years there has been rapid shift in the management of the academic libraries. Scientific management has come to play an important role in the development of the libraries. There have been discussions in the scientific management in all the spheres of the library, including the academic libraries. There have been talks on the standardization of the various activities of the libraries, management surveys and analysis of their different functioning. Interest has been aroused recently in the librarians to apply the theory and methods of scientific management in administering the libraries. Increased attention is now being paid to the subject of library administration and management. Leigh observes, "while librarians, like other professional groups, are not quick to accept the changes suggested by outside specialists, it is of great importance that the skills of management analysis and scientific personnel administration be assimilated within the general administration of libraries and professional training of librarians rather than occasionally presented as an intrusion of outsiders to measure work, to analyze and classify positions, or to establish salary grades" (Quoted in Wilson and Tauber: *Ibid*: 123). The implications carried by this observation are noticeable. In their new programmes and planning, the library schools now attempt to provide courses dealing with organization and operation of problems of different types of libraries. To elaborate the programme and promote the ideas of library administration, workshops and other institutional programmes are organized. Such short-term courses provide background knowledge to the librarians to deal with the administrative problems and accept the new challenges in the field.

A Difference

The university library, however, differs from other libraries in various respects and therefore the characteristics of its organizational pattern and the problems are also different. The factors like the historical growth of the library, its building, resources of finance as well as the staff together with their quality, the support of the authorities in the administration and kinds of clientele the library has to attend to, the variety of the subjects offered at the university are a few to quote which account for and influence the diversity of the library organization and the depth of the principles of the management of that library. For a successful organizational pattern to be achieved, the librarian should combine scholarship together with his skill of administration. Absence of any one of these qualities results in disorganization of the institution. A librarian having been installed on the post just by virtue of his professional skill and scholarship and with no administrative skill and experience may find it difficult to translate the theoretical principles to the practical problems which the situation warrants. The library should be operated by an individual who may be accountable for the administrative efficiency. This does not necessarily mean that efficiency is the sole criterion of a successful librarian. Coney observes, "it hardly seems necessary to add that management is only one of the aspects of librarianship, and that 'library work' and an appreciation of the uses of books are of even greater importance" (*Ibid*: 125).

The Staff of Administration

The success of appropriate library functioning depends, to a large extent, upon the nature of the staff. With the new courses coming up at the university and increase in the enrolment of the students, the character of the library's clientele as well as the services have changed. The library's working has, therefore, to be attended to the changed needs and requirements and the librarian has to adjust functioning accordingly. These discussions lead us to conclude that the administrative efficiency as well as its effectiveness depends upon the skill, knowledge, characteristics and the administrative acumen of the librarian and his administrative and principal staff who help him in the administrative functioning. It is, therefore, imperative that the librarian and his supporting administrative staff should be selected on the basis of their merit which implies higher academic pursuit, experience in the field of library administration, keenness in the organizational and administrative work of the library and the aptitude for its development and progress.

Nomenclature of the Administrative Staff

There have been different nomenclatures, designations and titles for the chief administrative officer of the university libraries at different places and there is no uniform pattern in this respect. In most of the libraries, the head is designated as chief librarian, university librarian and librarian etc. In the institutions where there are departmental libraries under one jurisdiction, he is called 'Director of Libraries'. The supporting administrative officers are called associate librarian, assistant librarian, head of the acquisition department or order librarian, head of the catalogue department; readers' service department; circulation department; periodical department; photographic department; bindery department and the head of the departmental libraries. There are many variations of titles in the librarianship, even involving the names of curators, custodians and superintendents. Titles like college librarian, map librarian, reserve book librarian and archivist are used to designate those who do some administrative function. The departmental libraries in different subjects are supervised by individual persons who are designated as geography librarian, physics librarian, law librarian and commerce librarian. Where several like departments are grouped together in one faculty like faculty of arts, science, humanity, social science or commerce, the librarian is called by the respective titles like social science librarian, humanity librarian and science librarian. There are endless possibilities in this regard. Sometimes designations are invented by combining two or more types of work together which a traditional librarian has to do—or, in true sense, look after. In a small traditional library, regrettably. The librarian is named drogativety as a clerk and asked to look after the collections of valuable books. He is designated in various forms as clerk-cum-librarian, accountant-cum-librarian or steno-cum-librarian or sometime even as an Upper Division Clerk-cum-Accountant-cum-Librarian. There are certain inherited designations found in the profession. There is a prime need for making all these designations uniform as standard nomenclature is the characteristics of a profession.

Duties of the Librarian or Director of Libraries

The duties assigned to the Librarian or the Director of Libraries differ from library to library in different institutions and organizations. However, looking at the duty-charts of different libraries, a pattern emerges for the Chief Executive of the library which is more or less like the following:

1. To formulate the policies, rules and regulations governing the functioning of the libraries and secure their optimum use by the students, faculty members and other members of the community.
2. To direct the activities of the university library committee and participate in its deliberations as a member (usually Secretary or the Chairman) of the committee.
3. To bear responsibility to the President of the library committee (who should usually be the Vice-Chancellor) for the effective administration and satisfactory functioning of the library.
4. To make necessary recommendations to the Vice-Chancellor on all matters pertaining to the status, promotion, change in position or dismissal of the members of the library staff.
5. To select proper and qualified technical and other kinds of staff of the library and make recommendations for their employment.

6. To guide and implement the process of selecting books and procuring other reading materials for the library to build up a useful book collection.
7. To prepare the annual budget plan of the library and get it executed.
8. To procure gifts and other such donations for the library from the benevolent donors and the library patrons.
9. To present the report of the library to the library committee, board of trustees or other such body.
10. To participate in the formation of the educational policies and take part in the activities of the various university bodies like academic council, senate and syndicate as their member.
11. To maintain relationship with the faculty members, deans of the faculties, administrative staff and leaders of the university union regarding the functioning of the library.
12. To extend professional advice and exercise administrative control over the staff of the faculty and departmental libraries of the university.
13. To represent the university library to its users, general public, the educational and library groups.

The success of the working and the functioning of the library depends on the active formulation and carrying forward the duties and responsibilities by the librarian. The librarian is assisted by his deputy librarian and assistant librarian in the discharge of his duties.

The duties of the Deputy Librarian or the Assistant Librarian are the following:

1. To assist and help the librarian or the director in matters of library administration and functioning.
2. To prepare the work schedules for the staff and supervise the task assigned to them. To have a close control over the progress of the different departments of the library.

3. To formulate the administrative and technical policies of the library and present them to the librarian.
4. To supervise the technical and service departments of the library and make a report to the librarian/director regarding the work done.
5. To help the librarian/director in preparation of the annual budget of the library for the routine items as well as the future development.
6. To assist and help the librarian in preparing an agenda for the staff meetings and prepare the report.
7. To help coordinate the instructional and research programmes of the university from the library point of view and bring to the notice of the faculties and the student members.
8. To act as a liaison officer between the staff members and the director/librarian.
9. To look after the upkeep of the library building and its organizational work.
10. To represent the librarian/director during such meetings in which he is deputed to do so.
11. To act as a principal administrative officer during the absence of the librarian/director.

The assistant librarians and the sectional heads should also be accessible to the staff members for consultation. All the general sectional and administrative officers, even if they are not actually trained in the librarianship, should have knowledge of the library's functioning—may not be with greater details. By their participation in their plans and programmes, they derive knowledge and function which make direct bearing on their working as well as on the institution. The duties of the sectional and departmental heads are similar to those of the assistant librarians, since they are derived out of the elements of and based on the fundamental principles of the administration like, planning and programming, budgeting and accounting and the staffing pattern etc. However, when their duties are actually applied to the specific departments or sections, they differ.

The duties of the sectional departmental heads are generally the following:

1. To lay out the different items of work of their sections and to assign duties to the respective staff for implementation.
2. To ensure the actual implementation of the work assigned to the staff.
3. To see that factual statistics and the records relating to different items of work is maintained in the section.
4. To coordinate the items of work in the library and to cooperate with the different sectional heads.
5. To make recommendations concerning the appointments, promotions, grades of pay and other personnel problems.
6. To prepare annual reports and other necessary memoranda for the deputy librarian (assistant/deputy director) and the librarian (director).
7. To evaluate the performance and working of the different staff of the section and make a report to the higher authorities.
8. To provide instructions, directions and advice to the individual staff working in the section in their work.
9. To elaborate, develop and improve the procedures and routines of the departments to meet the needs of the clientele more effectively.

Integrated Lines of Responsibility

The organizational system of the university library administration is an integrated one. It indicates the lines of the descending responsibilities through which the responsibility from the superior officer rolls down to other officers below him. For example, it shows, how the responsibilities descend from the library committee or the board to the librarian or the director and other administrative officers. It indicates the relationship between the librarian (director) on the one hand and the various other subordinate officers like the deputy librarian, assistant librarians and others.

Relation between Librarian and President

In the university library administrative set-up of developed countries, the university librarian is directly responsible to the President (Vice-Chancellor). But in certain universities and mostly in the underdeveloped countries, the librarian is made immediately responsible to the senior academic dean. In some cases, he may be made responsible to the Vice-President, Provost or the Pro-Vice-Chancellor.

The experience speaks that the most workable arrangement, from the viewpoint of the interest of the library, is the direct relationship of the librarian with the President or the Vice-Chancellor. There may be exceptions due to a particular condition prevailing in any specific institution, but in all cases it would be advisable to delegate the authority of the administrative control of the library to the librarian. This strengthens his authority to exercise better control.

Relation between Librarian and Deputy Librarian

The associate or deputy librarian is responsible to the librarian to translate his policies into action. The active operation of the policies, processes, and the services is the responsibility of the deputy. Being the second-in-command after the librarian in hierarchy, he makes supervision over the work of his subordinate staff and serves as a link between the departmental heads and the librarian. In certain developing libraries, an organizational pattern has emerged in which the areas of administrative control and responsibilities have been divided, between the librarian, deputy librarian and a few assistant librarians. Attempts have been made to design and develop, through experimentation, the effective plans of organization. Local factors like the physical condition of the library, the environment, general condition and the nature of the university library system as well as the personnel of the institution play an important role in the organizational set-up. Where there are two or more deputy or assistant librarians, the librarian is spared from dealing directly with the various service units.

Administrative Council

In certain university libraries, 'Administrative Council' or 'Library Council' has recently been set up. At California, this body is known as administrative conference. It consists of the librarian as chairman, and three others as assistant librarians. The meetings held by this conference are informal, which deal with the future plans, policies and problems which involve the whole or a large section of the library organization. It is a forum through which the general matters concerning all the departments can be discussed. It also serves as a means for keeping each of the administrative officer informed of the development of the work in other areas.

Departmental Heads

The departmental heads are given freedom to control and supervise the work of their specific areas. In general matters they seek advice or direction from the assistant librarian or the librarian. The departmental heads usually delegate specific operations to the subordinates to make the functioning easier. One of the simpler but effective ways of the administration in a large library is to select certain qualified individuals from different areas of the work and give them full control of those sections. This delegation of authority to the sectional heads, if chosen carefully on the basis of their professional expertise and competence, stimulates the working of the libraries in different areas and developes responsibilities.

Sometimes there is unwillingness on the part of the university librarian to allow the sectional heads to go ahead with their new ideas and devices in the field of operation and to experiment and adopt the innovations borrowed from other libraries in case they have been found useful in those libraries. Such an attitude on the part of the librarian is unhealthy for the working of the library. In fact, the librarian should appreciate and encourage such initiative and activity taken up by the subordinate staff. At the same time, the librarian should have stricter control over the staff and exercise effective supervision by looking into their work-schedule, asking them to submit their daily or weekly work-reports, insisting upon them the use of up-to-date equipments and routines. Studies of costs, use and return should be kept in constant view.

Assistant to the Librarian

In certain universities, some official is attached to the office of the librarian who is designated as 'assistant to the librarian', 'administrative assistant' or 'research officer'. Duties of this official depends on the nature of the particular library organization. It varies from library to library. In general, the duties involve problems concerning personnel, finance, building matters and other special projects. The assistant librarians and other sectional heads of the library should work in close co-operation with this official.

Organizational System

It is a wrong notion to believe that the organizational system has no bearing upon the quality of service. This view is not only not true, but, in fact, a better and improved kind of administration and the changes made towards that end steps up the efficiency considerably. Thus, the organizational pattern is an important factor. Its form should be simple. It should cover the whole staff including the staff raised for the new service or for any departmental library. The whole library setup should be covered under one system. Each person should fit into the system to avoid any personnel problem. The other influencing factor on the organizational pattern is the nature of the building. If the building is a poorly planned one, contrary to its being a functional one, a well-coordinated supervision becomes more difficult.

Complete or Partial Centralization

These are the two different systems of organization followed in the university libraries. There are certain libraries which are partially centralized in which the central or the main library and departmental libraries are placed under the control of the chief librarian but certain special collections and professional school libraries retain their autonomy. If the whole institution is under a single authority, complete centralization may be possible. It is important for the university librarian to be aware of the organizational patterns which may cause expensive or inadequate service to the clientele. In such cases, the librarians should be in a position to make necessary changes readily. The external administrative organization of the university library affects the internal organization.

Functional Arrangement

The functional type of arrangement makes provisions for the departments of acquisition, classification, cataloguing, circulation, (periodical or serial), reference and documentation etc. Other departments like those of business or finance; divisions of departmental libraries, professional school libraries; textbook and special reading-rooms and collection may also be set up.

Critical Analysis

One of the main disadvantages of this functional arrangement is the lack of close coordination between the related activities like the acquisition and cataloguing departments. The other point of criticism is that the area or the span of control is too wide to allow efficient administrative control. This is more true when the librarian works directly with the supervisory officers of the departments without having any joint link with the assistant librarian.

To counteract and mitigate the disadvantages of the common form of the functional arrangement a different system is adopted. Under this system, three officials viz. (i) the assistant librarian incharge of public service; (ii) assistant librarian incharge of finance; and (iii) the assistant librarian incharge of technical processes place their reports to the librarian; five officials dealing with (i) departmental, school and college libraries outside the main building; (ii) departmental libraries in the main building; (iii) special reading-rooms and collection; (iv) reference department; and (v) circulation report to the assistant librarian incharge of public service and four officials dealing with (i) order department; (ii) catalogue department; (iii) binding department; and (iv) photography section make their reports to the assistant librarian incharge of technical services. Although the officer incharge of special collections and school libraries possesses wide area of control but direct supervision is usually limited to the special reading-rooms and collections and the departmental libraries in the main building.

Rising Cost versus Administrative Advantage

The multiplication of the posts of the assistant librarians in the university library system no doubt carries economic responsibility and the cost of establishment increases. But as compared to the additional cost, the advantages are found to be more and apparently these outweigh the increased economic burden. Firstly, the unwieldy area of control of the librarian is reduced to a practical minimum with the result that he is able to pay his attention and give more time to other important work like planning, promoting the activities of faculty-library, improving student relationship, meeting the faculty members and engaging himself in the work of a scholarly nature. However, we must also mention that the assessment of the achievement of the divisional organizations is a difficult one; although it is increasingly accepted during the recent years. In fact, it needs close examination and assessment.

Classified Arrangement and Open Shelf System

In big libraries, the different service departments are set up in an organized form. Swank mentions, "the traditional organization by forms of material, such as periodicals and maps, and by types of service, as reference and reserves, is giving way to organization by subject divisions" (Swank : 1952 : 41-42). This practice is being followed in other libraries as well. Wilson and Tauber also state that the Johns Hopkins University Library and the University of Chicago Library used subject departments as a basis for organization even before it was applied in public libraries. In the last fifteen years or so such institutions as Brown University, the University of Colorado, the University of Oregon and the University of Nebraska, among others, have introduced subject divisions (Wilson: *op. cit*: 146). These divisions have been organized on open-shelf system, with adjacent stack and equipped with typewriter and conference rooms. In most of the universities the division has been as arts, social sciences, humanities and pure science This is generally for the use of postgraduate and research students. An undergraduate reading-room is also provided. The work of the circulation department is reduced.

Questions relating to reference are directed to the reference desk where specialist of the subjects help the questioners. With their specialization in one or the other subjects, together with the professional training, the reference librarians help the readers find out answers to their problems, and, thereby they support the class-room work. Swank observes, "the educational significance of the subject-divisional plan derives from the association of library services with specific departments of the instructional programme. The library divisions are given subject content and circular motivation. Their efforts are focussed on a definite clientele, with whose projects and problems the library staff can become familiar. The library's services are varied to satisfy the widely different needs of physical scientists, social scientists and humanists. Definite parts of the library belong to them, Library staff members specialize in their divisional subjects, identify themselves with the faculties of instructional departments and may in fact become active members of those faculties" (Swank: *op. cit*: 42). From the administrative viewpoint, the divisional plan arrangement is found to be more expensive to operate than the traditional functional organization. In fact, for a smaller university library, which is making endeavour to reduce or eliminate departmental libraries, the divisional plan may be more economical. The implications of the subject arrangement from the educational view point are inescapable.

Departmental Library System

It is erroneous to consider that university possesses one central library and that is all. In a university where teaching and research units are dispersed and located separately over a large geographical area, in the city or state, it is necessary to make provisions of library resources in each of such units. In such cases, complete centralization or consolidation of the library at one place will be impracticable. The educationists and the university librarians have debated and discussed for long the administrative and educational problems which emerge from having the book collection apart from the main library. The arrangements expressed by Miller are related to the factors of cost, adequacy, accessibility, efficiency, use of books, inter-relation of subject-fields and the educational significance. The arguments on efficiency and educational significance, however, can be made to serve the decentralist provided the institution has a budget which will afford service for both general and separate libraries and maintenance of a general collection of books for the correlation of the library needs of the collegiate departments (Miller : 1939 : 75-79).

Parry mentions that the terms 'centralized' and 'decentralized' refer to the collection of books and administering them in a university which may be housed either in a single repository or in a number of separate repositories. These collections may be administered either as a single unit or as a number of separate units (Parry: *op. cit*: 92-93).

Wilson and Tauber say that although recent reports indicate that there is a tendency towards centralization, there is still a strong belief, particularly on the part at the faculty members that separate faculties are important for educational programmes. In some cases such a movement has been influenced by the creation of new buildings. However, no uniform pattern has so far emerged regarding the setting up of the departmental libraries.

The departmental library, which is sometimes called a branch library, is a collection of books and other reading materials related to the particular school or college or a part of the university system. The organization of such a library varies in different institutions. In many universities, libraries for the departments like Philosophy, Geography, History, Hindi, Sanskrit etc. are set up separately. Similarly, the professional school libraries such as those meant for Journalism, Law, Medicine, Pharmacy, and Engineering are also separated from the central library administration. The factors to be considered in this regard are the line of responsibility of the departmental and professional school librarians, the amount or the income derived from the general budget of the library, centralization of acquisitional and technical services, procurement of books and other reading materials and appointment and control over the personnel.

The chief reason for creating a departmental library is a matter of convenience for members of the academic staff, for the students and the other users. They would like to have such a library close at hand involving only five to ten minutes' walk from their department. Secondly, such a library is small and therefore proves to be-easy and more convenient for the use as compared to the large and complex central library situated at a distant place.

However, there are disadvantages too with the setting up of the departmental libraries. Firstly, the faculty members and the staff of the department may not look to the collection beyond their departmental libraries which ultimately narrows their area of knowledge and learning and results into lack of both depth and breath. Bryan refers to the university library as "perhaps the last bastion of general education in an age of galloping specialization" (Bryan : 1966 : 120). Secondly, if the departmental library happens to be a small one, there is likelihood of its either having no librarian or the necessary qualified staff, the organization of the library will be poor without any guarantee of the conveniently available material stocked there for use. If the departmental library is fairly large, it might prove to be less economic in matters of staff than what it would have been just for the one central library. Neal mentions that at Liverpool, where every departmental library is controlled and staffed by the main library, the size of stock of each such library ranges from 20,000 to a mere, 2,000 : such a dispersal of staff raises problems of morale, supervision and communications (Neal: 1971: 12). Then, there are chances of the stock being overlapped or duplicated between the central and the departmental libraries. There are certain interrelated, like and near-common subjects. A library on applied science needs materials on the basic sciences too, and this leads to unnecessary duplication. Further, the building of the departmental library is found to be unusually inadequate and small with less number of staff made available. These factors limit the hours of functioning of the departmental library. It remains open only for a short period. In many cases, the rules, opening hours and other circumstances in which the individual departmental library functions also differ with the result that the readers using more than one library has to accustom themselves with the variety of rules.

Position in Great Britain

The three British universities viz., Oxford, Cambridge and London have decentralized their book collections. Here, quite a substantial portion of the book collections are both housed and administered in the libraries of colleges and other institutions. In Oxford, these collections are entirely separate from the Bodleian Library and London, it is separate from the uinversity library. In other British universities, the book collections are centralized in the sense that these are administered as a single unit by the university library but decentralized too in the sense of being housed in varying numbers of separate repositories. The characteristic of two-sided decentralization prevalent in Oxford, Cambridge and London has of course sprung from the circumstances in which these universities developed. Similarly in other British universities, the varying degree of decentralization in housing their collection of books have again been due to varying circumstances. Some of the factors responsible for such a situation are : shifting of a department or the faculty to a distant place from the university central library necessitating the transfer of books; the department receiving donations of books and periodicals to be housed in a particular department in terms of gifts; availability of a private gift of money for the purchase of books; assistance received from the University Grants Commission for a specific newly established department outside the campus of the university; availability of research grant for a departmental purchase, etc.

It may, however, be noticed that the decentralized system of libraries at Oxford and Cambridge is not prevalent in all the British universities generally. Parry mentions that in the great majority of British universities their collection of books are decentralized only in the sense of their being kept in separate repositories. Otherwise, they are administered as a single unit. The university librarian possesses overall responsibility for them all and their organization is governed by the policy adopted by the library committee of the university as a whole. "In other words, in most British universities, the relationship between the university library and the faculty or departmental library is more comparable with that prevailing in the United States than that existing in Germany" (Parry: *op. cit*: 98).

Kinds of Repository Libraries

(i) Sub-Library or Branch Library : It consists of a large collection of books to serve the members of faculty like engineering, law, medicine or a combination of more than one subject like biological science etc. This library is administered under the control of the university librarian and it functions under full-time staff members of the university library. This type of library is usually set up for the reasons of distance of the faculty or department from the central library.

(ii) Sectional Library : This kind of library usually consists of unique items, including the duplicates relating to a particular subject. These are housed in a department or faculty building. Usually the size of this library remains small and it is managed not by a full-time staff but looked after by some other members of the staff. Generally, it remains open to every member of the university. The books and periodicals of this library are normally processed in the university library and the stock is given entry in the catalogue of the university library.

(iii) Departmental Library : The stock of this library usually consists of the duplicate copies of books and journals in the central library of the university. The supervision over this library is exercised not by the library staff but by the staff of the departmental library. The university librarian maintains control over it. The processing of books of this library is done at the level of the central library whose catalogue carries entries for them.

In nature and content, the stock of this library is mostly the text-books, the multiple copies of which are kept reserved for the students' use and to ensure their availability for consultation by the students all the time, these books are generally not issued for home lending.

(iv) Class Library : It is a collection of students, text-books with a few reference books like dictionaries etc. added to it. The collection is commonly housed in a professor's room for the use and benefit of the students. Entries for these books are not made in the general catalogue of the university central library and the collection does not remain under the control of the university library.

(v) Institute Library : In the university, sometimes special institutes are set up to meet the needs and requirements of study and research in a particular area of study. For example, the library of the Institute of Education falls under this category. This library remains outside the administrative control of the university. Sometimes, such libraries are set up with special financial aids and grants sanctioned by the Government, the University Grants Commission or other such agencies, for setting up centres or institutes to promote specified studies and research. The Institute of Oriental and African Studies is an example of such an institute. In India, quite a good number of such institutes have been set up, viz., the Institute of Economic Growth, University of Delhi, New Delhi; the Institute of Economic and Social Change, Bangalore; the Indian Institute of Education, Pune and the A.N. Sinha Institute of Social Studies, Patna (Bihar). These libraries are staffed by such persons as are able to render specialist service on the subjects to the members of the Institute.

In British universities, sub-libraries are smaller in number considering the expansion of the universities. Their sizes vary from 1,000 to 1,50,000 volumes and coverage of subjects is smaller. They commonly relate to law and medicine followed by social sciences which include economics and business management and pure and applied science. Other subjects in these libraries are agriculture, veterinary science, music, art, education, geography and geology. These are manned by adequate staff and they remain open usually till late in the night.

The sectional libraries are mostly devoted to pure and applied sciences. Arts subjects rarely support such a separate library excepting in some larger universities like Glasgow. Edinburgh and Manchester. The most common subjects for these libraries are physics, chemistry and geology. Engineering and metallurgy are also popular. These libraries usually function between 9 a. m. and 5 p. m.

The departmental libraries are fairly high in number as compared to the previous two types of libraries. The sub-libraries and sectional libraries taken together may not be more than 10, the departmental libraries in the universities like Aberdeen, Manchester and Edinburgh are more than 60 each. They represent almost all the subjects of the faculties with emphasis on science, technology and medicine. The collection goes up to several thousand volumes, depending upon the library and they possess seating accommodation for about 300 readers. They remain open generally during the departmental hours.

The class-libraries are often termed as seminar libraries and they are set up in many universities. They usually remain outside the librarian's control but sometimes books for them are bought through the university library. Each department at the university is allocated a sum of £ 10 per annum for purchase of books for these libraries. The majority of the class-libraries provides benefit to arts students and they hardly possess any seating accommodation for the members.

The institute libraries are increasingly becoming common in the universities. Presently it is the largest in the University of London. The establishment of centres or institutes by the

University Grants Commission for Oriental, African and Slavonic Studies may become a pattern of development for the future.

The Oxford, Cambridge and London libraries offer library facilities on three levels, viz., the central library, college libraries and libraries in faculties, departments or institutes.

Position in the United States of America

Certain campuses of the American universities have independent libraries, The book-purchase is not always wholly centralized. Comprehensive union catalogue is not available everywhere. In most of the American universities the library collections are placed under a single administration. Students and the faculty members have the opportunity of making use of the entire book resources. During the past fifty years, there has been a tendency in the direction of a decrease in the number of independent book collections, improvement of union catalogues, centralization of acquisitions and appointment of professional library staff to man the libraries of the departments and the institutes of the universities (*Ibid* : 97).

Position in France

In the universities of France, institute libraries function side by side the university library. In 1945 their co-ordination was strengthened by the establishment of the Direction des Biblio-the ques de France within the Ministry of National Education. The Board exercises its jurisdiction over all the university libraries and all the libraries serving the faculties, and university colleges are treated, for all interests and purposes, the university library even if these are set up and dispersed among several cities.

Position in Austria

In Austria, before 1955 there was some measure of co-operation between the university library and the faculty libraries.

After the said date, law regarding the functioning of the institute of higher learning was laid down, which governed the libraries of the institute as well. Under this law, the university librarian has the responsibility for the acquisition policy, cataloguing and the services of all the libraries within the jurisdiction of his university.

Position in Spain and Portugal

In Spain and Portugal the administration of academic libraries is completely decentralized. Seminar, faculty and institute libraries function independently of the university library. In Portugal, only the University of Coimbra possesses a university library in addition to the faculties and institutes libraries.

Position in Italy

Similarly, in Italy the administration of academic libraries is completely decentralized. The resultant situation has been described by the librarian of the University of California at Los Angeles as presently "a great variety of jealously autonomous, uncoordinated and selfish, parochial institute libraries" (Parry: *op. cit:* 97). There seems to be little prospects of changing the situation at the moment.

Attempts have been made to appoint trained librarians to look after institute libraries, but the number is insufficient and surprisingly their duties are supervised not by the university librarian but by individual departments without reference to the central library.

Position in Soviet Union

Over the past few years the centralization of the library network in the large university of the Soviet Union has been increasingly high. But still, there are many universities where departmental libraries function independent of the main library. These libraries often duplicate their book collection and in certain cases, these departmental libraries do not look for any sort of guidance from the central library of the university. Such a decentralized system results in duplication of collection and consequential wasteful expenditure of resources. It also creates difficulties in organizing a union catalogue and hampers the bibliographical work and reader's service. The university opinion actively favours the centralization of the acquisition and processing, preparation of union catalogue for the university collection, developing a unified system of the library's role making it responsible to the university library.

Position in Germany

The library system prevalent in Germany especially the relationship of the main university library with other libraries has created a great impact in the European countries. The collection of books in the German universities are decentralized from both the view points—they are housed in a number of separate repositories and are also administered as separate units. Although there are certain variations, separate funds are allocated to the university library and to the institute or the departmental libraries. The ratio of share of the institute libraries to that of the university library ranges; from 1: 1 to 4 :1 to enable the institute libraries as a whole to receive four times as much as the university library. This has strengthened the collections of the institute libraries which have become not only more comprehensive in their subject-areas as compared to the collection of the university libraries, but "the institute libraries have often become the most outstanding in their subject in the whole of Germany" (*Ibid*: 94). The libraries of the institutes make appointments of their own staff, order their own books (without reference to the university library) and maintain their separate catalogue, independent of the university library. The students and teachers of the university are not expected to use the institute's catalogue. The books are not made available to them even on inter-library loan. "For these reasons there is often, to British eyes, a surprising lack of adequate seating accommodation, very little open access to books, and only very rarely a classification system, in the German university library. Its staff too is organized on a subject-specialized-basis since there is not the sort of liaison on book acquisition between university teachers and the staff of the university library which is normal in Britain" (*Ibid*: 94). The existing system has grave disadvantages. The excessive duplication of the titles results in waste and the resources remain uncoordinated. Wissen Schaftsrat has made the following proposals:

(i) Between the funds allotted for the purchase of books in the university library and the institute library, a reasonable relation should be established.

(ii) Between both kinds of libraries there should be co-operation in acquisition and cataloguing. For this purpose, the libraries within a single university should be considered as belonging to one entity.

(iii) To serve as a guide for book selection and more so for the convenience of readers, union catalogue of holdings of all the libraries within one university is necessary and be prepared.

(iv) The membership card for one departmental library should be valid for admission to all other libraries in the university.

(v) All technical processes for all the libraries within the university should be carried out centrally and, on an experimental basis, an office be set up in the existing university library.

It is expected that the above proposals which have already been accepted in many of the new German universities will have strong impact on the future development of German university library organization.

Position in Scandinavia

The dual system of library provision viz. university library and institute libraries normally prevalent in Germany has a strong and profound impact on the academic library service in Scandinavia. Almost all the older universities have department or institute libraries which are fairly large and are treated completely separate from the university library.

Position in India

The report of the Library Committee of the University Grants Commission (1965) deemed it necessary to consider the problem of separate libraries for the several departments. The Commission says there are varying practices. In certain universities the departments possess their own independent libraries and, in others, the departments are served by the university central library only. In some universities, the departments are given a small working collection on a permanent loan basis. Still, in the certain cases, such loans have to be renewed periodically, say, once in an academic year. Such practices were established at a time when the university libraries were not properly organized or even established. As such, the time has now come when this question be reconsidered by the universities and colleges; giving due weightage to the local problems as well as to the principles. Two moot points should be considered here: (a) library routine of an impersonal kind; and (b) factors concerning personal judgement and convenience of the members.

(a) The Impersonal Work : Under the category of items of impersonal work, the important point is the centralization of all impersonal work done in the libraries of the university or college. Such works are acquisition, classification, cataloguing, binding and maintenance of books of all the collections irrespective of the fact whether they pertain to the central library or the departmental libraries. If these jobs are decentralized and passed onto the department concerned separately, this will result into the increase of the total over-head charges of the library system as a whole. The modern trend in the librarianship is to centralize the work of classification and cataloguing for the linguistic region or even for the country as a whole.

Great Britain has already made a beginning in this direction. Denmark and Germany are also experimenting on it. Ranganathan's Heading and canors (1955) indicated a saving of 79 per cent of the cost in a library system on these two items alone centrally. The university libraries are, therefore, taking up seriously this fact of adopting the centralized classification and cataloguing system. In some countries like Norway, the centralization of even the purchase and binding of books for the public libraries in the country has been adopted and this system is working satisfactorily. The committee, therefore, recommended that every university and college should leave to all the impersonal items of work discussed above to the sole care of its central library.

(b) The Personal Work : *(i) Book Selection :* It is an item of work which should necessarily be decentralized because the particular department is always in a better position and is rather competent to scrutinize and finally decide the quality and priority of the books and journals they actually need. But at the same time, it is also necessary to co-ordinate at the level of the central library, the selection of the books for the departmental libraries so that unnecessary and duplicate titles may be avoided. This co-ordination is desirable at the different areas like the locality, region, state and finally the country as a whole. The agency to perform this task is the college or the university library.

(ii) Service to Students : The committee mentions that generally speaking service to students is best entrusted to the central library with regard to the reference work, loan and making the provision of studies within the library premises. This is certainly true for the undergraduate students, as experience

shows, that they feel less prohibited in the central library in using the books and other reading material than in a departmental library. The class-room restriction prevails in its department's library as well which mars their reading interest and habits. In case of postgraduate students, at present they generally expect all the books they need to be available in their departmental libraries. The reason being that the environment and atmosphere of the central library is not found to be quiet and peaceful, conducive for the serious reading by the postgraduate students and also that the central libraries remain mostly ill equipped and poor physically. But actually this should not be the position. In fact, the central library should be equipped better with all necessary facilities and present more conducive environment to attract readers.

Permanent Loan for Teachers and Research Scholars

The teachers and other scholars engaged in research work, however, need special service. Since they need the materials very often for the teaching or research work, they should be provided with this facility close at hand viz. within their department where oft-needed works should be kept separately for use. Some of these reading materials may have to be kept permanently in the department depending upon their frequent needs. Another point for consideration here is the number of such volumes to be fixed for the departmental library. The UGC Committee mentions that 2,000 may be a satisfactory figure. The committee further suggests that if these materials are also likely to be needed by students or by other departments, they should be duplicated for the departmental collection so that one set is available in the central library. The works needed and loaned to the department should be treated as permanent loan (UGC: 1965: 59). But when the loaned material of the departmental library becomes irrelevant because either of the completion of the research or the change of the subject-area, there is no use allowing them to remain there as it would be advisable to shift them to the central library for use by other readers. Such a provision will also result in saving of the space in the departments.

Short-Term Loan

Sometime, the exigencies of research work in departments need a liberal short-term loan, say about a hundred volumes at a time, from the central library. After the work is done, the collection is returned to the central library. It would be convenient for the users as well as the department and the central library if the period of such a loan is fixed for one academic year of the term.

Availability of Prescribed Text-Books

The teachers of the academic library need the text-book for the full term or the academic year. If there is only one copy of the text-book in the collection and that is issued to the teachers, the students have to suffer on that account. They are not able to make use of the said text-book. The college or the university should, therefore, provide wherever necessary the text-book to the teachers quite independently of the collection in the university central library. The UGC Committee recommends that "such a copy of text-book should be treated as on par with the material equipment furnished to a teacher" (UGC: 1965: 60).

Issuing of the Current Periodicals

This is a debatable point in the functioning of the college or the university library. Generally, a research scholar or reader of a particular issue of certain periodical assumes that issue is needed by him alone and none else. He, therefore, insists for getting it on loan for home reading. Since only one copy of each periodical is subscribed in the library, this practice deprives other readers of the use of the issue. The contention that the issue will not be of interest to other readers is wholly incorrect as even the specialized periodicals contain certain articles which are of equal interest to the specialists in different fields. This would lead to conflict of interests between the majority and the minority. This can be solved only with plenty of money by duplicating the issues, which no library can afford to have during the present age. "Even the richest university in the world does not have sufficient finance to take single copies of even a tenth of the world output of periodicals" (*Ibid*: 60).

The possible solution is to keep the current issues of periodicals for a week or two at least in the periodical reading-room of the central library so that they come to the notice of everybody and they may have an opportunity to glance through them. After a week or so, they may be released on a short-term loan. Photostat or microfilm copies of a particular article desired by the research scholar may be supplied. The issue of bound volumes of periodicals to a department may be allowed on the condition that the volume will have to be returned or allowed to be consulted within the department whenever a reader needs that. Duplication should be avoided as far as possible.

Advantages of Departmental Libraries

(i) The Parry Committee enquired of the Association of University Teachers as well as the individual teachers to know their attitude regarding decentralization of libraries in their respective universities. The committee approached some smaller libraries and some larger ones in sizes. In smaller libraries, the result was two to one (20: 10) in favour of maintaining departmental or faculty collections in addition to the main university or college library. In larger ones, they were nearly six to one (48:8) in favour. The distance of their departments from the central university library was the most often quoted reasons, besides a variety of some others.

(ii) The science teachers considered the departmental

libraries absolutely essential for quick consultation of the reference and research materials required by them, especially the abstracts and the research journals. Even they desired the highly specialized periodicals to be kept in their departments as they were of no use to general readers and non-specialists. Some of the teachers even viewed that the central library was an obstacle to research and teaching and the departmental libraries were the most important asset in stimulating study and research.

(iii) The science teachers also argued that the departmental libraries provide an opportunity for the undergraduate students to have a look at the larger collections and get encouraged for intensive reading.

(iv) Some teachers desired that their libraries should be close to the lecture-rooms. Further, if the keys to the libraries were with them, they could use it for informal borrowing any time they liked and had quick approach and consultation of the reading material.

(v) The Parry Committee further mentions that although there was a divergence of opinion about the use of departmental libraries, especially those belonging to science departments, most of the faculty members believed that such a library was necessary to stimulate intensive reading in the graduate students. However, the members mentioned, such a subsidiary collection should be carefully integrated with the main collections, which should be fairly comprehensive. It should possess essential works of reference and multiple copies of text-books which are prescribed reading for lecture courses. The staff of the main library should exercise control over them because the growth of departmental libraries can lead to unnecessary duplication. It sometimes leads to a situation in which neither the university nor the university finance department knows how much is spent on books by departments and that what books exist in these libraries. The collection of such libraries should be catalogued by the main library. Competent and skilled assistance should be provided to the readers of all subjects and faculties.

Disadvantage of Departmental Libraries

(i) On the other hand, certain faculty members and students complain that if the system of departmental libraries is maintained in university, the books and periodicals get dispersed geographically throughout the university. This causes inconvenience to them in consulting the collection.

(ii) The departmental libraries remain open for short hours and their timings do not suit to the members outside that department.

(iii) Generally the collection in the departmental library is so small that it does not provide full-time job to the person employed. The service here is not found as adequate as that of the central library. Therefore, its use is very limited and the maintenance uneconomical.

(iv) In the departmental libraries, books and periodicals are purchased in multiple copies for a small number of readers confined only to the respective department. If this collection is not catalogued and classified by the central library, its existence remain unknown to the library authorities and cannot be made known to the rest of the university community.

(v) Setting up of separate libraries, independent of the central library, proves more expensive to administer and it is comparatively a difficult task to protect the valuable books. There is further danger of waste by duplicating the books and the staff.

(vi) The grant for purchase of books for the central library is normally found unequal to the pressing demand. In such circumstances, purchase of books for creating a separate departmental library is just a wasteful expenditure. The Conclusion.

According to the Parry Committee, the university library being the heart of the university serves as the most important extra-departmental means of educating students. It should make available books and periodicals on a wide variety of subjects and render service on open-shelf system to all students. The collection and service should be such as to make them experience the added stimulus of publications relating to disciplines other than that of their own curricula. It is not in the interest of readers to confine to a small collection, rather they should have larger view of the subjects.

At the same time, the committee also expresses its awareness of the necessity for conserving the time and energies of both staff and students. It says, "the departmental libraries are an effective method of meeting that need has been sufficiently proved by the long experience of university generally. The committee is, therefore, in agreement with the view put forward for the maintenance or establishment of libraries in departments and regards such libraries as recognized features of the academic library system" (Parry: 1968: 103). The committee has also mentioned that, in the past, the prime factor in preventing the creation of book resources at more than one place had been the lack of funds. The committee recommends that no library should be set up outside the central library unless there are sufficient funds to support it—both the initial purchase of the stock and its continued maintenance. A large and important department situated at a considerable distance from the central library will require a library containing basic reference works, current periodicals and monographs for the use of postgraduate students and staff members. All such libraries should function under one library authority and one union catalogue should be compiled for the holding of all of them.

References

1. Bryan, H.A., 1966, A critical survey of university libraries and librarianship in Great Britain. Library Board of South Australia.
2. Miller, Robert A. 1939, Centralization versus decentralization, ALA Bulletin, V. 33, pp, 75-79.
3. Neal, KW, 1971, British university libraries, published by author at 7 Church Road, Cheshire.
4. Parry, Thomas (Chairman) 1967, Report of the committee on libraries, University Grants Committee, Her Majesty's Stationery Office, London.
5. Swank, Raynard C, 1952, The educational function of the university library Library Trends. V. 1, 1952, pp. 37-38.
6. University Grants Commission, New Delhi, 1965, University and college libraries, containing the report of the library committee of the University Grants Commission and proceedings of the seminar from publisher to reader held on March 4-7,1959.

7
LIBRARY STAFF

Service of a library depends largely on the kind of staff at work. It is second only to finance, as an essential pre-requisite for a good library.

Today, librarianship is a highly complex profession warranting specialised and technical knowledge of various sorts like personnel administration, financial management and different bibliographical and bibliothecal techniques. The personnel responsible to render library services are expected to know both the objectives of this institution as well as the potentialities to achieve them. This can be possible through harnessing properly the library tools and means in an adept and skillful manner. The situation suggests that even an illustrious writer or scholar of a very high repute cannot be successful to direct the functioning of a library unless he has acquired the professional skill in librarianship. As such, under the modern personnel management in the library greater emphasis is laid on appointment of trained staff.

Nature and Size of Staff

During the recent past, the nature and size of the staff in a university library have undergone considerable change. The increased collection of books and other reading materials, the phenomenal increase in the number of students' enrolment and the faculty members, change in the nature and content of the library services are some factors responsible for the present change in the style and functioning of the staff in the library.

The present conditions of professional service in the university library necessarily demand that the staff should be precisely trained, equipped with technical skill for the job. Unfortunately, there is an acute shortage of trained staff in the university libraries especially in the developing countries and also in some of the developed countries. It is, therefore, a problem to be solved not only by the profession of librarians alone but also by the Government. It is both the authorities of the university as well as the Government individually and jointly which can help set up standards and norms and create conditions to encourage the highly qualified graduates to enter the library profession and adopt it as a career successfully.

University Librarian

Selection of a qualified university librarian is a matter of prime importance in the staffing pattern of a university. To a considerable extent, the selection of university librarian in the whole academic milieu of the university is even of greater importance than that of a university professor of one single department, as the former plays a more effective role in creating a healthy and scholarly environment on the campus conducive to the study and research. The university should, therefore, fully ensure the capability of the incumbent's role, performance and eminence to contribute to the library services; a complex problem these days. Danton says, "expediency and a desire to acquire or enhance prestige may suggest the selection of a distinguished scholar or an outstanding scientist, but such a selection cannot be too strongly condemned when the individual concerned is without familiarity with modern librarianship and is not in any sense a librarian" (In Gelfand: 1962:50). Further, even a small university library needs a highly competent librarian. It is wrong to think that a small library can be managed by anybody since its problems are not complex. Initially, a university may be small in size but it is bound to grow and develop when different faculties for study and research are added. This should be clearly borne in mind from the very beginning.

Formal Training

Formal training for a university librarian is necessary. It is wrong to argue that because some librarians, even without formal training, have been successful in organizing libraries and building them up, so formal training of librarianship for persons incharge of university libraries could be done away with. It is true, in some cases that "formal training in the most literary sense may not have been required by some individuals, who, after a long apprenticeship in learned libraries and many years of close identification with library administration have reached the point where their accumulated experience and contributions to librarianship have established them in positions of authority and respect" (*Ibid*). It is also true that some of the great librarians of olden days were scholars without formal training in librarianship. They achieved distinction, however, because they studied the problems of librarianship and contributed to library literature and thought that in that way they might thereby promote and enrich scholarship generally (*Ibid*). Such instance are only exception than general rules. The effective as well as complex administration of university library today demands steady application of training and the experience to the various academic and technical problems. The librarian has to face many complicated problems, and it is incumbent upon the university authority to make proper selection of the university librarian. He should possess, says Wilson and Tauber, "a through knowledge not only to methods and purposes but also of the subject matter of instruction and research and of the techniques of librarianship, broadly conceived" (Wilson and Tauber: 1958:262).

In designing the training programme for the university librarian, the following three important factors should be taken into consideration : (i) the nature, kind and extent of the demands which the university administration is likely to make upon the university library and his staff; (ii) the complexity and nature of the job involved in the position of the university librarianship which he has to face and (iii) equipping the librarian adequately and appropriately to discharge his duty and responsibility effectively in the library, in relation to the faculty members, students as well as the administrative authorities.

There is a fairly well-defined and established pattern of training for the university librarianship in Europe and North America and the training pattern is making its impact on the university library scene in the developing countries as well. The training embraces three levels viz (i) Undergraduate professional course leading to the award of a Bachelor's degree: (ii) Postgraduate professional source leading to a Master's degree in library science and (iii) Advanced professional course leading to the award of a Doctrate degree. The key staff in the university library are the graduates. The non-graduates are employed as semi-professionals.

The Academic Requirements

The qualifications for the job of a university librarian should be equal to the task. His training should obviously be extensive and specialized. He should at least be a postgraduate, with a doctorate (Ph.D.) degree as a desirable qualification. The librarian has to perform both administrative and technical responsibilities. He is required to frame and outline the overall policy; prepare and pilot the library budget at different levels and see that it goes through the various bodies of the university and participate in various non-library activities pertaining to university matters as do the other professors of the departments. Above all, he should aptly engage himself in personal contact with the departments of the university, the important faculty members and the decision-making authorities of the university.

It is necessary to develop definite understanding between the functioning of the faculties and the library and thereby maintain a strong liaison between the two. Parry mentions that as long ago as in 1921 the UGC said, "we are of the opinion that the Librarian should be an officer of professional status and emolument and an *ex-officio* member of the Senate, with the right of attending meetings of all faculties" (Parry: 1967:142). Parry has further mentioned that the above was reiterated in the report published in 1925. The first half of this recommendation has generally been implemented but the second half, attendance at faculty meetings, has been acted upon only in a very few universities. The Parry Committee has still reiterated its opinion in favour of the above provision. In India, except in the certain special libraries, the librarians have not been made members of the university bodies. In the British libraries, some university librarians are also the active members of professional bodies, such as the Library Association and SCONUL (Standing Conference of National and University Libraries). By whatever means it may be possible, the librarian should essentially be kept fully informed of the plans for the development of new fields for teaching and research, the establishment of new research projects and, above all, the programmes and proposals of new buildings affecting the library policy. To this end, the librarians should be present at or be represented at all the university meetings where such matters are discussed, especially the meetings of the university budget where allocations for the different items are finalized and approved. The Parry Committee also states, "we further believe that senior library staff should be generally eligible for election or to serve on university committees including Senate on the same terms as teaching staff" (*Ibid* : 143). To co-ordinate the various services and improve the functioning of the university library, it is imperative that the librarian is vested with authority and powers equal to his position.

Professional Training

Unlike the other established professions such as medicine, law, engineering etc, librarianship till very recently did not prescribe or even require pre-professional training. Only recently, the library educators turned their attention to this aspect. The pre-professional training should consist of a broad general education. Through connecting well-designed courses in physical and biological sciences and in humanities and social sciences, the prospective trainee of librarianship should be introduced to various subjects within these broad subject-areas. During the first two years of college education, the students should acquaint themselves with the subjects and prepare themselves for specialization in the next two years. Such a course can prove to be of added advantage if it includes courses in ancient and modern languages, the principles of economics and statistics, elements of education-administration and university practices and their objectives. Courses in the use of the reference materials may enhance the value even more. Many of the most able librarians have first attracted towards this profession through part-time assistantship in the actual library services while being students. This provided them with the opportunity of a good grounding for the profession.

Wilson and Tauber have stated that the major objectives of the first year of professional training of the prospective university librarian should be the following: (i) to provide a broad overview of librarianship; (ii) to train in the principles and theories of major subjects in the librarianship and the library literature; (iii) to provide thorough knowledge of methods and techniques of library services and (iv) to acquaint and make fully conversant with the role of the university library, which strives to attain the university's objectives (Wilson and Tauber: 1952: 262). Gelfand, MA, describes that the general objectives for the training should be to acquaint the trainees with "universe of knowledge in allies forms; the historical as well as contemporary role of libraries as agencies for the selection, acquisition and organization of knowledge for effective use; the principles and practices of librarianship and their applications and the philosophy of librarianship in both its historical and contemporary aspects" (Gelfand: *op. cit:* 54). It follows that the candidate for the librarianship should be an educated person who should be fully acquainted with the history and culture of his country and region, should know the national language and literature, major languages of the country as well as one modern language other than his own. In a bilingual and multilingual country like India, the librarian's second language should be one that is most commonly used in the teaching, Government and diplomacy. His extensive knowledge of the modern language will help perform his professional task more appropriately and effectively. The academic librarianship needs a strong subject background as its base is laid on broad educational attainments.

The Library School Curricula

Period of Training

The length of the period of library science training varies from country to country. But the minimum period of training for this professional course consists of at least one full academic year in almost all the countries. In the USA, till the 1940's the library schools offered the Bachelor's degree courses. Now they provide Master's degree courses. The duration mostly covers a period beyond the two-semester or three-quarter programme. Some of the schools have scheduled orientation programmes prior to the beginning of the professional courses. Certain schools in the USA present doctoral degree programmes as well beyond the Master's degree. This programme is mainly for those who are interested in teaching and research and in the problems and subjects of a broadly historical and theoretical nature. The subject-areas contemplated for the Degree of Philosophy or the Degree of Library Science are: bibliography, history of libraries, history of books and printing, library as a social institution, public, college and university libraries, foundation of librarianship, communication research, library resources, organization of materials and library administration. (Wilson and Tauber: *op cit.* 266).

In England, the British Library Association controls the training of librarians to a large extent. It is much more than what is done by the American Library Association. In Britain, professional recognition can also be obtained through the attainment of the designation FLA (Fellow of Library Association). Certain universities also offer postgraduate courses in librarianship. India and the United Arab Republic provide Master's and Ph.D. courses. France, Yugoslavia, Taiwan, Nigeria, Poland and the Netherlands have also instituted postgraduate and advance level programmes. It has been observed that the training courses available in Britain, France and Germany provide the framework into which may be fitted, with variations, the programmes of practically all other countries where library training courses have been instituted. Interest in developing the training courses has been shown in the recent past in Switzerland, Belgium and Norway. Spain and Italy present the impact of the training programmes of France and the Latin American countries which bear the influence of American courses. This is also true in case of Japan. For the training of librarians in Russia, Moscow Institute of Library Economy is the chief base.

In countries where proper programme of librarianship was not available till the last world war, new courses of studies have been set up and those countries are now less-dependent on the overseas schools. These new schools have designed their programmes to suit the special needs and requirements of their countries and the region. Some of the countries where libraries have not developed and library schools have yet not been set up, send their candidates for training to overseas library schools. To them training under the close guidance of some able librarians in a well-stocked and properly organized library are imparted. Their practical experience gained at work stand them in good stead. In the selection of the candidate for foreign training, high academic standard and thorough know-edge of the language of the country in which the candidates are to be trained should be insisted upon. Poor or lack of knowledge of the language of the country often proves a great deterrent in successful training. Further, he should be strongly motivated towards the profession of librarianship. His professional activities are similar to those of other learned professionals who try to transmit and apply their knowledge for the furtherance and advancement of the knowledge in their profession.

India

The training of library personnel in India is based on the guidelines adopted by the University Grants Commission and the facilities provided to the universities to maintain the departments of library science. The report of the committee on university and college libraries appointed by the UGC stated that the universities should own up the responsibility of producing the required number of professionals. The development of library schools should be co-extensive with the needs of the professional librarians required to man the libraries.

The committee stressed the need of library personnel at different levels of attainments. At the top of the professional level in the institutions there is need for a few librarians with leadership and on the other extreme, semi-professionals are needed to do the routine jobs in the library. And, between those two extremes, there is need for the professional to attend to technical jobs and render reference service etc. to the readers in the library.

The training for the professionals should be at the university level. A graduate degree should be the pre-requisite qualification for admission to this course and the course of librarianship should be a postgraduate one. This can be possible only if the course is conducted by the university. The committee mentions that the analogy for such a course can be found in the courses conducted by the universities to train persons for the teaching professions. As in the case of education, there should be two degrees in library science also, which may be termed as Bachelor of Library Science (B. Lib. Sc.) and Master of Library Science (M. Lib. Sc.).

Further, there is need for research courses also in library science for creating a new philosophy and thought, forging and developing new techniques of service in the fields of classification, cataloguing and documentation work and analysing the various problems of readers to find out practical answers to them. It is, therefore, necessary that some of the departments of library science are brought to a higher level of educational attainment and are strengthened and equipped to take up operational research to meet the emerging needs of new library techniques and practices.

The UGC committee on university and college libraries (1965) mentions that the implication of the term 'professional' is the need for putting the candidates through an apprentice course before their undergoing formal training for the library science course. Without undertaking such an apprenticeship, the raw graduates would find it difficult during the library science course. The committee, therefore, recommends that the student should have "a preview of the daily routine and the know-how in a library." The idea is 'to filter out the persons who are not keen to enter the library profession'. (UGC : 1965 :78). Another implication of the term professional is that the librarians should be trained according to the requirements for the posts in the country, to avoid unemployment of the trained personnel. The supply should be comparable to the demand.

Department of Library Science

The UGC committee recommends that the department of library science set up at the university should not conduct the certificate course in library science organized for the non-graduates. This course being of a lower standard, should be left to the departments of libraries and the library association of each State. The department of library science of the university should only conduct the graduate degree course (B. Lib. Sc.). The better organized departments, whom the committee terms as first grade departments should conduct a course leading to the Master's Degree in library science (M. Lib. Sc.). The Diploma course (one year) in library science conducted by the university should be treated at par with the B. Lib. Sc. and gradually this Diploma course should be converted into the degree course of library science (B. Lib. Sc.).

The first grade departments of library science at the universities should have a minimum full-time staff of one professor, one reader, two lecturers and two demonstrators in library science. The second grade departments should have a full-time staff of one reader, one lecturer and one demonstrator in the subject. The ratio of full-time teachers (other than demonstrators) to students should not exceed 1 to 10 in the graduate degree course and 1 to 5 in the master degree course. The first grade departments should endeavour to conduct research in library science and train students for a doctorate in the subject. The B. Lib. Sc. course should be a postgraduate one and the M. Lib. Sc. course a post B. Lib. Sc. course. During the transitory period, the graduates with university diploma in library science should also be admitted to the B. Lib. Sc. course.

Attention has been drawn towards contributions of librarianship by the non-professionals i.e. by persons having no formal training in the librarianship. Several instances may be quoted in this connection. But the fact is that such contributions were made long before the days of systematic training. In the past, administration of major university libraries was much simpler than what it is at present. In future, it is likely to be all the more complicated. Wilson and Tauber mention, "recent surveys of university libraries have indicated that fundamental and costly errors were due to the lack of professional knowledge by non-professional scholars and library committees that have not been aware of significant changes in library administration and professional practice." They further state that "administrative boards and officers who are aware of the manifold complexities of university library operation will not make the mistake that some of their colleagues have made in the past in appointing non-professionals". In some cases, the result has been almost disastrous (Wilson and Tauber: *op. cit*: 272). In India, the views expressed recently by the UGC in the matter is that the office of librarianship of the academic and public libraries (including National Library) can be managed by any scholar of repute, even though he is not formally trained in librarianship. This erroneous view is being contradicted and fought by the library profession of the country from its various platforms.

However, Wilson and Tauber state that the above observations do not mean to close the door altogether to enter into university librarianships for the persons who may be able, eminent and scholarly in other fields. They say, "a scholarly director chosen from the faculty or an able administrator recruited from other fields may sometimes administer a complex, scholarly library with considerable skill" (*Ibid*: 273). They also observe that the probability of success depends on certain conditions. Young men who could adopt easily to the changed situations should be recruited. The person should be willing to use his intelligence, scholarship, tact and energy to tackle the major problems of librarianship rather than the narrow aspects of his former specialization. He should bring his entire ability to bear upon his work as a librarian.

Size of Staff

Provision of adequate staff is necessary for the proper and effective functioning of the library. Factors like number of students, size of the faculties, design and size of the university or college library building, size of the library collection as well as nature of the reading material and number of volumes added annually, nature and kind of the service rendered by the library and the kinds of students served, the number of hours for which the library functions, teaching methods of the faculties, the research programmes, and the number of faculty, departmental and institute libraries operating under the main library are there to condition and determine the numerical strength of the staff in the library. It is, therefore, necessary to prescribe guidelines for the staff composition in a library.

The library profession, Government and university authorities have endeavoured to establish some reliable and valid staff formula to calculate the strength of the library. This is based on classification of the professional and non-professional positions and determination of the number and grade of positions required in relation to the size and nature of the readers to be served. In United States the staff is divided under two classes viz. (a) Professional and (b) Non-professional. Against this, in Britain, the college and university libraries are classed into three categories viz. (i) Superior and professional staff; (ii) Middle or semi-professional staff and (iii) Lower or non-professional staff. The Ministry of Higher Education of the Soviet Union specified the professional staff in library of higher educational institution into the following four categories: Chief Librarian, Division Chief, Senior Librarian and Librarian. The strength of the staff in each category should be in relation to the size of enrolment. The Model Table of Organization of the Ministry provides for one chief librarian, two senior librarians and five librarians for an institution having an enrolment of 1,001 to 1,500 students. When the enrolment becomes higher and reaches 1,501 to 2,000 students, one division chief, one senior librarian and two librarians are provided additionally. The table does not provide for the technical, clerical, custodial and the non-professional staff but such provisions probably exist (Gelfand: *op. cit*: 52). In India, the library staff is divided between senior professionals, junior professionals and semi-professionals.

The American Library Association (ALA) brought out a comprehensive set of classification and pay plans for the guidance of libraries in higher institutions of education. The plan meant to set the minimum standards for the small and median sized institutions. The second edition (1947) of the plan gives the following standards for calculating the service-load :

(i) Each under-class (undergraduate) student other than honours student is counted as 1 unit.

(ii) Each upper-class (postgraduate) student other than honours students is counted as 2 units.

(iii) Each honours student is counted as 3 units.

(iv) Each graduate student is counted as 4 units.

(v) Each faculty member is counted as 5 units.

Elaborating the application of these standards, Gelfand shows that supposing a university has an undergraduate enrolment of 500 in the first two years of its curriculum, 300 in the upper two years, 50 honour students, 50 postgraduate degree students and 40 faculty members, its library will have a total service load 1,650 units for its total readership comprising 940 persons. According to the above standards of the plan, such a library will require staff comprising of 6 professionals including the university librarian and 2 to 4 persons in the clerical cadre, 40 to 60 per cent of the total staff hours shall be in the non-professional service (*Ibid*: 53).

In the personnel administration of the library, ALA plans are helpful in describing and classifying the positions, but the plan is criticized on the ground that the assessment of service load alone should not be the basis for determining the size and need of the staff. It is also argued that the plan suffers from lack of inadequate provision in respect of non-professional and clerical staff. Highlighting the criticism, the ALA college library standards (1959) indicate that while the size of the library is an important factor, there are many other factors which should also be considered, and that with increase of the size of the library, the ratio of the non-professional to the professional staff should be larger (Quoted in *Ibid*: 53). AL McNeal prescribes a ratio of two non-professionals to one librarian—one professional staff member should be able to supervise or direct two non-professionals. Gelfand says that evidence is accumulating to confirm McNeal's view-point and that the fact is that there is a trend of even higher proportion of non-professionals to professionals in big libraries (*Ibid*).

In the underdeveloped countries, there is acute shortage of trained and qualified librarians and over-supply of non-professionals like clerks, typists, stenographers, book-keepers, book-binders, photographers, printers, messengers, book-attendants etc. In such a situation, it is impracticable to emphasize upon the workable ratio between professionals and non-professionals. Since it is difficult to get adequate number of trained personnel needed according to the prescribed standards, the library has to be organized with the help of the supporting staff (non-professionals). Under such a condition, the result can be achieved with proper supervision exercised over the non-professional staff. This arrangement proves to be economical also.

Staff Position in India

Looking back to the history of librarianship in the country, we observe that till recently our university libraries were small, both in content and functioning. The reason was that the teaching faculties of the universities themselves were limited and small. Therefore, the amount of work in the library was limited. The annual accession of books hardly exceeded two thousand volumes and the periodicals about five hundred. There were very few complete volumes of the periodicals. The number of books borrowed by the readers was small. Daily visitors in the library were only a few. There was no system of providing reference service to the members. The libraries remained open for a very limited number of hours daily and

Sundays and most of the holidays during the year were off-days. As such, the staff was not a big problem then.

Even after independence, the above situation continued for sometime. The administration of the newly created universities was in the hands of the teachers of the previously affiliated colleges whose conception of the college or university library was not broad and wide. They viewed that one clerk and a few cleaners were enough to manage the library. The designations like chief librarian, deputy librarian, assistant librarian, reference librarian, classifier, cataloguer, circulation librarian and maintenance librarian were not known here.

Gradually, with the development of the colleges and universities and the momentum of the academic pursuit gaining at the campuses, it was realized that the library is actually the heart of the academic institution. It should be kept open for longer hours daily for use by students and teachers. The stock of the library should be properly classified and catalogued in accordance with modern and scientific techniques. Its function should not be confined only to the issue of books but it should also personally help the students and teachers in selecting right material for their study and research by rendering reference service. Further, it should provide documentation service to disseminate specialized knowledge. The climate of the library should be such as not only a few but students in hundreds and teachers in dozens visit every day to make use of the reading material. It should have a big budget to purchase good number of books every week and make payment for them. Attending to all these items of work would need a good number of staff—this fact was lately realized. It was further conceived that the staff should not be provided in any arbitrary manner. It should be estimated on the actual quantum of work done in the library every day. This leads to the formulation of the staff formula for the academic libraries to ensure a uniform pattern.

Dr. S.R. Ranganathan has suggested that the estimate of staff should be based on the following criteria:

1. Annual budget of the library
2. Number of hours the library is kept open per day
3. Number of working days in a year
4. Number of gate-hours for a year
5. Number of reading-seats in the library
6. Number of readers in the library per day
7. Number of volumes added in the library during one year
8. Number of current periodicals subscribed
9. Number of entries prepared during the year for documentation work
10. Number of books added in the technical section
11. Number of readers attending the reference section
12. Number of issued from the circulation section and the new books added to the section.

Staff Formula

Dr. S.R. Ranganathan has formulated the staff pattern for the College and University libraries in India. He has reduced the pattern in the form of Staff Formula and has explained in following mathematical terms. (Ranganathan: 1959: 28-29).

Suppose,

A = Number of Volumes Accessioned in a year in the library.

B = Annual Budget allotment in Rupees.

D = Number of periodicals Documented (i.e. abstracted) and indented in a year.

G = Number of Gate-Hours in a year.

(One Gate = hour = one counter gate kept open for one hour).

H = Number of Hours the library is kept open in a day.

P = Number of Periodicals currently taken.

R = Number of Readers per day.

S = Number of Seats for readers.

V = Number of Volumes in the library.

W = Number of Working days in a year.

SB = Number of persons in Book Section.

SC = Number of persons in Circulation Section.

SL = Number of persons as Librarian and his Deputies.

SM = Number of persons in Maintenance Section.

SP = N umber of Persons in Periodical Section.

SR = Number of persons in Reference Section.

ST = Number of persons in Technical (Classification and Cataloguing) Section.

(a) Formula for the staff of different in the library.

$$SB = \frac{A}{6000} = \frac{\text{Number of Volumes Accesssioned in a year}}{6000}$$

$$SC = \frac{G}{1500} = \frac{\text{Number of Gates = Hours in a year}}{1500}$$

$$SL = \frac{HW}{1500} = \frac{\text{Number of hours library is kept open in a day} \times \text{Number of working days in a year}}{1500}$$

$$SM = \frac{A}{3000} = \frac{\text{Number of Volumes Accessioned during the year}}{3000}$$

$$SP = \frac{p}{500} = \frac{\text{Number of periodicals currently taken}}{500}$$

$$SR = \frac{(R)}{50} \times \frac{W}{250} = \frac{\left(\text{Number of readers perday}\right)}{500} \times \frac{\left(\text{Number of Working days in a year}\right)}{250}$$

$$ST = \frac{A + 40D}{2000}$$

$$= \frac{\text{Number of Volumes Accessioned in a year} + 40 \times \text{No. of periodicals abstracted and indexed in a year}}{2000}$$

(b) Formula for the total professional staff

SB + SC + SL + SM + SP + SR + ST

= {[3(A + 20D) + 2 (G + 3P)] + [2W(H + 6R/50)]}/ 3000

(c) Formula for the non-professional skilled Staff

B/30,000 + [SL /100]

(d) Formula for the unskilled staff

SB/4 + SC/2 + SL + SM/4 + SP/2 + SR/8 + A/20,000 + D/500 + B/60,000 + (S/100)/4 +V/30,000 = {[27A + 2 (B + 120D) + 40 (G + 3P) + 30,000 [S/100] + 4V + 2W (40H) + 3[R/50]}/1,20,000

The UGC Committee (India) recommends that the strength of the staff for the different sections in the library should be determined on the following basis (UGC: 1965 : 72) :

(a) *Book Section* : One person for every 6,000 volumes added in a year.

(b) *Periodical Section* : One person for every 500 current periodicals subscribed.

(c) *Technical Section* : One person for every 2,000 volumes added in a year.

(d) *Circulation Section* : One person for every 1,500 hours for which one wicket gate of the library has to be kept open in a year.

(e) *Reference Section* : One person for every 50 readers (other than the users of text-book collection) in a day.

(f) *Documentation Section* : One person for every 1,000 entries prepared in a year.

(g) *Maintenance Section* : One person for every 6,000 volumes added in a year, one person for every 500 volumes to be replaced in a day and one person for every 100,000 volumes in the library.

(h) *Administrative Section* : Minimum of one library accountant, one stenotypist and one correspondence clerk.

(i) *Supervisory Section* : One chief librarian and one deputy or assistant librarian.

(j) *Unskilled Staff* : One cleaner for every 30,000 volumes in the library, one attendant each for every 6,000 volumes added in a year, for every 500 current periodicals taken and for each of the shifts in the circulation section, besides unskilled and the semiskilled workers normal to any institution.

Leave Substitute

University libraries unlike ordinary offices should be kept open all the days of the year to render service. The committee observes that as a hotel cannot function even for an hour without servers, the train cannot run even for an hour without a driver, guard and other staff, similarly the library cannot function even for an hour without staff in the supervisory section, reference section and circulation section. But the staff put on the job normally works for about 250 days in the year. On remaining days, he enjoys his weekly holidays, notified holidays, casual leave and earned leave. Therefore, it is necessary to make provisions of staff for deployment of staff for the remaining days in the library. This should be done by making provisions for leave substitutes. In other sections, it would suffice if provisions are made for the leave vacancy at the rate of one month in a year for each member in it.

It is a matter of regret that the staff formula is not strictly followed in a majority of college and university libraries (exceptions may be few) due to several reasons—the chief being lack of funds and the indifference of the administrative authorities towards the library to accord sanction for the posts. The library profession is hardly doing anything in this regard. The old-established libraries have been the greatest victim as they still suffer from the tradition of honorary librarianship which cuts to the very root of expansion and development of the libraries. Therefore, this institution is not getting the attention, it deserves, at the hands of the university and Government authorities.

University Grants Commission's Role

Development of universities and their libraries in India depends largely on the University Grants Commission's interest. The UGC sanctions funds in the form of capital grants for building, fittings and furniture as well as annual or plan grant for books and journals of the library. It is, therefore, for the Commission to ensure that the grant is not spent for the sake of merely spending it as a ritual but the books and journals so purchased are processed and put to use and the library as a whole is transformed into an active workshop. This can be possible only when the library is adequately and properly equipped with qualified staff. The Commission should prevail upon the administration and management of the university to provide qualified staff in the library in accordance with the staff formula. The Commission should also subsidies the salary-fund of the library staff so appointed, as it does in case of the teaching and research staff. To find out the facts whether the universities are strictly adhering to the prescribed staff formula or not, the Commission may ask the universities to submit the annual returns showing the staff appointed, their qualifications, scales of pay and the quantum of work in the library in the light of the staff formula prescribed. To ensure the strict adherence of this formula, the Commission should make it a pre-condition on the universities to equip their libraries with the staff properly to become eligible for the book grant. This will ensure proper development of the libraries and their improved service to the university community. At present most of the universities hardly view the existing deplorable condition of the staff in their libraries with any seriousness and their interest is only to obtain book-grant from the UGC and spend it without any proper planning. Such a situation affects the functioning of the library adversely.

Transfer of the Staff Members

In a large university library it is necessary to make periodical transfer of the staff in which the positions are interchanged from one section of the library to another without affecting any change in the salary of the persons concerned. Transfers are made, when it is felt necessary by the librarian, to take care of the increased amount of work in certain sections, to correct faulty assignments, to tackle the personality problem of the staff, to create renewed interest in the staff member and to provide leave substitutes. Transfer is a positive method to stimulate interest, maintaining morale of the staff and making the administration of the institution economical. It should be done with care; in the best interest of the institution.

Demotion and Dismissals

This is infrequent but happens in case of staff members found ineffective. Ordinarily, promotion and annual increments in the salary of the persons are withheld. In rare cases where the guilt is severe and the person is not found to be improving even after warning, recourse to demotion and dismissal is taken to save the institution from further damage by the person. In every university, there are certain rules and action has to be taken as per rules prescribed on the subject.

Orientation Programme for Staff

The orientation programme for the staff of the library consists of tours to the different libraries in the country, organization of lectures by the departmental heads and other library scientists on invitation, study-programmes of the working of the different sections in the library to gain practical knowledge and detailed study of the library texts and publications like staff mannuals etc. The staff in the library on appointment possesses basic knowledge. But the orientation courses refresh the memory and provide them with more practical information and opportunity for gaining experience.

In-Service Training

This training is designed for the staff, professional as well as non-professional, in their particular job for increasing the efficiency in work and for preparing them for promotion and taking up new responsibilities and positions. This service also assists the members to qualify for different and higher examinations. Tucker defines in-service training as, "management process of aiding employees to gain effectiveness in their present and future work assignments by providing, planning and organizing a programme of systematic instruction and practice on the job in order (i) to point out to the employee the way to apply, the body of knowledge gained in pre-entry education and training to the concrete duties of a specific job, and (2) to develop appropriate habits of thought and action, skills, and knowledge, essential to effective performance" (Quoted in Wilson: *op. cit:* 309). In the recent past, the university librarians have increasingly set up in-service trainings for their staff, both professional and non-professional. It has become a deliberate function of the management. It becomes more effective when the programme consists of imparting the skill by the senior staff members to the junior ones.

Student Assistants

In the university library, there are many works of supplementary, clerical and technical nature. For example, delivering books from stacks; returning them to the shelves; working at the issue counter and attending to the loan work; pasting and labelling of books, simple book mending and repairs, typing work, messenger's service, attending to duplicating machines and filing of catalogue cards etc. These are comparatively simple jobs which can be performed by the undergraduate and graduate students of the institution. The students may be engaged on these works to help them with the financial aids. Such aids should be given usually to the needy but meritorious students and they should be paid at the prevailing rates of salary at the university.

The practice of providing student assistants is increasingly adopted by the university libraries these days, specially in the developed countries. These libraries set apart a sizeable amount of the budget for this purpose and the system has proved successful. Care has to be taken in the selection, engagement and training as well as proper supervision of the students put on the job. Sometime administrative laxity leads to failure of the programme. Adequate training for these persons should be organized. Better efficiency can be achieved if few students for a longer period are engaged instead of employing large number of students for a short duration of time.

Wilson and Tauber have outlined certain principles for supervising the student-assistants' work. There should be close cooperation between the supervisor and the students assigned to him; the work should be interpreted to the students and they should be impressed upon showing good results. To guide the students properly, the supervision should formulate the objectives of his section clearly and specifically which are intended to be achieved. Gelfand, however, mentions that the students' aids and assistance is more useful as supplementary rather than principal source of help. In general, these students do not represent a reliable source of assistance and, as such, they should not form the sole supporting force for the professional staff. The chief reliance should be placed in the regular staff of the library whose tenure of service is for a longer period and who have received proper training for the job (Gelfand: *op. cit.*62).

Besides its utility in the functioning of the library, this practice has been found advantageous and useful for the profession as well. The young student assistants are encouraged to take up librarianship as career. Selection and recruitment from amongst these assistants for the graduate course and eventually their appointment in the library have been found to be beneficial for the institution and, as such, this practice of student assistantship need to be encouraged.

Library Personnel

Many of the universities in India remained only examining bodies for several decades. The teaching and research functions in such universities remained absent for a long time and, therefore, they did not possess any organized library; just they did not feel any necessity for it as there was no demand for the library service by the staff and the students. However, these universities did gather collection of books in their premises which were surprizingly left to the care of the staff like cleaners, care-takers and some clearical persons to keep the books listed in the registers and clear the dust occasionally. This situation brought forth a wrong tradition in the universities where the library staff meant to consist of cleaners, peons, book-lifters and some literate clerks alone.

Honorary Librarian

About sixty years ago, new universities with teaching function attached to them were set up in the country. Such universities required help in their studies and teaching activities by the libraries. To co-ordinate the services of the library to various faculties, honorary librarians were appointed in each university. To do this job some professor of the faculty was designated honorary librarian as a rule will all powers vested in him to run and control the library. He was placed over and above the existing staff of the library.

Only about fifty years ago, the university authorities realized for the first time the need for a professional man to be appointed as librarian and given the powers, status and responsibility to develop the library. But such idea was conceived by only a few, very few universities. The UGC Committee Report (1965) in India mentions, "till recently this had happened only in about three of the older universities and four of the leader ones. Most of the other universities are still under pressure of old tradition in respect of the function, the qualifications, the status, and the strength of the library staff. As for responsibility, some universities are still looking on the university library as a section of its general administration and continue to get it administered by the registrar of the university and to make its staff interchangeable with that of the registrar's office, not realizing the specialized professional nature of the work in a progressive library" (UGC: *op. cit*: 63). In fact, nothing has done more harm in the progress of the academic librarianship in India, than the above two facts viz. tradition of appointing honorary librarians and interchangeability of the staff between the library and the registrar's office. The Committee has, therefore, very rightly recommended the abolition of this practice of appointing a person, without the prescribed qualifications, even as honorary librarian. The Committee says, "this old practice inhibits and kills the enthusiasm and initiative of the professional librarian and his staff. It clips their wings. It degrades them to the level of clerical assistants. It has been all along suppressing the functioning of libraries. It will make the library continue to be a mere collection of books instead of an intellectual workshop and the heart of the university and college" (*Ibid*: 69). This discussion amply proves that the tradition of appointing honorary librarian should be abolished forthwith and the UGC should put a compulsion on every university to appoint a full-time professional librarian in the grade of university professor in all the universities. Similarly, the staff of the library should be placed completely under the control of the university librarian, independent of the purview of the registrar and the inter-transfer of the staff of the library and the registrar's office should be disallowed. Except for a few clerical posts like establishment clerk, stenographer, accountant and the storekeeper, all other staff in the library perform the professional and semi-professional work of some kind or the other. This staff should, therefore, be left entirely under the control of the university librarian without making their service transferable to the office of the registrar.

Qualification of the Library Staff

We have discussed in the previous pages that the academic requirements of the library staff has since greatly changed. The library staff no longer consists of merely book-lifter who could only read and write the title of the book or the clerk to maintain the entries of the books on the register. Today, the academic qualifications of the library staff need be at par with those of the professors, readers, and lecturers. Further, the librarian, reference librarian, classifiers and the documentalist in a university or college library should be fully aware of the modern literature and development of knowledge and the new subjects emerging in different areas. There should be subject specialists also available amongst the staff. In fact, the awareness of the staff of the library should be in many subjects unlike the professors who are specialists in only one subject. They should keep themselves abreast of the growth of knowledge which is multi-dimensional.

Besides possessing the general academic qualifications of a high order, the librarian and his professional staff should also acquire professional qualification of an equally high order.

The standards of professional qualifications indicated by the UGC Committee (1965) are the attainment of doctorate, M. Lib. Sc.and the B. Lib. Sc. degrees. The higher staff in the library should also pursue research on useful projects of librarianship. The universe of knowledge is growing and expanding with a terrific speed. To march with it, it is necessary for the library profession to modernize its techniques and standards and adopt new innovations in the field of library services.

Academic Status

The librarians and their staff working in colleges, universities and research institutes have been struggling the most to achieve their professional recognition, in terms of parity, with the teaching staff. The argument is that with their close association with the students and teachers of the university, they contribute to the furtherence of educational and research programmes in the faculties and, therefore, they should reasonably be included in the ranks of the teaching staff of the colleges and universities or in other professional or scientific classifications done by the research institutes. Further argument in this regard is that the contemporary libraries need well-educated library staff and their academic attainments and training are quite comparable to those of the members of the teaching staff. As such, they object, and very reasonably, to any other classification done to differentiate them form the academic community. With the expansion of colleges and universities and the consequent need for more staff to organize and disseminate the world's knowledge, this demand is gaining strength.

The academic status implies grant of formal recognition to the professional staff of the library as members of the teaching and research staff in the form of assigned or equivalent faculty ranks and titles with corresponding grades of salaries and other privileges. Gelfand mentions that the lack of such a recognition is one of the major obstacles for recruitment of competent staff in the library profession. The meritorius and qualified graduates cannot be attracted to the librarianship unless they are assured of a respectable, promising and satisfying career in this profession. The Regional Seminar on Library Development in South Asia (1960) recommended that the following ranking schedule should be adopted in respect of the staff working in the college and university libraries.

Description of staff member	*Nature of duties*	*Equivalent to faculty post and enjoying scale*
Librarian	Supervisory	University Professor
Deputy Librarian	Senior Professional	University Reader
Assistant Librarian	Junior Professional	University Lecturer
Senior Library Assistant in any section	Professional Assistant	Assistant Lecturer
Technical Assistant	Professional Assistant	Assistant Lecturer

This is one approach to grant the academic status to the library staff. Another approach, mentioned by Robert, B Downs, Director of the University of Illinois Libraries (US) is that followed in his library in 1944 for transfer of staff from civil service administration to the academic staff of the university. All the existing professional positions in the library were classified on the basis of their educational and technical character and placed in the academic categories of associate professor, assistant professor, instructor and assistants. They were made entitled to the salary of their respective ranks, with all other benefits like retirement benefits, leave, tenure etc. The library staff received the same privileges as those of the teaching staff in the university. For work schedule, however, they were covered by the rules of the working conditions of administrative officers. Thus, to grant the academic status to library staff, each university should make its own provision in the statutes.

The library should provide adequate avenue for training and promotion of the library staff. This opportunity should be equal to those of the teaching members of the faculty. Degrees, advance studies, scholary and research contributions and scientific publications are the basis for the promotion of the teaching staff. For the staff of the library, it would be desirable to be flexible as the library personnel do not get much time for the scholarly and academic contribution either by way of acquiring higher degrees or through contributing to the learned journals. They are frequently transferred from one position to another of greater responsibility depending upon their experience and performance. Therefore, the criteria for promotion of this staff should be prescribed with understanding of the factual position. Age, educational attainments, experience in the profession, professional contribution and opinion of the librarian are some of the factors which should also be taken into consideration.

It is quite a difficult job for the university administrator to select the chief librarian. The problem is whether the local assistant or the deputy librarian should be promoted as the chief librarian or a new person should be selected. Wilson and Tauber mention that an analysis of the library appointments indicate that only in exceptional cases the local assistant librarian succeeds in getting promoted to the position of the chief librarian. Although, the assistant librarian might have worked de facto and officiated as chief librarian during his absence on leave, his actual or de jure appointment to the office is rarely made and he is usually passed over in favour of an outside individual. The reason given is that the university authorities would like to secure a new view-point and look in the library (Wilson and Tauber: *op. cit*: 314). In turn, the university librarian also faces such a situation while making selection of assistant librarian or the other professional staff of the library. Wilson and Tauber suggest, "when one of these individuals is as fully equipped as any outside candidate, it would be a sound principle of personnel management to promote him to the position of assistant librarian" (*Ibid*).

The Salary

The University Grants Commission (India) appointed a committee under the chairmanship of Dr. S.R. Ranganathan in 1951 to give new scales of pay to the staff of university and college libraries in India. This committee recommended the following structure of the library staff, their functional designation and professional status, qualifications and grades in the university libraries.

The committee also recommended and made it clear that the salary scales of the staff of the library should be changed to concide with those of the teaching staff, whenever the latter is changed (UGC: *op. cit.* 66).

The idea and the principle enunciated by the philosopher and library scientist Dr. S.R. Ranganathan were taken up seriously by the University Grants Commission under the stewardship of Dr. C.D. Deshmukh, a distinguished educationist. The foundation for the integration of the college and the university librarianship in the maintream of the academic community of the institutions was laid during his chairmanship of the University Grants Commission. It provided fresh impetus and new life to the library profession (academic) in India and enhanced its prestige. In the report of the UGC Library Committee the faculty status of the librarian was accepted and the pay scales similar to those of the teachers were implemented.

The Third Five Year Plan showed a significant development towards this end. It actually created a landmark in the history of the enhancement of the status and position of the academic library profession by revising their scales of pay by the University Grants Commission. The UGC revised the following scales of pay for the professional library staff in university libraries and also prescribed the qualifications for them :

Designation, qualification and salary-scales of the technical staff of the library

Sl. No.	Designation	Professional Status	Qualification Minimum	Desirable		Grade Scale of pay
1	2	3	4	5	6	7
1.	Librarian	Professional Senior	M.Lib Sc II class or MA or M.Sc II class and Dip Lib.Sc or B Lib Sc I class; prescribed minimum experience in a research or university library	Doctorate in library science or any other subject	1	800-50-1250 (Professor's)
2.	Documentalist	-do-	-do-	-do-	2	500-25-800 (Reader's)
3.	Deputy or Assistant Librarian	-do-	-do-	-do-	2	-do-
4.	Reference Librarian	-do-	-do-	-do-	2	-do-
5.	Chief Classifier	-do-	-do-	-do-	2	-do-
6.	Chief Cataloguer	-do-	-do-	-do-	2	-do-
7.	Maintenance Librarian	Professional Junior	Dip Lib Sc or B.Lib Sc I class and BA or B.Sc or B.Com II class		3	250-20-500 (Lecturer's)
8.	Assistant Classifier	-do-	-do-		3	-do-
9.	Assistant Cataloguer	-do-	-do-		3	-do-

10.	Accession Librarian	-do-	-do-	3	-do-
11.	Periodicals Librarian	Professional Junior	Dip Lib Sc or B Lib Sc I class and BA or B.Sc or B.Com II class	3	250-20-500 (Lecturer's)
12.	Circulation Librarian	-do-	-do-	3	-do-
13.	Senior Library Assistant in any section but not the reference section	Professional Assistant	-do-	4	150-10-250 (Assistant Lecturer's)
14.	Junior Library Assistant in any section but not the reference section	Semi-Professional	Cer Lib.Sc and good Higher Secondary Certificate	5	80-5-150-10-250

Note : The above information has been drawn, with acknowledgement, from University and College Libraries by University Grants Commission, New Delhi, 1965, pp. 66-67.

Designation *1*	*Equivalent academic status* *2*	*Qualifications Prescribed* *3*	*Scale of Pay Recommended* *4*
1. Profess-ional Junior	Lecturer	(a) First/Second class BA/B.Sc/B.Com degree plus Ist or 2nd class M.Lib.Sc degree (Two year's course) or (b) First /Second class MA/M.Sc/M.com degree and Ist or 2nd class M.Lib Sc or one year diploma course in Lib.Sc.	400-30-800
2. Professional Senior	Reader	(a) First/Second class BA/ B.Sc/B.Com degree plus Ist or 2nd class M.Lib.Sc. degree (two year's course) or First/Second class MA/M.Sc/M.Com degree and Ist or 2nd class B.Lib.Sc or one year diploma course in Lib.Sc. (b) Five years' experience as librarian or of working in responsible professional capacity in a Library	700-40-1100
3. Professional Senior	Professor	(a) First/Second class BA/B Sc /B Com degree plus 1st or 2nd class M Lib Sc degree (two year' course) or First/Second class MA/M Sc/ M com degree and 1st or 2nd class B Lib Sc or one year diploma course in Lib.Sc. (b) At least 10 years' experience as librarian or of working in a responsible professional capacity in a library (c) Recognized research experience of work on special projects	1000-50-1500

The Ministry of Education, Government of India, revised further the scales of pay of the university and college library staff vide their letter No. F. 29-20/66-41 dated September 6, 1968 (Sharma: 1977: 158).

Designation	*Equivalent academic status*	*Scales of pay recommended by UGC*	*Remarks*
1	*2*	*3*	*4*
(A) University Library Staff			
1. Professional Senior	Professor	1100-50-1300-60-1600	Subject to the fulfilment of the conditions regarding education qualifications and experience prescribed.
2. Professional Senior	Reader	700-50-1250	In the case of existing staff, however, the revised scales of pay may be given to those who are already getting the scales of pay recommended by the UGC during the Third Plan period irrespective of the prescribed educational qualifications and experience.
3. Professional Junior	Lecturer	400-40-800-50-950	But in the case of professional junior the qualifications prescribed must be insisted upon and the revised grades may be given to persons who, as and when improve upon their qualifications. Their placement in the revised scales must be subject to the screening by a duly constituted committee of experts.
(B) College Library Staff			
1. Professional Junior	Lecturer	300-25-600	Must possess an MA/M Sc/M Com degree and a diploma in Lib Sc or B Lib Sc. In the case of existing staff persons with BA/B Sc/B Com degree and a diploma in Lib Sc or B Lib Sc with ordinary

at least five years' experience as librarian may be given the revised scales. The qualifications prescribed above must be insisted upon and the revised grades may be given to persons who as and when improve upon their qualifications. Their placement in the revised scales must be subjected to the screening by a duly constituted committee of experts.

The Third Pay Commission, Government of India, recommended revision of scales of pay of the teachers from 1973. The revised pay scales were duly implemented in most of the states in the country. But the committee on governance of universities and colleges in its report on "Teachers" said, "the Committee is not making any recommendation regarding the revision of scales of pay of librarians and other staff in the libraries and physical instructors in universities and colleges and suggests that this may be considered along with the revision of scales of pay of non-teaching staff. However, when teachers are appointed in the universities/colleges for teaching in the departments of library science and physical education, they should be treated on par with the other teachers provided they fulfil the qualifications". The University Grants Commission (India) appointed a committee under the chairmanship of Dr. S.N. Sen, Vice-Chancellor, Calcutta University, Professor Nihar Ranjan Ray; Professor GR Sharma, Department of Ancient History and Culture Allahabad University; Professor MRN Prasad, Zoology Department, Delhi University; Dr B Anderson, Librarian, Madras University and Sri RS Chitkara, Director, Ministry of Education and Social Welfare. This Committee said that the academic aspect in a university/college library was relatively more important than the service aspect. The library staff in a university or college was expected to keep abreast of a large part of the growth of knowledge in different subjects. It should, therefore, be the endeavour of the universities and colleges to attract people, with high academic background, to their libraries. The following scales of pay were recommended for the library staff : (i) Librarian Rs 1500-2000; (ii) Deputy Librarian Rs 1100-1600 and (iii) Assistant Librarian Rs 700-1300.

Thus, the earlier long-established parity with those of teachers, accepted and granted by the UGC in India, was overlooked and the scales for the library staff were downgraded. Besides this, the UGC also provided for appointing a scholar of standing in any discipline, other than library science, as university librarian. The downgrading of the scales of pay as well as making non-professionals eligible for the highest office in the academic librarianship (university librarian) was viewed by the library profession in India with the greatest concern. In fact, there has been intense simmering and great agitation in the library profession over this step taken by the UGC and the Government of India. The XXI All India Library Association Conference held at Bhubaneswar on January 16, 1975 debated this point with vehement opposition from the members. The librarians argued and urged the Government to place them on par with the academic staff in the college and the university as was done at the time of the revision of the pay scales during the years 1961 and 1968. A convention of the All India Librarians, Documentalists and Information Scientists was held on April 15, 1974 which impressed upon the Government of India to adopt a uniform national wage policy for different categories of library personnel in the context of the revision done with regard to pay scales of the teaching staff of the academic institutions. The Conference of the Indian Library Association held at Delhi in 1975 and at Srinagar in 1976 passed similar resolutions to emphasize upon the demand for the parity. The views of the UGC in this connection was such that it issued a D.O.No.F. 1-41/7441 dated 13 September

1979 which suggested the following scales for the staff of the academic libraries (Sharma: 1977 : 170).

S.No.	*Designation*	*Existing Scale of Pay*	*Revised Scale of Pay*
(a)	**University Library Staff**		
1.	University Librarian	1100-50-1300-60-1600	(i) 1500-60-1800-100-2000-125/2-2500
			(ii) 1500-60-1800-100-2000
2.	Deputy Librarian	700-50-1250	1100-50-1600
3.	Assistant Librarian	400-40-800-50-950	700-40-1100-50-1300
4.	Documentation Officer	(i) 700-1250	(i) 1100-50-1600
		(ii) 400-950	(ii) 700-40-1100-50-1300
(b)	**College Library Staff**		
	Librarian	(i) 400-950	(i) 700-40-1100-50-1300
		(ii) 400-800	(ii) 700-40-1100
		(iii) 300-600	(iii) 550-25-750-EB-30-900

The UGC has prescribed the following conditions for implementing these grades:

(i) The scale of pay of Rs 1500-2500 for the librarian will be admissible only in case the university decides to appoint a scholar of standing in any of the disciplines as university librarian. For eligibility to this scale of pay, the essential qualification would be :

(a) Good academic record with first or high second class Master's degree in a subject other than library science with a Doctorate degree or equivalent published work of high standard and preferably with experience of guiding research with knowledge / experience of library science and management.

(b) At least 10 years' experience of teaching postgraduate classes and research; or of research in an independent capacity in an organization of higher learning and research or in a responsible post in a library for advanced students and research workers.

Such existing university librarians as fulfil the above qualifications would also be eligible to the scale of pay, Rs 1500-2500.

The UGC took three long years to announce the revised pay scales for university and college librarians. The great concern of the library profession was that the UGC in India had thrown overboard the principles of natural justice and equity by creating two grades for the university librarians and three grades for the college librarians. Further, a new class of professor-librarian had been created in the scale of pay of Rs 1500-2500. The professional qualification had been downgraded for the librarianship which is actually a job of an expert. Such a step taken in this country was a violation of the internationally accepted norms of granting the librarians the scale and status equal to the teaching staff. The executive councils of the leading universities in the country like those of Delhi University, Jawaharlal Nehru University and the Jamia Millia Islamia has passed resolutions endorsing the principle of parity. The librarians all the world over are enjoying faculty status.

Professor M.V. Mathur, inaugurating the first national conference of INDAAL, said that the librarians are the non-formal teachers and Professor Sarup Singh expressed the need that the academic librarians should have an active mind and linking of Ph. D. for restoration of parity of pay scales with the teachers in university and colleges was undesirable. This convention also adopted resolution for the restoration of parity in respect of pay scales for the academic librarians with the teachers in the universities and colleges.

Also the joint convention organized by INDAAL, ILA, IASLIC and DLA urged the UGC, the Government of India and the State Governments to restore parity in the pay scales and status with teaching staff to the professional library staff (librarian, deputy librarian, assistant librarian and professional assistant) working in the university and college libraries with retrospective effect. The convention further recommended that the principle of "Parity in pay scales with qualification" should be delinked. The revised qualification, if any, should not be applicable to the existing incumbents as has been in the case of teachers. With a view to providing incentives and scope for future promotions, the Convention recommended that the UGC/Ministry of Education/State Governments and other bodies concerned should extend the scheme of personal promotion as being provided to teachers in the universities and colleges (INDAAL Newsletter: 1977).

At long last, the UGC accepted the parity in pay scales of the librarians of universities and colleges and revised their grades as: Librarian Rs. 1500-2500, Deputy Librarian/ Documentation officer Rs. 1200-1900, Assistant Librarian/ Documentation officer Rs. 700-1600 and College Librarian Rs. 700-1300-Assessment 1600 under UGC letter No. F-1-96/81 (CP/MP) dated 31 August 1984.

Now, with the revision of the teacher's grade from January 1986, the Ministry of Human Resource Development (Department of Education) Government of India, has considered the librarians grade as well and keeping these on par with those of the teachers, the Ministry has revised the grade of University Librarian from Rs. 1500-2500 to Rs. 4500-7300 (Professor's grade), Deputy Librarian from Rs. 1200-1900 to Rs. 3700-5700 (Reader's grade) and Assistant Librarian from Rs. 700-1600 to Rs. 2200-4000 (Lecturer's grade) under letter No. F. 1-21/87-U-I dated 22 July 1988.

Ministry of Human Resource Development, (Department of Education) Government of India, considering the scales of teachers and other academic staff, decided the following modified scales vide its letter no. F.1-22/97-UI dated 6th November, 1998.

(a) Scales of Pay of Teachers and other Academic Staff in Universities and Colleges.

Relevant extract relating to the library staff

S.No	Category	Existing Scales of Pay	Revised Scales of Pay
For Universities			
8.	Librarian	4500-150-5700-200-7300	16400-450-20900-500-22400
9.	Dy Librarian	3700-125-4950-150-5700	12000-420-18300
10.	Assistant Librarian Assistant Documentation Officer (Sr. Scale)	3000-100-3500-125-5000	10000-325-15200
11.	Assistant Librarian Assistant Documentation Officer	2200-75-2800-100-4000	8000-275-13500
For Colleges			
12.	College Librarian (Sl.Grade)	3700-125-4590-150-5700	12000-420-18300
13.	College Librarian	3000-100-3500-125-5000	10000-325-15200
14.	College Librarian	2200-75-2800-100-4000	8000-275-13500

(b) Pay Scales Recommended by the pay Review Committee Appointed by the UGC.

S.No	Category	Existing (Rs.)	Revised (Rs.)
8.	Librarian	4500-150-5700-200-7300	14300-450-22400
9.	Dy Librarian	3700-125-4950-150-5700	12000-375-18000
10.	Assistant Librarian	2200-75-2800	8000-275-13500
16.	College Librarian	2200-75-2800-100-4000	8000-275-13500
18.	College Librarian (Senior Scale)	3000-100-3500-125-5000	1000-325-15200

Association's Responsibility

The library association in the country owes its responsibility in this regard. The academic content of librarianship in this country is going down. The remedy for improving the conditions lies in restoring position, dignity and the scales of pay to the librarians treating them as non-formal teachers. And, along with this, the librarians should also improve their content and style of functioning and bear the full responsibility towards the clientele.

The Indian Library Association field representation to the Chairman, UGC Committee to Review Pay Scales of Teachers of Universities, submitting, *inter alia* detailed proposal for rationalization of the designations of the Library Staff and providing them parity with those of teachers (See Newsletter; Vol, 25 ; No. 4-6 ; April - June p2).

The library staff were, infact, placed at par with teachers till the Fourth Pay Commission. Thereafter in the Fifth Pay Commission, even though the Library staff of University Libraries were given the academic status, they were discriminated in respect of the pay benefits, as given to the university teachers. The Association Pleaded when the respective educational qualifications, selection criteria and other requirements for recruitment and appointment of the library staff in Universities and colleges are the same, as those prescribed for the teachers; then such discrimination does not stand to reason. The Association asked for restoration of the faculty status; giving complete pay parity to the library staff, as provided for, earlier.

Further, the Association also demanded change in the designations of the library staff, saying that the designation of University Librarian, Deputy Librarian, University Assistant Librarian/College Librarian, Documentation Officer, Information Scientist be changed as Professor, Associate Professor and Assistant Professor respectively.

That, the circulars, as and when issued by the University, in respect of teachers should be applicable equally to the Library Staff as well. And the library staff should be made equally to eligible to research etc. and work as guide for M.Phil./ Ph.D. students in the Library and Information Science subjects.

The proposal outlines various other issues also concerning the staff of the libraries (*Ibid*: pp2-7).

Working Condition

While good physical conditions are conducive to the

efficient work, the bad conditions make adverse effect on working of the staff. The library should endeavour to provide comfortable office for the staff to work. The workrooms should be adequately large and open, well-ventilated and well-lighted, equipped with comfortable furniture and equipment. There should be staff lounges. Air-conditioning is increasingly demanded these days more so in the tropical countries. Besides providing comfort to the readers and the staff sitting in the building it also helps preservation of the reading materials, its collection and equipments.

The staff should also be provided reasonable amount of opportunity for their professional writing and advancement of knowledge. Provision should also be made for medical aid of the staff and for their security in retirement.

In American university libraries provision for tea-break for fifteen minutes has been provided specifically for the staff. The staff-rooms are equipped with kitchens and supplies for the purpose. The use of working-time for tea is permissible there on the ground that such brief rest causes beneficial effects and it is important. However, it is for the departmental heads to see that this provision is not misused and the teabreaks do not transform into uncontrolled social gatherings.

Hours of Work

Unlike the teaching programme in the college and university, library work is an year-round activity. It is generally kept open for a longer period every day and it knows no holiday. The hours of work, however, vary from one region to another, depending upon the climatic conditions. Keeping the library open for longer hours enables the students and the teaching staff to make use of it according to their convenience for study and research. The librarian has to regulate its timings according to needs of the classes.

Leave

To make the library function effectively all the year round, it is necessary that the library staff, though entitled for leave, as per rules of the university, avail it at different times than those for the teaching staff. The library staff should be given medical leave with pay and offs during other local and national holidays. Necessary arrangements be made to continue the library services of the different sections of the library during the period of absence of staff members.

Further, librarianship is a rapidly changing profession and to keep abreast with modern development in the field of knowledge and to acquaint himself with the new techniques in his own or related fields, the librarians should be provided with opportunity to get study leave for a year or so and avail travel grants etc. Library staff should also be entitled to the sabbatical leave.

Fellowship

The meritorious members of the library staff should be granted fellowship or grants-in-aid for undergoing graduate or postgraduate training in librarianship or to take up research study like the faculty members. However, there should be compulsion on the recipients of such awards to return to their position for a stipulated period after having undergone the course.

So, the staff is an essential factor in running the whole show of the library. In fact, the efficient functioning of the library depends upon the quality and quantity of the staff. And, unless the library is equipped with adequate qualified staff, proper administration of the library will become well-neigh impossible. It is really a matter of pity that such an important factor is overlooked in the planning of the library services and the scheme of things in the academic institution, especially in India.

References

1. Gelfand, MA, 1962, University libraries for developing countries, UNESCO Manual for Libraries,-14, UNESCO, Paries.
2. Parry, Thomas (Chairman) 1967, Report of the committee on libraries, University Grants Committee, Her Majesty's Stationery Office, London.
3. Ranganathan, S.P., 1959, Library administration, Asia, Bombay.
4. University Grants Commission, New Delhi 1965, University and College libraries, containing the report of the library committees of the University Grants Commission and the proceedings of the seminar from publisher to reader held an March 4-7, 1959.
5. Wilson, LR and Tauber, MF, 1958, The University library, 2nd ed., Columbia University Press, New York.

8

LIBRARY SERVICE

The prime objective of organization and administration of the university library is to facilitate the academic community to exploit and harness fully the resources of the library for the maximum use. To this end, the library invites the reader, guides him and provides him with literature. William S. Dix says the library's ability to make available the book, a reader needs, is its basic test of the quality. He suggests further, "this is the first principle and from it stem nearly all the things we do or ought to do in libraries." (In Gelfand: 1962: 95). It is necessary, therefore, that the library should provide planned service to make its stock easily accessible and conveniently usable; fulfilling the reader's needs.

Kinds of Service

Generally, the university library performs the following services to its reading community : (i) all kinds of reading materials are acquired, organized and displayed in classified order using the techniques of classification, cataloguing and shelf-arrangement; (ii) circulation work in the library is planned providing lending services of books, periodicals and other reading materials so that the teachers and students could make use of them at their convenience; (iii) documentation service is provided so that the readers may have pinpointed access to the information and data they need; (iv) readers' guidance is provided for efficient use of the library materials; and (v) the stock of the library is widely displayed and publicised for use by the largest number. All these are termed technical services undertaken by the library. These steps prove to be stimulant to the members for making use of the library resources. The main objective is to bring the documents and the readers closer for productive results.

Broadly, there are two principal services which the library renders to its clientele viz. (a) Circulation Service and (b) Reference Service.

(a) Circulation Service

This is a major service rendered by the library. The aim is to facilitate physical access to the library resources and to help encourage optimum use of the reading materials for purpose of study, teaching and research in the institution. This implies the acquisition of books and journals in the library; their technical processing like classification, cataloguing and arrangement on the shelves; identification of prospective borrowers; compiling of reading tests; conducting inventories, circulation work; assisting the readers in use of library catalogues and searching out the needed document and allied activities to help the readers; re-shelving of books on return from borrowers and organization of loans as per rules of the library framed for the purpose. The test of efficiency of this section is the quick service to the readers.

The allied jobs done in the circulation section are : maintenance of all records of loans, maintenance of files of registered borrowers, keeping records of overdue loans for their recall, reservation of titles on demand and to supervise the arrangements and shelving of documents on the library stacks.

The reading material is loaned (from the library) for being taken away from the library building. The library adopts a set of procedures for this purpose. The material is loaned to the registered borrowers for which a registration record is maintained in the library. The intending member has to fill in the library registration card. The student has to show his identity card. Certain university libraries in America maintain a visible file of registration at the circulation desk. This helps in finding out whether the borrower is a registered member of the library; in verifying his signature and checking up whether he owes any fine already. The idea is that the library must satisfy itself, before loaning any material, that those who borrow are actually entitled to the privilege and that they are suitably identified. This is necessary for the library to fulfil its obligation to safeguard the collection. In libraries of larger institutions the identification assumes greater importance. In a small university the students and teachers are likely to be known to the staff. Here the identification is not a big problem.

The organization of the circulation section in college and university is done with a view to enhance the instructional and research programmes. Its planning depends upon the size of the library. The staff working in this section should have fair knowledge of books, periodicals, reference work as well as the organizational techniques of the library. They should also be fully conversant with the rules and procedures of borrowing in the library. Above all, they should possess the qualities of orderliness, accuracy, good judgement, patience and tact. These qualities are particularly important to the staff working on loan-desk. Besides getting along well with the members of the library, the staff should meet them pleasantly.

Restricted Documents

Most of the libraries possess certain restricted documents which need special attention to deal with in the circulation section. Generally they form the following classes : (a) Reserved Books; (b) Reference Books; and (c) Rare Books. Treatment of documents of these classes vary with the nature and characteristics of the library. In academic library, the reserved books mean the collection earmarked for assigned or required reading. Most of the popular and heavily sought for text-books in school, college or university libraries are marked reserved and kept in one separate section called Reserved Text-Book Section for use by the students in the library. Such books are not allowed for home-lending. Reference Books are such documents as are needed by the readers for consultation. They are generally dictionaries, directories, yearbooks and encyclopaedias, standard bibliographies, printed catalogues, abstracts and indexes etc. Rare Books are organized and maintained in a separate room or the department depending upon the size of the library. Also it is not necessary that all the libraries possess rare books, again it depends upon the budgetary position of the library.

The items like incunabula, manuscripts, letters, old newspapers and periodicals, old maps, gift books, association records and typography and out-of-print works etc fall in the category of rare books. The university library frequently becomes a collector of rare material because of its being the beneficiary of private collection. Sometimes, special provision in the library budget has to be made for maintenance and development of the rare-collection. Powel mentions : "because of their historical significance, their intrinsic value, their beauty, and sentimental associations, rare books, when intelligently grouped, have power to excite the imagination and stimulate the intellectual curiosity of the student." (Powel : 1939 : 101). The collection of rare books should be built up with a purpose. Home-lending of the items of this collection is not permitted. They need special care for their preservation and maintenance. A set of rules is prepared for service to users, borrower's privileges, inter-library loan privileges, fines and lost books and other such activities done by the section.

Charging System

The mechanics of charging and discharging routines in the library have undergone revolutionary change during recent years. Various devices have been adopted in the routine to dispose of the readers within the minimum possible time. 'Save the time of the readers' has been the motto. Besides, the accurate recording of loans is also of prime importance. Some of the devices adopted are: ledger system; dummy system; indicator system; temporary slip system and the permanent slip or card system.

Nina E. Browne proposed a system in 1895 which was adopted by many libraries. It used a borrower's pocket (or envelop) instead of a card. Each borrower was issued the number of pockets or envelops equal to the number of volumes he could have on loan at one time. While issuing the book, the library assistant inserted the book card into the envelop of the borrower, projecting the card above the top of the envelop. The call number was filled in behind a date guide. There was no mention of borrower's number on the book card. Similarly, the number was also not mentioned at the borrower's card.

After five years (in 1900) another routine called Newark System was introduced. Under this system, the cards of the books. lying on the shelves, were kept in the book-pocket and the cards for books on loan were kept in files by call number each due date. Each borrower also carried a card of the same size. The library assistant recorded every issue by writing the borrower's registration number on the next line of the book card and by stamping the date due on the same line of the book card. He also stamped on the date due, on the next blank line of a date due slip in the book and on the next blank line of the borrower's card. The discharge of book was done by stamping the date of return opposite the date due on the borrower's card in the book pocket. The book card was returned from the file to the book.

Mostly the readers select the books themselves from the shelves provided the library maintains open-shelf system. He selects them either to read in the library premises or to get them issued for home reading. In a closed-shelf library, he reaches the books via catalogue—he results the library catalogue first to find out the desired book. Then a call-slip (requisition form) is filled in for each title he wishes to borrow. The call-slip is a printed requisition form in which the borrower fills in the author, title and call number of the book, his name, address and any other information required by the library. The call-slip is presented by the borrower at the issue counter, from where it is sent to the book-stacks. Then the desired book is obtained by the library assistant from the shelves and sent to the issue-counter along with the call-slip.

In case of the book being not available at the shelves, it is marked 'not available' and returned to the issue counter. The returned call-slip is then checked up from the records of issued and the outstanding books to ascertain whether the book is on loan and if so, when it is due back in the library. The borrower is informed accordingly.

In case the borrower intends to have the said book reserved for issue in his favour, on its return in the library, he has to put in a request so that he may be notified when the book is returned. In such a case, the borrower is required to fill out a self-addressed postal card for which he is required to pay the cost. The library informs him through that postcard the arrival of the book.

The call-slip system is the simplest method of issuing a book to the borrower. But it can work well only in a small school or college library. For university library where issues are fairly large it proves unsuitable inasmuch as the borrower has to wait for long at the issue counter where crowds could become unmanageable.

The common system adopted in most of the university libraries is the use of a book card and a due-date slip. Every book in the library, which is meant for home-lending, is provided with a book-pocket and a due-date slip, pasted on the book. A book card of 3"× 5" in size and designed to fit into the book-pocket is also prepared. Author's name, title, the call number of the book and its accession number are typed on the book card. The same information is typed on the book pocket as well. Thus, each book is provided with the full details of its loan records. On issuing the book, the borrower is asked to sign the book card or his name and the identifying number is stamped on it. The book card is also stamped with the due-date. This date (on which the book is due for return) is stamped on the due-date slip also. The book card is then filed either alphabetically by author, or by the due date or by the call number of the book, as per requirements of the library locally. In this system, the entries made in the book card presents the cumulative record of the use of the book.

The period of loan varies in different libraries. Mostly it goes with the local conditions. For such books as are in very great demand, the loan period may need to be three to four hours only, especially during the examination hours when such books are segregated from the general collection to regulate and control their issues. Faculty members are, however, permitted to borrow books for longer periods as compared to students. All the books whether borrowed by students or the faculty members are subject to recall. The reference books, rare and precious books, manuscripts, other restricted items and journals are lent for use within the library premises. The archival materials are also treated as restricted documents for purposes of lending.

All libraries do not provide identical loan privileges. It also varies according to the status of the user undergraduate, postgraduate, research scholar and academic staff. Thompson says, "borrowing privileges mirror this ascending order precisely." (Thompson : *op. cit*: 90). In fact, the number of volumes and the period of loan allowed are matters of wide variation from library to library but the essential distinction between the status and categories of the borrowing members is everywhere observed. The library committee frames rules for the purpose. Certain amount of discretionary power is also left in the hands of the university librarian.

Overdue Charges (Fine)

Fine is charged for each day the book remains overdue, if the borrower returns it late. The idea behind realizing the fine is to use it as a deterrent and to discourage late returns. However, the imposition of fine over the borrowers is not considered a satisfactory method. Firstly, it proves expensive for the staff time. Americans say, "it is spending times to collect nickels" (*Op. cit.* : 91). Secondly, if the fine accumulates quickly and mounts up equal to the cost of the book, it becomes all the more a reason for not returning the said book and the very purpose is defeated. Thirdly, most of the readers start thinking that the collection of the library is being built up out of the fine realized from the members, which is not a healthy idea. Fourthly, the percentage of such members who abuse the borrowing privileges in the library is usually small for which the majority of the members and the whole system of the library should not be greated up. And fifthly, the fine system does not work equitably because all the members are not financially uniform. It is better to persuade the defaulter for return of overdue books by sending him reminders. Thompson says that the absence of fine system helps create an atmosphere of trust and co-operation. He cites the example of the University Library of Reading stating that this library does not charge fines and has one of the lowest book-loss figures in the country (*op. cit* : 92).

(b) Reference Service

It is an activity of the reference department of the library for the benefit of the students, faculty members and other such readers of the library. The aim is to assist the members in finding out the information or the document they need. It involves two-fold activities viz. (i) to assist the students and faculty members in getting acquainted with the nature, content and scope of the library and its collection and (ii) to work as a guide to the members for providing them instructions in the most effective use of the library materials and the reference tools. This is done by rendering personal service to the clientele by providing bibliographies, reading lists and documentation service etc. The idea is to provide a consistant, informal and systematic personal service to the readers for interpreting the holding of the library for purposes of study and research.

Organization of the Section

There should be a separate reference department in the central library. In small college and university library circulation and reference sections are combined in one department but it fails to serve an adequate purpose. Therefore, in most of the libraries these two sections function separately, headed by an assistant librarian each. The organization of the section is based on one of the following patterns:

(a) Division by Form : In certain libraries the reference section is organized by a form of reading material. The publications of Government, the manuscripts, maps, periodicals etc are kept separately. This system requires separate reading rooms for the different kind of the publications. It also fails to help the readers looking for the materials on a particular subject.

(b) Division by Subject : Under this system, the documents pertaining to different subjects are kept separately regardless of their form. The resources of the library is divided on the basis of subject-groups (sometimes broadly) like physical sciences, biological sciences, social sciences and humanities and technology etc. The groups are physically co-ordinated for the convenience of readers. This arrangement needs fewer departments. All types of documents viz. books, journals, government publications, manuscripts and microfilms are brought together by subject of one area of study and research. The journals and newspapers are received in the technical section first for being processed for use and they are sent to the relevant subject departments. The overlapping subjects, however, create some problems in organizing the subject departmentalized sections.

In certain university libraries, reference service is proved by (a) creating a central reference department in the main library building; (b) providing a central reference department as also the divisional or the faculty libraries and (c) setting up decentralized departments either within the central building or in separate departmental libraries. The predominantly known system, however, is to organize the central reference service reinforced by the subject departmental libraries or the special reading rooms.

In such a case, the central reference collection maintains general encyclopaedias, directories, handbooks, indexes, trade and national bibliographies while the specialized reference books are maintained in the departmental libraries of the respective subjects. Thus, the central reference section functions as an information centre and clearing house of enquiries in the university and co-ordinates the various activities of reference and inter-library loan services with the library. In a large university where there are several departmental libraries and units, endeavour should be made to obtain co-operation between the units and co-ordinate their activities by the central reference department of the university.

It is necessary that the reference collection in the library is made well-equipped and strong. To this end, the collection should be built up gradually all the year round as a continuous process. The reference librarian should find out the significant gaps in the collections of the general books and make a note of it for acquiring such documents to fill the gap. The reference section should also collect circular letters, bulletins and accession lists of foreign, national and local libraries containing details of their existing and newly added library materials. The section should also consult the catalogues of Government and institutional publications and serials as well. For proper growth of the section, the obsolete materials should be discarded periodically.

There are three essential pre-conditions to provide adequate reference service viz. (i) availability of the materials, (ii) accessibility of sources and (iii) co-operation in the libraries of the region. General reference books like encyclopaedias, directories, dictionaries, almanacs, atlases, abstracts and standard translations etc should be readily available in the library for reference purposes, Besides, the standard works of different subjects should also be available. Other source-books like bibliography and index are also necessary. Proper organization of the reference section is important. The room should be calm and quiet. The reference desk should be placed just at the entrance of this room. The staff should assist the readers in use of the library catalogues and guide them in selection of proper reading materials.

The reference librarian need be an exceptionally well-qualified and energetic person with an inquiring mind. He should be well-conversant with the various reference works and tools available in the library. He should also have the knowledge of the programmes of study and research being pursued in the university. He should be capable of working effectively with the students and teachers of the university. This department should itself conduct literature-search on the research topics pursued by the departments and prepare special bibliographies. It should be equipped with the provisions of photostating and translation services.

Library Guide or Handbook

By implication, the system of open access suggests provision of assistance to the readers in locating the materials. This can be done by providing various directional guides. The library handbook is the first necessity of this kind. It should contain the following information for the reading community of the library.

(i) A diagram and general layout of the library building, descriptions and details of the various sections and rooms, description of branch library, if any;

(ii) A list of staff members, their position, room number and the telephone number, service and area of responsibility;

(iii) Detailed account of the arrangement of the collections, underlining the special collection;

(iv) A full account of the different kinds of services offered, loan facility, book reservation and photostating service available;

(v) Reference service provided to the readers;

(vi) Official text of library's rules and regulations;

(vii) Hours of opening and closing the library, the list of holidays;

(viii) Arrangements of classification, cataloguing and shelving in the library; and

(ix) How to use the library.

This will be a sort of general guide for the users readily available to apprise them of what and how of the library. Besides this, there should be subject to guides prepared for each of the faculties separately throwing details of the material, bibliographical tools and reference works available in the discipline. Catalogues and book-lists of new assessions of different subjects should be prepared. Hand list of current periodicals as well as back volumes of journals should also be prepared for circulation among the readers. Notices like 'Do Not Smoke', 'Ask Me For Book You Need' and 'Use Me' should be displayed at proper places but their number should be minimum.

It is a matter of common knowledge that the students are generally found to be ignorant regarding the library catalogues and bibliographical tools available in the library. The Parry Committee mentions that widespread ignorance among students about the use of bibliographical tools, of closed access material and about the availability of inter-library loan service is apparent among the students (Parry: 1968 : 117). This need be tackled.

The National Union of Students (UK) said, "the encouragement in the case of books should be the attitude throughout and that such encouragement was particularly needed by the 'bad' student. The librarian could be of great help if the lecturer was not providing adequate guidance on the books in his subject and, in particular, the library staff should advise students about catalogues, indexes and how to consult books." (*Ibid* : 114).

Parry further mentions that "the proposition of undergraduates who claimed to know of the existence of bibliographical tools in their libraries was as follows: abstracts, 37 per cent; indexes, 33 per cent; 'others', 22 per cent. They were then asked whether they had been taught to use such tools. Only 14 per cent said that they had, 74 per cent claimed that they had not, and 12 per cent were in the 'can't say' category. Twice as many students in the humanities and social sciences as in the pure and applied sciences said that they had received instruction in the use of bibliographical tools." (*Ibid*: 114). If this could be the position in the British libraries, the condition in India is miserable.

Library Instruction

To overcome the above deficiency, the library should impart instructions to the readers at the various levels. The new students should be introduced and attracted to the library. There are various methods of doing this. (i) By talk—In the students' first week, an introductory and welcoming talk may be arranged for the new and coming students in the form of groups by the university librarian. (ii) By supplying printed instructions—the talk should be supplemented by supplying printed instructions to the students by the library in the form of guide or handbook. (iii) By conducting tours—a series of tours of the libraries in the batches of the students may by arranged to apprise them of its functioning. The staff of the library should act as guides for these tours. (iv) By showing film—a film of the library and its functioning may be shown to the students. (v) By audio-visual devices—these may be used as substitutes for the introductory talks or as a supplementary programmes for general information. (vi) By seminars and lectures-general information should be imparted about the organization of the library and the skills of using the catalogue, bibliographies and reference books should be demonstrated to the students. The objective is to induce the students library oriented. All these will entail the library undertaking additional work. The Parry Committee appreciates this fact that such instruction will involve additional work for the library staff, for which financial provisions should be made for engaging additional staff to carry out these duties. (Parry : *op. cit* : 118). This would necessitate appointment of senior library staff of high ability and knowledge for this work.

The university library should make every effort to ensure that the resources of the library are fully known to its clientele—the students and teachers of the university. The use of data-processing equipment is helpful in this regard. It simplifies the use of catalogues, encourages the compilation and preparation of bibliographies and thus helps the investigator find out his information with ease. The current awareness service is another method to be applied to keep abreast of the new and coming researches. This is done by issuing the weekly list of the recent publications and displaying them items for the knowledge of the intending readers. Certain libraries also provide contents-lists of periodicals. But such facility is not available in all the libraries. In most of the libraries the readers themselves browse through the current periodicals and reports and other such literature. There should be a systematic current awareness service to inform the research and teaching staff of the current publications as and when they are received in the library.

Open Assess System

Woledge and Page mention, "direct assess to the shelves is the keynote of the sweeping changes which came over library service to readers in the last generation". (Thompson : *op. cit* : 94). In support of the statement, they quote the study carried by Friedman Jeffrey which found that out of 51 libraries, which responded to the questionnaires, 44 (86 per cent) followed open access and only the rest 7 (14 per cent) had partially closed access (*Ibid* : 95). The resources of library planning and administration have now been directed towards making the collection easily available to the readers by observing the open access system; this is now an universally accepted dictum. F W Radcliffe has, however, opened a debate saying, "unrestricted access does create serious problems of seating accommodation, efficient control and correct replacement of books and of ensuring that the library is reasonably quiet as unobstructed". (*Ibid* : 95). He argues that while the close access needs only accession order, the open access necessitates that the collection should be fully classified. The library building should be big and commodious to house larger number of shelves. Further, the chances for disarrangement of books, mutilation and the risk of theft are prevalent here. He also disputes the concept that the open access possesses educational value saying that the closed-access makes the librarian-reader confrontation obligatory. Further, the bibliographical skills like use of catalogues etc are not encouraged in open-access: the reader gets confused and lost in the shelves; researchers rely on only borrowing and accurate maintenance of statistics of the library—use by the readers is not possible. There are certain sections like special collection and store of the library which cannot be made accessible to every reader. And, "there is an optimum size beyond which open stacks are liability, a luxury and a decided disservice to readers to say nothing of staff." (*Ibid* : 96).

Assistance to Readers

Mackenna says for a university librarian, the assistance to readers is to provide them with necessary facilities to solve their problems on their own. He subscribes to the view that the development of trained mind is the primary function of a university and, therefore, search for the piece of information assumes more importance than the information itself. While the library staff should help the readers, they should not sit to work for him by doing their (reader's) job. "Such service is disservice", he maintains (Quoted in Neal : 1972 : 106). The readers themselves are the experts of their disciplines. They know the relevant documents, literature on the subjects of their interest as well as the sections and shelves where these are to be found in the library.

Information Explosion

But the conditions have been changing fast. Reader's needs as well as their demands have been growing considerably in recent years. The different classes of readers have now come up and, on the other hand, there has been much information explosions during the last fifty years. With this the size of the stock of the library has also increased which is creating problems of providing easy access to the material. Yet another factor is that some readers get used to the kind of bibliographical services offered by the special libraries and on coming to the university they look for same type of assistance to be made available to them. But, in fact, the conditions of the two types of libraries (special library and the university library) are quite different. The scope of subjects and the range of reader's interest in a university library are greatly wide and large.

Forms of Reader's Assistance Service

Following are the forms of reader's assistance service which are generally provided : (i) Publication of list of recent additions in the library, (ii) Publication of abstracts of articles and papers, (iii) Circulation of new and coming periodicals, reports and other such documents of micro-literature as they are received in the library. Certain universities offer current awareness service in particular areas for the benefit of readers. Under this programme they bring out the xeroxed copies of the content pages of periodicals in the selected areas. Sometime, translation service is also provided by the libraries in limited areas of subjects and languages.

Modern research needs largely the literature of nascent thought-more so in the field of pure and applied sciences. In these disciplines, heavy reliance is put on the literature published in periodicals, conference papers and reports. In social sciences also interdisciplinary studies are now getting popular which demands search of literature cutting across the boundary of a particular discipline. The literature-search has, therefore, become complex in the modern age. To facilitate the process, libraries are providing information retrieval service, literature searching, dissemination of information and compilation of bibliographies for the readers. Line concludes saying, "information services are not an ideal; they are ultimately a necessity". (*Ibid*: 113). In developed countries several methods are employed to render this service. In certain cases machines are installed which answer bibliographic enquiries like location of the documents etc. Cavy suggests, "there should be information stations, that is taped information with explanatory visual aids situated at strategic points in the library to be used without library staff assistance." (*Ibid* : 113). Whatever the methods are employed, it is essential that the university library provides reader's assistance service to its clientele.

Supplementary and Auxiliary Service

To augment its basic services with a view to enhancing the library's contribution to the university community, the library undertakes certain supplementary and auxiliary services. These relate to preservation and storage of the library documents, photography and reproduction services, microfilming, communication facilities needed for inter-library lending, audio-visual service, extension activities and the services for advanced readers etc in the library.

Preservation and Storage

This begins right from the acquisition of the reading material and applies to their handling, preparation and processing, maintenance and use by the readers. For this purpose physical setting of the place of storage is also relevant and important. It should be adequate, well-ventilated and protected against the intense sunlight, dust, dampness, fungi and book-destroying insects. WJ Plumbe says that the library materials are best preserved in a relative humidity of between 40 and 65 per cent. Above this, micro-fungi are likely to grow on book covers particularly in the areas of warm climate. The air temperature is less important. In a temperate climate 60 degrees F. or there abouts is regarded as suitable; in the United States and tropics 85 degrees F. is regarded, as not too hot, although 70-75 degrees F. combined with relative humidity of about 50 per cent is the best temperature range for permanent preservation of paper (Plumbe : 1963 : 318).

While shelving the book, convenient spacing should be provided; there should be no over crowing. Adequate space should be left on the shelves to admit of future additions of the books. Periodical inspection of the shelves should be done and the books requiring treatment should be withdrawn immediately and treated adequately. This is all the more necessary in a country like India where inspects and fungi are prevalent in the libraries. Use of bactericidal equipment for disinfecting the air in stack-rooms is also necessary. The Lenin State Library in the USSR has used pentachlorophenol sodium salt as a fungicide successfully. The Scientific Research

Laboratory of this library recommends that for disinfecting the air in the stack-rooms bactericidal equipments should be used. And, for controlling the insects, the laboratory mentions, the most convenient, safe and effective insecticide is DDT. It can be used in the form of powder, suspension or solution as the need be. Observing the conditions of African and Asian libraries, Plumbe reports that varnishes and lacquers may be used on books, library shelves, furniture and fittings as safeguard against silverfish, cockroaches and bookworms. Periodical inspection of the materials should be done and those requiring special treatment need be identified. It would be advisable to keep the suspected materials in a fumigation chamber. The paperbound books should be sent for binding. For careful hauling and preventing losses, the rare books, manuscripts and other such materials should be segregated from the general collection and kept under suitable atmospheric conditions under the safe custody. Preservation of the library document is an important aspect of the library service.

Binding and Repairs

In certain libraries there is a small provision for simple mending and repair work. Most of the libraries, however, do not possess their own bindery and they depend on the commercial binders. If the volume of binding work is large enough in a particular library, establishment of a separate bindery of its own in the library should be considered as that would be an economical proportion.

Where the binding work is to be done by a commercial binder, complete plan should be drawn well in advance. The plan should specify the details of the binding—its type, the kind of materials to be used, other specifications and details to be followed. The work should be assigned under the charge of a professional who is conversant with the work and techniques of binding and is capable of imparting necessary instructions to the binder for the quality work and later evaluation of the finished job.

Reproduction Service

Quick-copying methods are a recent phenomenon. The photographic and the other reproduction services have revolutionized the library services during the modern age. The microphotography has made it possible to bring within the reach of even the smallest libraries copies of costly and even rare books, journals, manuscripts and other documents, which were otherwise impossible to acquire. With the developed microfilm printing, it is now possible to reproduce the pages of books and the whole article of journals within no time. Photography combined with xerography reproduces quickly and at a lower cost. To reproduce the bibliographical works, reading lists and catalogues, xerography can be well used. This method has improved the transmission of knowledge and the inter-library lending service in the libraries.

Audio-Visual Service

Being more popular in public libraries, this service is gaining popularity in academic libraries and its use is increasing gradually. Motion picture films (documentary type), filmstrips, sound tapes, picture files, gramophone records and lantern-slides are the present day devices which supplement the instructions in colleges and universities. To provide these facilities, physical setting of the room as well as appropriate projection and listening equipment should be procured and made available to the readers.

Extension Service

This service is provided to make readers aware of the holding of the library and its activities. The programme includes arranging additional lectures, holding exhibition of reading materials, concert and dramatic performances. The activities are organized in collaboration with cultural organizations in the college or the university comprising of students and teachers.

Service for Advanced Readers

The advanced readers like scholars, students, professors and specialists of different disciplines, need special care and treatment at the library. Firstly they need a quiet-corner equipped with modern facilities of light and air, where they can sit with comfort for study and keep their books, writing equipment and supplies safely. The space should be provided near the book-stacks and the adjacent rooms. Besides this physical setting, they should be also provided with source-documents like bibliographies, abstracts and translations helpful for study and research.

Library Co-operation

Ours is an age of literature explosion. It is well-night impossible for one library to be absolutely comprehensive in all the subject-fields. Even in one particular area of study, no library can be fully self-sufficient. This condition applies to the libraries of not only underdeveloped countries but also to those of highly developed countries. Thompson mentions, "in view of the highly specialized nature of some of the research work done, the age and scarcity of some of the material required in the humanities and the ever-increasing amount of information (largely in periodical form and from foreign countries) demanded in the sciences, no university library can contemplate attaining self-sufficiency" (Thompson : 1970 : 117). Discussing the conditions of British Libraries, which are so rich in their resources, MaColvin and Review state, "there is no library —not even the British Museum—in which a reader could find everything he might require, and, if there were, only a infinitesimal proportion of readers could go there". (MaColvin: 1984: 44). The remedy is library co-operation. The Regional Seminar on Bibliography, Documentation and Exchange of Publication in Latin America, held under the auspices of UNESCO in 1960 recommends, "in view of current developments in science and technology, which make adequate and efficient bibliographical and documentation services a necessity...there should be a co-ordination of and broader co-operation among the university libraries, documentation centres and specialized libraries of each country." (Quoted in Gelfand : 1962 : 113-14).

Similarly, the Regional Seminar on the Development of University Libraries in Latin America (1962) concludes, "insufficient co-operation between libraries in Latin America is detrimental to the standard and development of library service and that Latin American libraries should make co-operation their watchword on all fields of library, book and development work" (*Ibid* : 114). In the field of library service, co-operation is all the more a necessity as the library deals with the universe of knowledge which is a dynamic continuum.

The Scope and Function

The scope of library co-operation is vast. The most important type of library co-operation is the inter-library lending. In Britain, the National Central Library performs this activity. Parry Committee Report has described the National Central Library as the pivot of this service. It maintains union catalogue of the holdings of university libraries, regional libraries and the special libraries which participate in the scheme. There are about two and half million entries in this catalogue. The request for the loan is submitted to the National Central Library which forwards the same (loan request) to the library possessing the item (located through the union catalogue). The loaning library then sends the title direct to the borrowing library.

In addition to the inter-library lending and exchange of information, the following areas also need to be covered.

(i) Co-operative Acquisition : Before making purchase of expensive and specialized publications, consultation within and amongst the university libraries should be made. By centralizing the book purchase activities and co-ordinating it, we can avoid the duplication of books. This will lead to better book selection and better economy. This method is all the more beneficial and useful with regard to procurement of foreign documents and literature, which otherwise present a lot of difficulties. In the United States, the Farmington Plan has been drawn to make sure that at least one copy of each new foreign publication of book and pamphlet, which is of interest to the research workers in that country, should be acquired by an American library. On acquisition, such a document is quickly listed in the Union Catalogue at the Library of Congress and that is made available through the inter-library loan or photographic reproduction service. This is a kind of voluntary agreement among the research libraries of the United States. In the Federal Republic of Germany a more comprehensive plan has been drawn since 1949 with similar objectives. It is the programme of the Deutsche Forschungsgemeinschaft (German Research Association) for co-ordinating the acquisition policies of the research libraries in that country. Denmark, Finland, Norway and Sweden have also set up a joint programme of international system of co-operative acquisition, known as the Scandia Plan. Under the programme, which is operated at the expense of the participating libraries each library decides independently, on its own, its acquisition and exchange policy. But in the area of special subjects, a comparative evaluation of the existing collections in the libraries is made and the acquisition policy is framed depending upon the areas of interest in the different libraries.

In addition to these acquisition programmes which are national and international in character, there are certain co-operative acquisition programmes sponsored jointly by the neighbouring libraries. These include co-operative acquisition of newspapers, microfilms, historical documents and manuscripts, scientific reports, reference and bibliographical publications and translations. In India, these problems were discussed at the Regional Seminar on Library Development in South Asia, held at Delhi in 1960. This seminar recommends for the creation of a national system for centralized purchase of foreign documents in the country. It further says that in respect of the university libraries, a co-operative acquisition plan should be drawn on the lines of the Farmington Plan. Such a plan should, however, keep in view the subjects of specialization in different libraries.

The Government of the country should own up the responsibility in this regard and take a lead in co-ordinating the activities. The participating agencies should be association of university libraries, special libraries, documentation centres, other professional library associations and the national libraries.

(ii) Co-operation and Centralized Cataloguing : Duplication is more likely within and amongst the university libraries. A particular title is purchased in several university libraries of the country as also in the various branch libraries of one university. All these libraries classify and catalogue the book separately. This results into the wasteful duplication of labour. If one library does it and distributes the copies of the catalogue to all other libraries, the process will result in a good deal of saving of human labour as well as expenditure. Further, it will bring greater uniformity in the cataloguing work and maintenance of records. Services of the language experts, specialists and classifiers can be made available for this purpose for the common good of the libraries.

The US Library of Congress has introduced since 1902 a centralized system of catalogue-card production service. But in respect of the university libraries it is still desired that co-operative cataloguing is done by a centralized agency on the lines of Library of Congress.

In the USSR, there is a one All-Union Book Chamber which has undertaken the work of preparing union catalogue and publishing the printed catalogue cards for all the titles published in the USSR, in Russian or in a foreign language, for all the articles published in the reviews and for all documents, articles and abstracts published in the newspapers of the capital.

All the university libraries should be permitted to participate in the programme of co-operation and centralized cataloguing both at the national and university levels. The faculties as well the university libraries should take full advantage of the programme.

(iii) Bibliographies and Union Lists : There are several faculty or branch libraries in one university. If these libraries combine their activities of cataloguing and bring out jointly union catalogue of their periodical holdings, and distribute the same to the faculty members and students, it would be of great help to them. Similarly several universities in the region or the state could join hands together and bring out a consolidated union list. On similar lines the union list of special materials like manuscripts, rare collections and newspapers should be compiled at the local, regional or national levels. In preparation of the union catalogue and bibliographies, co-operation of all the university libraries in the area is necessary.

(iv) Union Catalogues and Bibliographic Centres : The union catalogue in respect of the holdings of all the units or branch libraries of the university should be maintained. This will facilitate location of the required document in the units of the university library. The main university library can also function as bibliographical centre. Such activities can be combined together by a group of university libraries in the region or by the national library. In Europe and United States, such a service is widely available. In Asia, Latin America and Africa, it needs to be developed.

(v) Documentation Centre : The university library should serve as a documentation centre. In case it is not possible, it should participate in the documentation programme undertaken by other universities in the region or the country and make use of the services. This can be done by lending documents and reading materials to the documentation centres and by providing the photocopies of the articles, when needed. This kind of service is extremely useful as resource centres for the journals and other periodical publications in pure and physical sciences as well as in social sciences and humanity. Gelfand mentions, "through affiliations was similar agencies and research libraries throughout the world, and their indexing, abstracting and translation services, they are capable of becoming strong allies of university libraries in supporting university research." (Gelfand: 1962:119). The UNESCO Science Co-operation office convened a regional meeting of national research organizations in South East Asia in December 1961 which concluded that the universities should participate in the research programmes actively. The students should be trained in the research methodology and its application. A close link and collaboration should be set in between the national research organizations and the university. This will lead to the university occupying a better and more important place in national research programmes.

(vi) Co-operative Reference Service : It is generally found that the reference collection of the university main library is a strong, rich and comprehensive collection of reference materials. As such, it becomes the source for reference services not only for the readers of the main library but also to those coming from the faculties or unit libraries in the university. It should encourage and invite the faculty librarians to draw upon the resources of the central library and seek assistance from it. Similarly, the main library should also call upon the specialists of the faculty libraries for information and guidance in the areas of their specialization. Similar steps may be taken to set up inter-university and nation-wide reference service programmes which should create conditions for free flow of information in the country as a whole.

(vii) Co-operative Photographic Service : Setting up laboratories at every place is not possible as the photographic equipments are very costly. The photographic section of the university main library should, therefore, serve its faculty libraries and the neighbouring libraries and cater to their demands. A kind of co-operative relationship linked with well-equipped documentation centres should be created.

(viii) Subject Specialization : While the duplication of the material in the libraries should be avoided as wasteful expenditure, it is necessary to ensure that at least one library in the area is equipped with the basic documents and materials on a given subject. The different unit libraries should possess specialized collection on different subjects and cooperate for inter-lending the materials among themselves.

(ix) Co-operative Publication : To avoid possible duplication in the printing of reference documents like the union catalogues, bibliographies and current awareness lists etc the participating libraries can cooperate with each other in bringing out such publications on a lesser cost. A significant work published under the joint-duplication programme in Britain is "British Union Catalogue of Periodicals; a record of the periodicals of the world, from the seventeenth century to the present day in British libraries." It is in 4 volumes (1955-58) with a supplement to the year 1960 (published in 1962).

(x) Co-operative Storage Centre : The rare works, documents of special nature and fragile materials like manuscripts, historical documents out of print books need special care and place for storage, preservation and security. All libraries cannot afford to provide such a storage. As such, a new library coming up with spacious accommodation and modern facilities can provide space for storage to its unit and neighbouring libraries as well, which may not possess such storage facilities. The problem of storage is more acute in the libraries of the developed countries than in the underdeveloped and developing ones.

(xi) International Co-operative Services : There are a large number of co-operative activities in the libraries at the international level, in which the libraries can participate. Such activities are translation services, abstracting work, copying services, inter-library lending work, documentation service, compilation of union catalogue and preparation of bibliographies, gift and exchange of library materials and holding of seminars and international conferences.

The participation of libraries can be of two kinds : (a) direct participation in which one library can enter into co-operative service with another library and (b) indirect participation in which the cooperative problems are executed through some agency like national libraries, library associations or other international organizations.

There are certain international organizations helpful in this area. These are : UNESCO (United Nations Educational, Scientific and Cultural Organization), IFLA (International Federation of Library Association), FID (International Federation of Documentation), ISO (International Organization for Standardization), ICA (International Council for Archives) and certain other such organizations. The publications brought out by these organizations prove to be immensely useful in apprising the librarian of the recent trends and developments in different areas of knowledge, new and coming publications in the field of specializations, scope of the cooperative activities in the various branches of disciplines and finally in assisting the readers and other libraries in solving their problems through co-operation.

(xii) Exchange of Annual Reports : This is another area in which co-operation may be sought. The annual report of progress should be circulated and exchanged amongst the libraries to have an idea of the developments and progress made by different university libraries.

(xiii) Exchange of Library Professionals : The staff exchange programme is a fruitful scheme of library co-operation which provides an opportunity to the staff to refresh their professional knowledge and skill and thereby to prepare themselves to serve the library in a more useful and effective way.

(xiv) Inter-library Facility of Reading : Another kind of co-operation among university libraries is the provision of reading facility for students, teachers and research scholars of one university by the other university library on a reciprocal basis. Such facilities should be granted liberally to the readers. This will help the students and teachers make best use of the vacations by exploiting the resources of knowledge in libraries other than their own. All the university libraries in the country should undertake to extend this facility.

Exchange of Surplus Reading Materials

The surplus volumes of books, periodicals, serials, monographs and pamphlets should be collected and notified for exchange with other libraries. Such an exchange is useful both to the beneficiary institution as well as to the beneficent institution. The superfluous material is disposed of and more useful and desired material is obtained at a little expenses and effort.

British Libraries

Co-operation among libraries of the universities in Britain began as early as in 1925. A conference on library co-operation was held under the auspices of the Association of University Teachers. It resolved to formulate a regular scheme of loaning books among the university libraries and to set an enquiry office at the Birmingham University to carry out the policy. In 1931, the National Central Library adopted the functions of the enquiry office. The Carnegic United Kingdom Trust helped the cause financially and a valuable publication entitled "The Union Catalogue of the Periodical Publications in the University Libraries of the British Isles" was brought out. This publication was supplemented by "British Union Catalogue of Periodicals" (BUCOP) in 4 volumes and a "World List of Scientific Periodicals". The National Central Library issues quarterly supplement to both these publications, with annual cumulations. Another important publication initiated by Library Co-operation Conference in 1952 is the "Background Material Scheme". The scheme envisaged that each of the participating libraries would undertake to acquire books published in certain periods between 1550 and 1869 and made them available on an inter-library loan. The catalogues of these acquisitions were maintained by the National Central Library.

There is another co-operative scheme launched by certain university libraries which ensure the availability of at least one copy of every book published in Britain since 1959 in some library of the country. These books are made available on loan. The Public Libraries and Museums Act (England and Wales) 1964 will have complete coverage of British Books and periodicals. The National Central Library runs a co-operative Book Centre since 1930 through which extra or surplus copies of books are made available to another library. This centre has become important at national and international levels dealing with over 1,50,000 titles annually. Through exchange of these materials, valuable books and periodicals are received by the British University Libraries.

India

India is a vast country possessing a large number of libraries. In every state, there are a good number of university libraries. There are certain cities in the states which have more than one university. The collection of one university library in the city is not known to another university library. The materials are, therefore, not exploited fully to the advantage of readers. This is because of the lack of any recognized record that could reveal the information of the availability of the desired document. Also, no access is provided to the readers of the other libraries as every university library functions separately in isolation. There is, therefore, a crying need for library co-operation in the functioning of the university libraries. This can be achieved by (a) producing an up-to-date union catalogue and (b) introducing inter-library lending services in the university libraries of the district, region and state.

(a) Compilation of Union Catalogue : The rich collection, in the form of books, journals, manuscripts and serials, possessed by the various university libraries need hardly any emphasis. These documents are of inestimable value. All these should be catalogued. The scope of such a catalogue can be local, regional or national. If there are more than one university library in particular city, all should combine to produce a union catalogue of the documents available in all these libraries. Similar union catalogues can be brought out for combining all the libraries in the state or region and then finally for the whole country as a National Union Catalogue. The objective is to provide at one place recorded information, in an organized form, of the entire book collection possessed by the participating libraries in the country to enable the reader to locate the availability of the desired document easily, which may not be available in the collection of some of the other libraries in the region or the country. This helps systematically inter-lending books from one library to another.

The preparation of union catalogue needs careful planning and funds. All the participating libraries should provide the information uniformally and regularly for compilation of the information.

(b) Introducing Inter-Library Lending : To increase the use of the available material and reduce the chances of unmet demand, it is necessary to pool the entire resources of the libraries in a given area together and allow its use by any of the other libraries needing the same on loan. Not only the college and university libraries but also the other kinds of libraries like the public, special and research libraries can participate in the scheme.

Such a scheme of library co-operation and co-ordination essentially helps conservation of book-fund and effective use of the available materials. The co-operative schemes operative at the National Central Library (NCL) and National Lending Library (NLL) for Science and Technology in Britain can be a guide for organizing similar programmes of co-operation in Indian university libraries. The first step in this regard is preparation of the union catalogue of books and serials. It should begin with the university libraries situated in the city. The scope should be widened and extended by including all university libraries falling in the region or the state and finally libraries of all the universities in any country should be covered under the national union catalogue. Compilation of the national union catalogue of India is a crying need for the study and research in the country and it has immense value for the students, teachers and research scholars alike. The Parry Committee recommends that "the entire resources of a geographical area should be regarded as a pool from which each individual library could draw. Co-ordination of the resources of libraries would facilitate the extension of coverage and the reduction of expenditure. University libraries within an area should avoid unnecessary and uneconomical duplication of effort and should investigate the advantages of all the forms of co-operation." (Parry : 1967 : 26). It is imperative that systematic schemes of co-operation in university librarianship are drawn and implemented to better advantage and improve upon the library services.

References

1. Gelfand, M. A., 1962, University library for developing countries, UNESCO Manual for Libraries-14, UNESCO, Paris.
2. Mookerjee, S. K. and Sengupta, B., 1977, Library organization and library administration, 2nd ed, The World Press, Calcutta.
3. Neal, K. W., 1971, British university libraries, (Author), 7 Church Road, Wilmslow, Cheshire.
4. Parry, Thomas (Chairman), 1967, Report of the Committee on libraries, University Grants Commission, Her Majesty's Stationary Office, London.

5. Plumbe, W. J., 1963, Climate as a factor in the planning of university library buildings, UNESCO Bulletin for Libraries, V 17 November-December 1963, p 101.
6. Powal, 1939, The functions of rare books, College and Research Libraries, 1 (1939), p 101.
7. Thomson, James, 1970, An introduction to university library administration, Clive Bingley, London.
8. University Grants Commission, Delhi, 1965, University and college libraries containing the report of the Library Committee of the University Grants Commission and the proceedings of the Seminar on "From Publisher to Reader" held on March 4-7, 1959.
9. Viswanathan, C. G., 1972, University Libraries of India : principles and policies, published by the author, New Delhi.).
10. Wilson, L. R. and Tauber, M. F., 1953, The University Library, 2nd ed, Columbia University Press, New York.